GYPSIES ❧ ❧

THEIR LIFE, LORE, AND LEGENDS

The Gypsies of Spain are the nobility of the road.

GYPSIES ❧ ❧
THEIR LIFE, LORE, AND LEGENDS

❧ ❧ ❧ ❧ ❧ ❧

By Konrad Bercovici

ILLUSTRATED BY CHARLOTTE LEDERER

GREENWICH HOUSE

Distributed by Crown Publishers, Inc.

NEW YORK

Originally published as *The Story of the Gypsies*.

Copyright © 1983 by Greenwich House,
a division of Arlington House, Inc.
All rights reserved.

This 1983 edition is published by Greenwich House,
a division of Arlington House, Inc.
distributed by Crown Publishers, Inc.

Manufactured in the United States of America

Library of Congress Cataloging in Publication Data

Bercovici, Konrad, 1882–
  Gypsies: their life, lore, and legends.

  Reprint. Originally published: New York: Cosmopolitan Book Corporation, 1928.
  1. Gypsies—Addresses, essays, lectures. I. Title.
DX115.B4   1983   909'.0491497   83-1647
ISBN 0-517-41290-X

h g f e d c b a

To

W. F. BIGELOW

because, because, because—

CONTENTS

The woman began to dance and sing.

FOREWORD

ACCORDING TO KONRAD BERCOVICI, THERE ARE AS MANY THEORIES about the origin of Gypsies as there are Gypsies. Fancy outstrips their memory, he writes, and this fact, together with the total lack of written records, renders the historian's task a difficult one. At one time, more than 30,000 Gypsies gathered in the Arabian desert to follow a prophet who was to lead them out of slavery. Unfortunately, there was no agreement as to where their homeland was, and the movement became a fiasco.

Who are the Gypsies? Where are they from? Why do they wander? Bercovici, among other scholars, believes they were originally the Sudras, or the fourth level of the Indian caste system, a downtrodden group of people reduced to the status of menial servants. That their language, the Calo, so closely resembles Sanskrit is primary evidence for this theory. He suggests that they were probably dispersed to the Balkans during Alexander's conquests and, later, having lived in Macedonia for several centuries, were scattered again by the Roman conquests. From that time they have wandered throughout the world, either by choice or to escape perpetual persecution.

Despite such persecution, they are a lively and colorful people. "Whatever Gypsies do, or wherever they are," writes Bercovici, "there is some instrument of music in their hands, and they are almost always engaged in producing music, melodies, accompaniments, dance and mirth." Once, he tells us, a band of Gypsies was being pursued by a company of soldiers. As the soldiers closed upon them, two young Gypsies, very much in love and knowing what could happen to them in a matter of hours, made preparations for their wedding celebration. Several other couples followed their example. The fires were lit, the singing began, the brandy was passed, the youngsters danced, and the fiddler began to play. Then the shots rang out. As the soldiers came nearer, the revelry heightened, until at last the pursuers were overcome by the merriment of the Gypsies and succumbed to the song and the dance. What better illustration is there of the infectiousness of the Gypsy spirit?

The Gypsy vocabulary lacks the words "duty" and "possession." This reflects their unwillingness to settle down, live in houses, obey the law, educate their children, be employed by others—and, helps to explain their almost universal persecution. Working at such occupations as cattle herding, horse trading, blacksmithing, entertaining, fortune telling, and basket making, they are the "conscientious objectors to factory work, to all the soul-killing inventions of a haphazard civilization," he says.

There is no country on earth where one cannot find a Gypsy tent, but "they have accepted no religion, no customs, no laws, no traditions from the world outside their tents; and they have kept their own language, though they have been subject to a hundred differences in every generation." They were enslaved in Roumania; forced to submit to Christianity and, later, accused of cannibalism in Hungary; outlawed in France; endured Gypsy hunts in Germany; exiled to Barbados from England; and suffered tuberculosis when forced to live indoors in America. On the other hand, some of the best violinists in the world have been Gypsies from Roumania and Hungary; the best Spanish matadors have been Gypsies; members of some of England's most elite families have traveled with them at one time or another; and in many countries they are highly esteemed for their great skill in metalworking.

The author did much of his research and wrote this book in the period between the two world wars. It is a praiseworthy gathering of the history of a people, but it is also lively entertainment. The author spent much time living among these spirited folk, and tells an anecdote of his early years when a close Gypsy friend, thinking Bercovici abhorred schooling as did most Gypsy children, presented him with enough money to pay the authorities to allow him to go unschooled— a common gypsy practice. His friend thought he was too poor to pay his own bribe! Fortunately, the offer was rejected. Had it been accepted, we would have been deprived of the fine story these pages contain.

There is no denying that somewhere within most of us resides a bit of the Gypsy spirit—if not the blood—which longs to trade in the automobile for a horse; which can respond with Bercovici to this "passion for untrammeled freedom, and...sings the song of the wood to the rhythm of the pebble bottomed brook...." A thousand years ago, the world thought it had seen the last Gypsy. Not so. Believing themselves a superior race, they are today "as fierce, as passionate, as free as they have ever been."

ELIZABETH CONGDON KOVANEN

I—The Missing Words

I AM ATTEMPTING TO UNRAVEL THE STORY OF A people whose vocabulary lacks two words—"duty" and "possession."

For hundreds of years the Gypsies have lived beside us—in the Orient and in the Occident, in Egypt as well as in England, in Syria and in France, in Italy, in Germany, in Turkey, on the frozen plains of Russia, in the Pusta of Hungary, on the barren rocky mountains and in the fertile valleys of Wallachia, in Australia and in the Americas—and we neither know nor understand them.

What we know about them compared with what they know about us is like but a drop of water in the vast ocean. They do not live as we do because they do not consider our manner of living good enough for them . . . because they are not like the vintners who never get "half as good as the things they sell."

There is more joy and more happiness, there is more poetry and deep emotion in a Gypsy camp of three ragged tents than in the largest city of our civilized world. The range of the emotional clavier of the Gypsy is so wide that it reaches depths and heights to which no civilized human being has ever been attuned.

Duty and possession limit the emotional capacity of civilized man. They are the boundaries beyond which he cannot go. He must encompass his happiness within the limits of what he *must* and what he *owns*. He who has so much against him in his daily life, he who does not know or care where the morrow will find him and what it will bring, is free of the shackles of feasibility, and miracles become every-day occurrences.

Everything that is, is as passing as a glance from the eye of the beloved, as a ray of the sun, as ephemeral as a dewdrop on the petal of a rose at sunrise. Everything that cannot be, can and will be.

Sometime in the dark long ago the ancestors of the Gypsies undoubtedly experimented with the futility of possession and groaned under the heavy load. Behind them, thousands and thousands of years behind them, are the ashes of a civilization and a culture which, when the flame was blown out, demonstrated the falseness of its root and flower. The depths of the earth were not deep enough. The sky itself a threatening limitation. The ancestors of the Gypsies then learned to know that they who have nothing own everything without possessing anything; that possession is limitation . . . poverty; that the pungent odor of a rose is more than the rose. They who have no country of their own can call all ground under their feet theirs. They who have no complete language of their own can employ one understood by all the world. How inarticulate, how expressionless, spoken language seems after hearing Gypsy music!

And if Gypsies do have the ability to look backwards, if they do possess what is generally spoken of as "second sight," it is because the sense of time limitation has gone the way of all limitations. Past and future are poor inventions of childish minds . . . inventions as crude as the taboos of savages and the superstitions of fools.

In our dreams, when our time-sense is asleep, everything that would, in the wakeful life, take months to happen, happens in only a few seconds. Gypsies see things not one after another, but in a simultaneous way . . . the whole firmament at once and not the stars one by one. They listen to the music of the world not as if every instrument of the orchestra were playing separately, one after another, but as they do really play . . . all together. That, the symphonic perception, is the Gypsies' undeniable superiority over the white man. Compared to the Gypsies' tactile sense, ours is as clumsy as that of an elephant.

Yet, why do they insist on living in tents? Why don't they settle down anywhere permanently? Where do they come from?

Where do the swallows come from?

I am speaking of a people whose vocabulary lacks two words—*possession* and *duty*.

You who cannot fathom what would happen to your own life if these two boundaries were to disappear suddenly will never understand the Gypsies. What we own possesses us, jails us. The Gypsy has locked himself out of the gates of modern civilization and roams freely on the highways and byways of the world.

In the course of the year 1417 there appeared in Germany a horde of men, sunburned, dressed in rags of all colors, followed by a still greater number of women dressed even more immodestly than the men,

who thronged the roads and invaded vociferously the
homes of people, spreading terror everywhere and
begging or stealing everything they saw. At the head
of this mob there were a dozen men on horseback, who
distinguished themselves from the rest by wearing
scarlet clothes. These leaders had falcons perched on
their wrists, packs of hunting dogs at their sides, and
were comporting themselves with the airs and manners
of nobles. They bore letters from the Emperor Sigismund and other princes, permitting them to pass
through towns and provinces.

These people never remained in any one place
for any length of time. Passing rapidly over a
town or village, like colorful birds of prey, they would
split into separate bands, going in different directions,
trailing after them the native floating population
raised like dust by flapping wings. They formed
huge flocks, a plague upon the huts and houses which
they robbed, while the owners were in the fields.

At the fairs, while the men bartered and swindled,
the women practiced sorcery and magic upon the
credulous peasants and their wives, skilfully emptying
the purses of their foolish victims.

When questioned, the strangers claimed they hailed
from Lower Egypt; that they had been condemned to
a seven-year exile to atone for a sin committed by their
ancestors, who had refused to accept the Virgin Mary
and her Holy Son at the time of their flight from
Egypt. So great was the superstition these strangers
awakened in the German peasants, and so intense the
fear, that they considered it a crime to do violence to
the Gypsies, and left them to steal, rob, and cheat without hindrance.

An eye-witness of that period, Münster, in his "Cosmographia," says:

"About twenty-six years ago, I, Münster, happened to be at Heidelberg where I talked to several of these people, who claimed to possess letters from emperors and princes, permitting them to pass unhindered through cities and provinces. I saw one of these letters from Emperor Sigismund. It stated that their ancestors in Lower Egypt had once upon a time renounced Christianity to return again to Paganism. When they had reembraced Christianity and had done the penances of seven years' wandering imposed upon them, it was again commanded that each of their families must in turn wander for a like number of years. But since that time, their period of penance had expired, and still they do not cease to wander, to steal, to lie and tell fortunes . . . "

A Bavarian writer of the fifteenth century, Adventin, states that a "race of men, a mixture of the scum of various nations, living by prey, whose original home was on the borders of Turkey and Hungary, and whom we call Zigeuner, infested the countrysides, living by thievery, robbery, and magic."

A year later these bands appeared in Switzerland.

In 1422 they appeared in Italy, pretending to be on their way to visit the pope. The terror they spread in Germany and Switzerland was insignificant when compared to the hysteria they created in Italy. The sorcery and the miracles they worked upon the ignorant peasantry awakened in them the dormant paganism of the *vecchia religione*. The mere passing of the Gypsies shattered the fundamental teachings of the church.

These strangers were only a hundred and twenty souls when they had appeared in Germany. They claimed to have been reduced to that number from the thousand souls that had left Lower Egypt and perished on the wayside from hunger, cold, and disease. But they were more than a thousand souls when they reached Italy, their number having become augmented by additional bands of those who had followed them, and who spoke all languages.

When these Gypsies appeared in 1427 in France, they were in possession of real or apocryphal letters from the pope, who ordered his bishops to give them a definite sum of money upon their passing a diocese, and he forbade anybody to lay hands upon the poor repentant sinners, even when caught cheating or robbing.

Let us see what impression they made upon the Parisians, these colorful birds, when they swooped down upon that fair city!

In his book, "Les Parias de France et d'Espagne," V. de Rochas quotes a letter of a French theologist who was in Paris when the Gypsies appeared there for the first time.

"Sunday, August 17, 1427, there arrived in Paris a dozen feudal lords . . . a duke, a count and ten knights, all gaudily dressed and mounted on horseback. They said that they were good Christians from Lower Egypt, that not very long ago the Christians had subdued their land and forced all inhabitants, under pain of death, to become Christians. All complied readily; the lords of the country were baptized, and swore they would remain good Christians and keep and guard the Holy Faith even until death.

However, shortly afterwards, the Saracens overran their country, and the inhabitants accepted the faith of the Saracens, renouncing the Holy Faith they had accepted not very long before. Shortly afterwards, the emperors of Germany and other great Christian countries, learning how cowardly the inhabitants of Lower Egypt had behaved when the Saracens invaded their country, becoming pagans, idol-worshipers and traitors to the Faith, invaded the country and again reconquered the land.

"Having done so, they decided not to allow the inhabitants to remain in their own country until the pope should grant his consent thereto. And so, the Lower Egyptians were ordered to make a pilgrimage to Rome . . . all of them, great and small . . . and there they confessed their sins. The pope heard their confessions, held a lengthy council, and after long deliberation ordered them to wander seven successive years over the face of the earth, without sleeping in beds or enjoying any comforts. However, he ordered that every bishop or abbot should give them, upon passing, ten pounds in the money of Tours.

"They had already been wandering five years since their departure from Rome, when they arrived in Paris. The people following these dukes, counts, and knights were not allowed to enter the city, but were lodged in St. Denis Chapel. Then people came from far and near to see these strangers. Most of the men had their ears pierced, and in each ear a silver earring or even two. The men were very dark, with curly hair, and their women had harassed faces, and hair as black and coarse as that of a horse's tail. The clothing of these women consisted of a strip of cloth hanging from their shoulders by a cord. They were half naked, immodest, bare-legged, barefooted . . . the most wretched-looking creatures that had ever been known to visit France. These women made a practice of examining people's palms to tell their fortunes, and, claiming to be able to work magic, they emptied the purses of the folk who came to them.

"The news of such practices . . . this falling back to paganism on the part of the populace . . . reached the ears of the Bishop of Paris, who threatened to excommunicate any and all who would show their palms to these Egyptians. In September, that is to say a month after their arrival in Paris . . . they left for Pontoise."

Such is the graphic account given by this eye-witness of the arrival of the Gypsies in Paris. The picture is a marvelous example of French precision and aptness of phrase.

On June 11, 1447, according to the annals of Catalonia, thirty years after they had first appeared in Germany, and twenty years after their appearance in Paris, the Gypsies appeared in Barcelona, telling everyone who listened to them variations of the same story they had told in Germany, Italy, and France, from which last country they had probably crossed into Spain. From Barcelona they spread over the Spanish kingdom in small groups, each one conducted and ruled over by a duke or count who claimed to have received his orders from still higher powers.

They associated themselves with the wandering Calabreze, kettle-menders and coppersmiths, who lived in Spain, and by skilful use of the letters of the emperors and the pope, the "Egyptians" gained such power over the Spaniards that Ferdinand and Isabella issued an edict ordering them to settle in the cities or provinces and to allow themselves to be absorbed by the settled population and to work honestly for their living. Should the Gypsies be unwilling to do as ordered, they would be expelled from Spain, notwithstanding their letters from the pope and the emperors permitting them to roam at will.

What havoc the Gypsies must have wrought in Spain to induce Ferdinand and Isabella, the most Catholic of Spanish rulers, to ignore the orders of the pope regarding the Gypsies!

These letters and documents establish the official appearance of the Gypsies in occidental Europe. It is impossible to know whether the same band which appeared in 1417 in Germany also appeared in 1427 in France and in 1447 in Spain. It is difficult to believe that a small band of a hundred and twenty people could have created such a sensation by their appearance anywhere, at a time when there were many wandering hordes of native people in every country.

There were more than one hundred and twenty wandering Calabreze in Spain at the time, and yet they had not caused any law to be issued against them. There were also thousands of wandering families in France, in Italy, and in Germany. But the Gypsies gave the impression of being more numerous than they really were by traveling at a rapid pace. Who goes a-visiting instead of being visited multiplies his presence by the number of visits he makes. The Jews, too, have created the impression of being ten times more numerous than they really are.

II—THE ORIGIN OF THE GYPSIES

N 1780, H. M. G. GRELLMANN, A GERMAN PHIlologist, collected a number of words spoken by the Gypsies, and found that a third of them were of Hindu origin. Comparing the grammatical construction of the language of the Gypsies with the dialects spoken in India, he arrived at the conclusion that these wanderers came originally from India. Pursuing still further his studies among the principal dialects of India, Grellmann discovered that the Surat dialect, spoken in the northwest of India, was very much like the language spoken by the Gypsies. Subsequent studies pursued by other philologists and travelers confirmed Grellmann's opinion that the cradle of these wanderers, known over the world as Tziganes, Zigeuner, Gypsies, Czigany, Zingari, Bohémiens, was also that of the tribe of the Jats, living near the mouth of the Indus River.

Pott, Bataillard, Trumpp and Sir Richard Burton arrived at the conclusion that the relation between the language spoken by the Gypsies and the language spoken by the Jats tribe in India today was so close that there could be no doubt that its root, in spite of all changes, lay in the dialect spoken in the north of India, and is entitled to claim parenthood with Sanskrit.

Today the unanimous verdict of most philologists is that the language of the Gypsies is the daughter of Sanskrit and sister of the neo-Hindu dialects deriving from the same source, just as the Romance languages are derived from Latin.

Attempting the solution of the same problem from a historical angle, de Goeje, another investigator, noticing that in Mohammedan chronicles there recurred frequently the name of wandering tribes called Zotts, deduced that they were the same as the Jats, and the Gypsies.

According to Arab authors and geographers, there lived long ago at the mouth of the Indus a tribe of roaming cattle-breeders, who raised their tents wherever their black water-buffaloes were grazing. The Arabs tried several times to conquer them, but were driven back every time, with heavy losses.

Under Walid I, these Zotts agreed to terms of peace. The Arab ruler, however, realized after his alliance with these wandering tribes that their faithfulness was not to be relied upon; that they would neither obey nor follow of their own volition. In the year 710 he took a great number of them captive and led them forcibly to the borders of the Tigris in Kurdistan. Six years later, under Yazid II, a still greater number of captives were transported to Antioch with their cattle and tents.

A hundred years later, in 820, these Zotts had become so powerful, so insolent, they revolted against the Arab rulers who had imposed upon them. For fourteen years the rebels fought against the armies of the Arab princes sent to subdue them, inflicting the heaviest losses upon their erstwhile allies who had become their masters, raiding, pillaging adjoining territory and capturing great booty. Men, women, and children fought with equal valor against their oppressors and betrayers who, after forcing them into an agreement of peace, had forcibly transported them hundreds of miles away from their home and attempted to break their independent spirits.

Arab chroniclers admit the great valor of their foes; these Zotts were no mean fighters. Finally, in the year 834, Prince Motasim subdued the enemy after long and bloody warfare. Bagdad celebrated for three days the great victory over these wandering cattle-breeders. Motasim passed through the gates of the great city 27,000 prisoners, men, women, and children, who were deported first to Khanikin, northeast of Bagdad, and then to Ainzarba.

In 856, the "Roums," as the Byzantians were called, took Ainzarba from the Arabs, taking the Zotts, with tents and cattle, as prisoners.

The year 856 is the approximate date of the appearance of the Gypsies upon Byzantian territory. That the Byzantians were called Roums and that the Gypsies later called themselves "Roms" is of great importance to those who want to know something about the Gypsies. Did the Zotts take the nickname of their new masters as their own? Are the Zotts and the Gypsies one and the same people? Who knows? Arab chroniclers are not very trustworthy. Accounts of battles and numbers of hosts are frequently very fantastic tales.

Is it not strange that a people should have lived in the occident of Europe for almost four hundred years before its origin should have been inquired into? Is it not strange that the civilized world should have disbelieved everything else they said except their assertion that they were from Lower Egypt? It is almost incredible that the mob of a hundred and twenty which had first appeared in Germany should have multiplied so that they should today count close to a million! The Gypsies must have known the truth about their origin. Why have they not told it? What dark past were they so carefully hiding?

However, here they are. You can find them everywhere you go—driving automobiles in America; on foot in England; on donkeys in Arabia; everywhere in Spain; in large and small caravans over all the roads and in the market-places of Roumania and Hungary; hiding in the mountains of the Tyrol and Switzerland; camping beside the fiords in Sweden and Norway; bartering with Laplanders in the Reindeer Country; fishermen on the coasts of France and Spain; occupying whole sections of Russia; in Egypt, Palestine, and Italy. . . .

Infiltrating themselves everywhere, they allow little infiltration from the outside. Humbled and despised by everybody, they consider themselves above all other nations . . . purer, cleaner, healthier, wiser . . . a race of kings and queens, with no peers on earth.

Grouped separately, power within power, a wheel within a wheel, they are led by their own rulers, and judged by laws entirely different from the laws of the countries they find themselves in. Accepting any faith, any religion, because they have inwardly rejected them all long ago, they are unwilling to suffer any pain or shed any of their blood for things that do not concern them. Unlike thousands of Jews, not one Gypsy died at the hands of the Spanish Inquisition. No Gypsy ever died voluntarily for a principle. Only absence of freedom kills them.

Catholics in Catholic countries, Greek Orthodox

here, Methodists there . . . five hundred years of life in the Occident have not succeeded in changing them one iota from what they were when they first appeared, from what they were two thousand years ago. No people have suffered what they have been made to suffer. No more Draconian laws have been issued against any people than have been issued against the Gypsies. Wolves have been treated better than these people have been treated! And yet they are far from having been exterminated, far from having been subdued, far from having been influenced, and have, as we shall see, brought gifts to the world which have given an infinitely greater measure of happiness than even the measure of pain and bitterness that has been poured for them by the world. I speak of Gypsy music, of Gypsy songs, of Gypsy dance, of Gypsy color and rhythm.

As for breaking the spirit of the Gypsy! Not in the least! They are still the happiest, gayest and the most light-hearted people in the world. They can sing and dance under all circumstances. And they are free . . . free. Instead of imitating the other peoples, they are being imitated now by all those who want to snatch an hour's happiness and freedom from the woefully civilized trap in which we live. More people travel today than ever did before. And if we only could . . .

But, again, why have the Gypsies kept the secret of their origin and history so long that they have forgotten it themselves?

The people in India are divided into four classes or castes, each one of which in turn has its own subdivisions. The first caste is that of the Brahmins, the second that of the Kshatriyas, the third the Vaishyas, and the fourth the Sudras. The formation of these classes is based upon the religious dogmas of the Hindus. Those who have no caste are to this day in Hindustan as well as in Malabar known under the name of Pariah.

The Brahmins believe that God ordained that the Brahmins should issue from the face of Brahma, the Kshatriyas from the arms of Brahma, the Vaishyas from the thighs, and the Sudras from the feet. Therefore, the Brahmins were to occupy themselves exclusively with the study of truth and the teaching of religion; the Kshatriyas, issuing from the arms, were to be educated as warriors; and the third class, issuing from the thighs, were to dedicate themselves to the study of sciences and especially those of agriculture and the breeding of cattle.

But the Sudras were to be the servants of the other three castes. They were and are considered impure and abject, and are employed to do the most impure and abject work. They are not permitted to touch the food to be eaten by the other three castes, or to touch anything that comes in direct bodily contact with anybody not of their caste. The Sudras are considered much lower than the lowest animals, and are required to turn their heads away when talking to persons of high caste, lest their breath pollute that of their masters.

Anthropologists have established by measurements of a number of heads that the Gypsies, the Sudras, and the Jats are of one and the same origin; that the measurements of their heads are totally different from the measurements of the heads of the Hindus of the other three castes. This leaves but little doubt that the

Gypsies, Jats, and Sudras are of a different stock from the other inhabitants of India.

If the head measurements alone were not convincing, the customs, morals, habits, and the great difference in diet would tend to clear up any doubts on the matter. It is improbable that the present inhabitants of India would ever have tolerated a people so alien in habits and so objectionable to settle amongst them, were it even for performing the most menial and abject services for them. I am therefore inclined to believe that these people were there long before the present inhabitants of India had conquered the country. Having conquered the Sudras, but unable to exterminate them, the invaders reduced their foes to the status of menial servants, denying them the teaching of their religion and the science of their faith, considering them unworthy even of hearing the words of the gods they believed in. Even the name Jats is one given them by the Hindus and is not the one by which they had called themselves; for in Hindustani and its various dialects, the word "jat" means robber, pirate, and abject creature. No people would call themselves by such names.

It is still unknown what culture, if any, these former inhabitants of India possessed. Some form of civilization had held them together. That they have been nomads is no proof of their lack of a firm organization. The Jats have been little more nomadic than other peoples three thousand years ago. The people who conquered India were also a nomadic people. Nomadic life may have been due to the nature of the land upon which they lived, which was more suited to the raising and breeding of cattle than for agriculture. The Arab authors speak of the Zotts as cattle-breeders. The whole world was once divided between roving herders in search of grazing-land, and staid and settled agriculturists. The Gypsies frequently pitched their tents upon foreign soil and grazed their cattle. This was not different from what other peoples, engaged in similar occupations, had done; other peoples who have since disappeared from the earth or have changed their mode of life.

The oppressor has always crushed whatever civilization and culture the conquered possessed, reduced him to the lowest and most abject form of life, enslaved him, and then despised him.

For how many thousands of years had these Jats lived in India before they were forced out of their cradle by the newcomers?

There are no written records, except the Arabic ones in which the battle between the Jats and Walid I and the other princes are related. Yet the Gypsies had existed as an entity before that time. The Arabs had had to make peace with them. No other people of Hindustan is mentioned in that record. If the Zotts, the Jats, and the Gypsies are of one and the same origin, they must still have been masters of a country they called their own . . . some land over which they were masters and which was not under Indian rule.

The three-day festival at Bagdad after the Gypsies' definite submission in 834, and the joy of the Byzantians who had taken them captive and brought them to Europe, indicate that at this time the Gypsies lived in tremendously large groups that were well organized and well disciplined.

Great masses of Jats, however, had long before that migrated into Asia and penetrated into Europe.

Homer speaks of them as the Sygynes, so beloved by Vulcan because they were so skilful in metal-work. The daring Phœnician seafarers had perhaps learned a great deal of their handicraft, which was recognized by antiquity to be the most superb one, from the traveling Sygynes camping in their towns and villages. Bataillard, the French writer, maintains that even the credit for introducing bronze into Europe is due the Gypsies, and not the Phœnicians, as is believed by many.

Grellmann, the German philologist, believed that the Gypsies had been driven out of India by Tamerlane at the end of the fourteenth century. This, however, does not square with records of the existence of Tziganes in the lower Balkans as early as the eleventh century.

In the "Miscellaneous Tracts Relating to Antiquity," published by the Society of Antiquarians of London in 1785, is the letter of Simon Simeon, who, after visiting the Island of Cyprus in 1332, tells that he found there a race of people who claimed to be of the origin of Cham. "These people," says he, "never stop in one place for more than a few days, packing up suddenly and running away as though God had blasphemed them. They live like Arabs in small low black tents, hiding in the hollows of mountains."

The Italian historian, Lusignan, attests that in the fourteenth century, the king gave as a present to one of his officers the revenue paid by the Zingari to the royal treasury. There is mention of the Zingari in a letter of Theophilactus, who lived in the eleventh century. Records in the archives of Bucharest prove that long before the eleventh century the Tziganes were recognized as an entity by the inhabitants of the countries they lived in.

The Gypsies were therefore in Europe long before Tamerlane or any of his ancestors knew of the existence of India. They were probably on the banks of the Danube and in the mountains of the Balkans and on the shores of the Black Sea and the Adriatic long before the present inhabitants had crushed the wild flowers of the plains under their feet. That there are still people in India of the same origin as the Gypsies means only that there have been a series of migrations which have not yet ceased, though they may have been interrupted for a long period of time. It would have been highly improbable for a people to traverse on foot all the countries from India to the west of Europe, after a long stay in Egypt and on the banks of the Danube, in less than a century, and the time elapsed between Tamerlane's invasion of India and the appearance of the Gypsies in Germany was even less than twenty years.

Yes, but what about their origin? It is possible for a single individual to deny and hide his origin. It is impossible for a whole people to do so. It is unbelievable that a people did not know its origin a century after it has left the native soil.

Had the Gypsies come so directly from India to Europe as Grellmann and other philologists and historians would have us believe, it would not have taken four centuries for the world to know their origin, no matter how well the others had tried to hide it.

The *Calo,* the Gypsy language as spoken today by the Gypsies of Roumania, Hungary, Russia, and Spain

—countries where they have kept to themselves more than anywhere else—still contains one-third Sanskrit root-words. Words, like people, struggle and fight before they are eliminated. Each word of a language has its own life, which it defends to the utmost. No foreign word is accepted willingly into the body of any language. It either forces itself into a place that has been left vacant, or it has to fight its way through and destroy another word in the ranks of the language it attempts to invade.

Two languages, opposed to one another, are like two inimical armies. In the language of the Calo, the foreign elements represent so many struggles against other peoples . . . so many long stays in the countries from which these words are derived. Each foreign word represents a generation born in the country where that word was spoken. A generation that has heard that word pronounced more often than its predecessor unconsciously adopts the new word. For every Greek, Roumanian, Spanish, or Hungarian word in Calo, you can count thousands of Gypsies who died or were murdered in the countries in which these words were first spoken. And if the world thinks there are too many live Gypsies, the Roms can call the world to account for their dead. All the languages of Asia entered into the present language spoken by the Gypsies, in exchange for the blood and the seed they have left in the countries they have traversed.

And yet what is Persia now? And Egypt, and Phœnicia, and Arabia, and Rome, and the Byzantine Empire? And what has become of Greece and the empire of the proud Macedonian?

A little trickle of water breaks through the most

solid rock. No solid mass can resist even the slightest
constantly moving force. History, like biology, teaches
that the length of life of a species can be measured by
its radius of dispersion. Well, then the Gypsies are
destined to exist until the earth grows too cold for
human habitation. What people has ever been dispersed on a wider range! There is no country on earth
where one cannot find a Gypsy tent.

Recently, a tribe of English Gypsies invited me to
come for a three-day feast with them.

"A wedding?" I asked.

"No, no. More important."

"Blood brothership?"

"No. I will tell you. Taro is coming home today.
He has been 'in' ["in" means "in jail"] for thirty days.
He is as thin as a rail and looks like a ghost, and we
want to make merry."

Having never refused such an errand, I was in the
camp that night. It was early in the fall. The tents
were ranged along a road backed by a forest of birch
trees. Fifty or more of the brotherhood sat around a
brightly burning camp-fire. The bottle passed from
hand to hand and mouth to mouth. Taro sat in the
center, and everybody toasted him. The hollowness of
the liberated man's eyes and the greenish pallor of his
face frightened me.

"But you are home, you are free, Taro. Why don't
you laugh? Why don't you help us be merry?"

Taro stared vacantly above his friends' shoulders,
but would not say a word. The thirty days in jail had
been too much for him. The women tried to amuse
him, to force him to dance. He shook them off apa-
thetically.

"Why, what is the matter with you, Taro?" I asked, taking his hand. "What are you thinking about?"

"Great sorrow, brother." The tears streaming down his face. He continued: "I have been there thirty days and then they let me out. But think of the jailer! He is there all his life. It's what breaks my heart."

Had the *"gelehrten"* tried to listen to legends of the Gypsies, they might have learned something that would have been valuable in tracing the history of this interesting people.

The legends of the Gypsies may prove to be the source of more information than the learned have been able to gather by examining minutely the frayed fringes of tales of travelers. Philological gymnastics of philologists with preconceived ideas, who turn words around, and replace syllables and vowels to demonstrate that such and such a word is of Sanskrit, Hebraic, or Arabic origin, do not teach anything. You can see such images as you wish when the moon is sailing through the clouds.

But here is a Gypsy legend:

"In the beginning we were all birds; we had wings; we flew high over trees and mountains to gather our daily food.

"And we were birds flying toward warm countries.

"We left one region for another when the season was about to change . . . when the leaves on the trees yellowed, when worms and other crawling things were beginning to burrow their holes.

"After a great hunger, we once came upon a region fat with grain, the like of which we had never seen. We swooped down, and ate ourselves so full we were too heavy to rise on our wings again. So we remained that night amidst the grass and grain-straw. In the morning, instead of flying away, we listened to our stomachs and ate again. Thus, remaining in that field from day to day, we became heavier and heavier, hopping instead of flying. Then the leaves began to yellow on the trees; the worms and other creatures of the earth crawled into their holes; the cold winter winds began to blow, but we could not fly away.

"The grass was thinning. The grain-straw was getting dry. We, too, watching the crawling things, began to shake the grain from the blade, gathering it in heaps with our wings and shoving it into holes. The fluff of our wings crusted, glued, and thickened. The wings took the shape of arms and hands. And as we were no longer able to fly, we dug holes on the shores of the rivers and on the sides of mountains.

"We are birds. Our arms are two stilted wings. We never can see a mountain without desiring to get to the top. But we cannot fly. We must crawl up there.

"The Calo People, the Gypsies, will get their wings back some day."

Birds again!

And if Gypsies are looked upon as crows and not as nightingales, it is because we paint them much blacker than they really are; because of our tendency to consider those unlike ourselves not as different beings but as of lesser value; because of our belief that a civilization that is not ours is barbaric and immoral.

The following legend tells the reason why the Gypsies left India:

"We were then living on the Ganges. And our chief

was a powerful chief . . . a man whose voice was heard over all the land, and whose judgments were final. And that chief had an only son whose name was Tchen.

"In the land of the Hind there ruled then a powerful king whose favorite wife had borne him an only child, a daughter, whom he named Gan.

"One day a sorcerer told this king that a man was to invade the Hind, at the head of a numerous host and overrun the land and destroy the king and his family, and become the master of the country. The sorcerer also told the king that this man was to be immune from every manner of death on the battle-field, but that it was written he would perish if he should do violence to the Gypsy.

"To save his newly born daughter, the king called our chief, Tchen's father, whose friend he was, and it was agreed between them that the child was to be taken secretly to the tent of the Gypsy chief, and only the chief's wife know who the child was.

"Three days later, our 'Barossan' announced to his people that his wife had given birth to a girl, and that her name was Gan.

"Tchen and Gan grew up in the same tent.

"When Tchen, the chief's son, was to be wived, they asked him to choose from the girls of his tribe. But there was no one he desired. Again and again the most beautiful daughters of our tribes were asked to dance before him, that he might choose one from among the loveliest. He found none to his liking.

"In the meantime the old chief died. The people urged Tchen to choose a wife immediately. Tchen then threatened to kill himself; for he loved his own sister. So the mother told Tchen that Gan was the daughter of the king of the Hind and not his sister.

"Our people were divided into two factions: one which agreed that everything the young chief did was right, and another faction which swore not to live under a chief who married his own sister. The truth could not be told, lest the invader destroy Gan; and so there was war amongst ourselves.

"Meanwhile, one of Skender's generals came like a cyclone upon Hind, devastating and destroying everything. As the sorcerer had foretold, the stranger killed the king of the Hind and his wives, and buried them underneath the heap of stones of their ruined palace. And still he continued at the head of his savage host, deeper and deeper into the land.

"One of our people went to the victorious stranger for judgment on the matter of a brother marrying his own sister. Still sitting on his horse, the conqueror hit the man a blow on the head. At that very moment, the great general and his horse burst and crumbled like an earthen vessel shattered upon a rock. The wind blew into the desert the remains of what had once been a great warrior.

"Those who opposed Tchen pursued him and his followers to the end of the land and beyond. Those who had remained faithful to their chief were called 'Tchen-Gans' . . . brothers who married their sisters.

"And a great sorcerer cursed Tchen and those following him, that they should forever wander over the face of the earth, never sleep twice in the same place, never drink water twice from the same well, and never cross the same river twice in one year."

I have heard the same legend with slight variations, timed for the invasion of India by Alexander the Great, three hundred and fifty years before the beginning of Christ.

The beginning of time, Alexander, Tamerlane, yesterday, or two thousand years ago means little to Gypsies. Time, as we understand it, is of little importance in the legends of most people, and of still less value in the legends and the lives of the Gypsies.

The Gypsies inhabited India long before the present population of that country had invaded it. They are not Hindus, but of pre-Hindu origin. Upon invading the country, the Hindus, the victors, despoiled the inhabitants they vanquished, not only of their wealth and land, but of all human rights. The invaders of the Hind decreed that the inhabitants they found there were outside the pale of humanity and outlawed them. Those who could saved themselves and spread over the Oxus into Persia and other lands. Driving their black water-buffaloes ahead of them, they dispersed themselves over Asia in small groups, tribes and families.

Old Persian legends tell of a people called Mutes coming from the Hind before Alexander's invasion of Asia.

Mutes! Even in our day persons are considered mutes when they do not speak the language of the country. Each people has two names: the one it calls itself by, which generally means, "We who know, who understand one another"; and the other name as given by inimical neighbors, which means, "They who don't know, who do not understand us." We always talk at the top of our voices when we speak to foreigners; as if not knowing our language were a sign of deafness! We refuse to believe that someone could speak intelligently of things we know, in another language than our own. . . .

Alexander's hosts were neither deaf nor mute. They were victorious vandals who imposed their language upon the vanquished. Alexander's army was mainly composed of Asiatic peoples who had had to learn the conqueror's language. The Sogdians and Bactrians were known to the Persians, as were the Phœnicians and Egyptians and Judæans. The Hindus were no strangers. Darius and the kings before him had signed treaties with the rulers of the Hind. Had the Gypsies been known to the Persians as Hindus, they would have spoken of them as such. Who then were these Mutes of the Persian records?

The exodus of the Gypsies might have happened at the time of Alexander's invasion of Asia, of India. There are too many Greek words in the Calo, the Gypsy language, and what is more, all Gypsies, whether living in Asia or Europe, still count in Greek.

No matter what new languages one acquires, counting is almost always done in one's own language, or in the one learned immediately after one's own. Why should Gypsies of Arabia, Russia, Roumania, Hungary, Spain, and England still count in Greek? Where and when have they learned it?

Did the Mutes appear in Asia when the Persian Empire was being shattered by Alexander? Were they caught between the invaders and the invaded? And did they side with the invader because he was the stronger, and work for him, selling him their skill at the forge and the anvil to repair broken weapons and shoe his horses? It is possible that they also served as guides to Alexander when he pretended to pursue Bessus . . . Bessus who had killed Darius, his strongest enemy.

Would that explain the intense hatred the Persians had for the Gypsies after Alexander's empire had been shattered? *Qui lo sa?*

There are Gypsy legends that curiously and strongly remind one of the story of Thalestris, the Queen of the Amazons, who appeared with her subjects before Alexander and did not leave before they had all been impregnated by him and his generals.

"The Gypsy men having been killed in war, the women withdrew into the mountains and captured men for themselves. When a child was born, it was examined closely. If it resembled the mother, it was allowed to live; if not, it was killed."

As a connoisseur of wines tells the vintage and the origin from the flavor of a single drop, so must one feel the source and the age of a folk-tale or a legend.

The history of the Gypsies is still so obscure, every ray of light has to be followed to its source. Legends, tales, words, habits and customs must be sifted carefully. What the Gypsies have once known has long since been drowned in the mass of falsifications and perversions caused by their mode of life, and by the primordial tendency to prevarication of a people who have neither "possession" nor "duty" in their language.

The deeper I delve into the matter, the more am I inclined to the idea that the first great exodus of the Gypsies from India happened at the time of Alexander the Great's invasion of that country. It matters not whether they were driven out and fell into his hands or joined him willingly.

Small groups had probably preceded the great exodus. The Gypsies were known to the Sogdians, Scythians, Bactrians, and Persians, long before Alexander appeared in Asia. There were mass exoduses as late as the fifteenth century. There is reason to believe that there is an incessant trickling into Asia Minor and from there into the rest of the world of people from the same race. There is more than one reason why they should have lied and should lie about their origin. Every historian has lied when telling the story of his own people, and lied again when telling the story of another people.

While the legend about Tchen and Gan may teach something of the history of the Gypsies, a wedding ceremony may reveal more about their former civilization.

Picture for yourself a large camp-fire within a wide circle made by tents and wagons. The women, young and old, occupy one half of the circle, the men the other. On a heap of rugs and untanned skins sits the bridal couple. The faces of all are lighted by the playful light of the flames.

The father of the groom pays the price of the bride to her mother, still wrangling over the last gold piece. The men, including the father and brothers of the bride, side with the other men against the women, accusing them of wanting to extract the last cent. There are even threats to break off the ceremony.

While the quarrel lasts—and it looks as if they would all come to blows—the bride and groom carry on a conversation of their own, as if the altercation of the others does not concern them. And it does not. This is just a manner of play; an occasion for the men and the women to express their opinions of one another. Husband and wife air their domestic quarrels, while talking in general terms.

"What woman is worth as much as is paid for her, eh?"

"No matter how much a man pays for a woman, he is cheating."

"That girl there . . . Why, she should have her mother pay a thousand ducats in gold to a seventy-year-old man for marrying her!" This from the father of the groom.

"The deal is off. Come, woman, let's go."

The discussion goes on for hours and hours. Not a copper goes down from the price agreed to long before. And that price! Really, if the groom and bride belong to the same tribe, paying for the woman is like taking money out of one pocket and putting it back into another. All moneys belong to the tribe; with the chief as custodian. If the bride belongs to another tribe, there will soon be another marriage between the two tribes to even matters up.

But daylight is breaking. The quarrel comes to an abrupt end. The oldest of the tribe is speaking to the groom:

"Swear that you will leave the woman you want to make the mother of your children, swear that you will leave her as soon as you discover you no longer love her!"

And after the groom has taken the oath, he turns to the woman and asks her to promise that she will leave him as soon as she discovers that she no longer has any love for him.

Then, they are made into blood friends. A little cut

is made on the left wrist of the man and on the right wrist of the woman. The hands are tied together in such a way that the two bloods mingle. No matter what happens afterward, whether they live together to the end of their lives or separate in a short year, they belong to one another; are brother and sister.

The blood-letting ceremony may have something to do with the Tchen and Gan legend, but the oath to free one another when love has left the heart is certainly based upon the long experience of a civilization that has ceased to exist.

I fancy that in the dark long ago the ceremony must have read to "cherish and obey and become one and indivisible." Experience has taught differently, and the contents of the oath have been reversed. An old Nuri legend says that a people in the Hind had lost its power because the women bore children from men they did not love. The Gypsies replaced the two words "duty" and "possession" by two other words: "love" and "freedom" . . . the freedom of love and the love of freedom.

"Worldly goods which you possess own you and destroy you. Love must be like the blowing wind, fresh and invigorating. Capture the wind within walls and it becomes stale. Open tents, open hearts. Let the wind blow." Thus runs a Gypsy song. . . .

III—THE MACEDONIAN GYPSY

HERE ARE MORE GYPSIES IN MACEDONIA, ONCE so powerful under Philip and Alexander the Great, than anywhere else in the world. Every second man or woman between the Pindus, the Olympus of Thessaly and the Rhodope, in the mountains, plains, and valleys of Macedonia, is Gypsy or of Gypsy origin.

There are so many Tziganes, they clog the roads and crowd out what is not of their kind. They are continually going to or coming from Syria, from Central Asia, from Egypt, the Caucasus, from Persia, France, and Bulgaria. They are always on the go, always there, speaking all languages, plying all trades, wearing the costumes of a hundred countries, and well versed in the intrigues, the politics, and the latent vices and peculiarities of the crowned heads and powerful men, from one end of the world to the other.

The homes of the pashas and viziers, and the harems of the sultans can keep no secrets from them. The Gypsy woman enters where no one else does, and one experienced, furtive look is enough for her to understand anything. Every time a pasha changes a favorite, some Gypsy woman knows it even before the pasha himself is quite aware of what he is about to do.

Macedonia is the one home of the Gypsies today. Unable, because so numerous, to live by the usual occupations of the race, they have skilled themselves in other trades. They are the best reapers, and are in great demand as farm laborers during the harvesting season. They are booksellers, tailors, shoemakers, mechanics, bricklayers, carpenters, barbers, besides being musicians, singers, dancers, bear-tamers, snake-charmers, acrobats, and unsurpassable showmen. A fair without a Gypsy showman's tent is unthinkable in Macedonia as well as in Serbia or Bulgaria. A Gypsy showman can give an interesting performance with only a mongrel dog, two fleas, and a fly as actors. The Gypsy can talk so entertainingly the audience forgets it has been cheated.

The mountains and plains of Thessaly are dotted and studded with villages of gaily painted mud huts and colored tents, helter-skelter everywhere, as though strewn by a giant hand of a playful god . . . villages of a thousand intense souls, feverishly active, imaginative, as noisy in sorrow as in joy, passing rapidly from one emotion to another; as if life were a musical composition with scherzos following adagios, and andantes merging abruptly with allegros and tempestuous prestos.

In one tent, a whole family is loudly mourning a son or husband who has failed to return at the appointed time. In the adjoining tent, four families are celebrating just as loudly the return of one of theirs from Siberia. Friends and relatives listen to the descriptive tales of the wanderer, to the new songs he has heard, and to news of the *pralos,* the brothers, he has met. The unfortunate family is called in to the happy one, to be consoled. Soon they all laugh and cry, embrace and fight one another.

"How are you, brother? Where do you come from?"

"Sar mai san, pralo! Katar avas?"

Everybody is welcome to the food, the wine, the songs—and the fight.

If a stranger happens to be in the camp, he is invited to cry with the mourning women if he looks good (*mishto*) and has the face of a *kako,* an "uncle." Any man who knows what sorrow is . . . who has suffered much . . . is a *kako,* brother to my father, brother to my mother. A true Gypsy recognizes such a man at a glance.

Such scenes take place in a dozen tents at one time, any day of the year. Births, funerals, weddings are celebrated in common, by all, in groups, while the smith stands with one hand on the bellows-handle and holds with the other the iron in the hissing fire, and another long-haired Gypsy teaches a newly caught bear to dance by compelling him to walk upon a large iron plate placed over a slow fire.

And what handsome men! What beautiful women! Clean-limbed, with faces as though chiseled out of a beautifully grained block of bronze in which there has been poured a generous quantity of copper. And the rhythm of their gait! The dignity of posture! What nobility! A race of kings and queens! No wonder the natives call them "Pharons," Egyptian princes!

The purest Gypsy is spoken in Macedonia. It is a complete language with a definite grammar and a full vocabulary, almost unspoiled by other languages, except for the slight sprinkling of Greek words. Neither Slav nor Arab words have squeezed themselves in the Calo of the Macedonian Gypsies. When a wanderer returns from distant travels, he is first *sitarit* . . . cleansed of the impure words he has brought with him, and loudly corrected by everybody when he introduces a foreign word in his speech: *"Calo, pralo!* Speak, Calo, brother!"* his friends call to him. Conscious of the purity of their language, they strive to keep it unsoiled by words brought from the outside.

Legends and stories tend to prove the Gypsies have been in Macedonia long before the appearance of the Roms in the west of Europe, . . . that they were there centuries before they crossed into Bulgaria and rowed themselves over the Danube into Roumania and thence over the Carpathians into Hungary.

The language of the other Gypsies has been corrupted with words of the languages of the peoples they have lived with, while the Gypsies of Macedonia still speak the purest Calo. Now, if it be true, that the cradle of the race is in India, all of them have had to follow the same route and share the same fate. How did it happen that the Gypsies of Macedonia have been able to keep their language pure, whereas the others have not?

Except for Gypsy legends, there are no facts to prove my contention that the first Gypsies have been brought to Europe by Alexander the Great. The great Macedonian genius, whose mind's eye could scan more space at one time than the eye of any other man has embraced, was a great admirer of Homer, whose works he always carried with him, everywhere, in a golden cassette, the gift of Aristotle. From Homer, Alexander learned of the existence of the Sygynes, "the people so beloved of Vulcan because of their skill at the forge."

Did Alexander first come upon the Sygynes in India, or did he discover them in Babylonia after defeating Darius, for whom they worked as artificers?

The Persians have never been skilled iron-workers. The Phœnicians had been made to work for Alexander, who had possessed himself of their arsenals. However, Alexander discovered the Sygynes somewhere, and dispatched them under friendly escort (for it is unthinkable that he should have behaved brutally to a people so highly recommended by Homer and beloved by Vulcan) to Pella, the capital of Macedonia. Alexander's victories had enriched his people beyond their wildest dreams. From a mud-hut town, Pella had become a resplendent capital. Wealthy merchants and retired captains had drawn much gold from Asia. But Persia had effeminated them with its luxuries and comforts.

Now the wealthy men desired to introduce the new things into Macedonia. Macedonians who had not taken off their animal skin clothes in years yearned for daily hot baths. If the truth be stated, hot baths destroyed Macedonia. Asia won its greatest victories by corrupting the primitive foes to cleanliness and hot water.

The Sygynes were skilled workmen. They had not been sent to Pella as slaves. They had traversed the countries lying between their homeland or wherever Alexander had come upon them, and their new home, so rapidly that they had had no time, and there had been no necessity, to learn new languages. Old Gypsies are certain that Alexander was one of their own blood, the son of Olympias by a Gypsy she had loved before she married Philip of Macedonia. Well, for all we know, it may be true, may explain many sides of Alexander's character.

There are Greek numerals in the language of the

Gypsies of all countries. "Seven, eight, nine, ten," are counted as *efta, ofto, enea, deca,* by the Gypsies of Russia, Spain, England, America, and Africa. Yet only the Macedonian Gypsies count in Greek altogether: *ena, dis, tris, tesra, penda,* and not *jek, duoi, tren, shtar, pantsh,* etc., as do the others.

The Gypsies of Macedonia are of a purer type and have more of their own unborrowed traditions than the Gypsies of other countries.

In Macedonia the Gypsies are a people and not a horde, and their speech is a language, not a local jargon. They do not feign the humility that other Gypsies feign, are cleaner, healthier, more courageous, and incline more toward highway robbery than toward beggary. They are feared, not despised. Macedonian Gypsies have served as mercenaries for hundreds of years in the Balkan wars, and were always preferred as body-guards by the old-time boyars and feudal lords.

Elsewhere, the Gypsies have mixed with the scum of every nation, and have absorbed large numbers of peoples who were Gypsy only in their trades, habits, and mode of life. When the Gypsies arrived in Macedonia—gently led there by the genius of Alexander, who loved to transplant whole populations and races from the mountains to the valleys, and from the seas to river shores—the floating population of the whole country was in Asia, fighting beside their young leader.

Physically, the Gypsies were superior to the native population whose able-bodied men were far away.

Macedonian families sought blood-alliances with the Greeks, who despised them; but they did not mix with this strange, barbaric, though capable, race who worked so well, and amused them with music and dance.

Thus the Gypsies were allowed to live their lives and speak their own language. That Greek numerals replaced their own was chiefly because of the communistic life of the Gypsies. The *barossan,* the chief, was the ruler, the law. What anyone got for his labors, or in barter, was communal property. There was very little counting necessary amongst the Gypsies themselves; but their dealings were with Greeks, sharp tradesmen whose wits had to be matched. One had to count four times when giving or receiving money. Numbers, figures, were the life of life! In the East, when a Greek arrives at a strange town, the merchants ask him how much money will persuade him to stay away from the market-place. If they can't induce him to leave the town or accept the bribe, in a year's time he owns everything the other Greeks don't already own. Sharp traders, the Greeks!

The Calo people multiplied rapidly in Macedonia, and began to spread out, more because of necessity than desire, tempted by great promises from other communities in the Balkans in need of skilled craftsmen. All blacksmiths in Greece, Turkey, Macedonia, Serbia, Bulgaria, Roumania, and Hungary are Gypsies. Wherever you hear hammer upon anvil, you are certain to find a *pralo.*

Who did the necessary iron-work in these agricultural countries before the Gypsies came?

How long did the golden epoch of the Macedonian Gypsies last?

Alexander dead, his empire crumbled. The bridge he had built from the Hellespont to India broke down because of its own weight, when death had flattened out the shoulders upon which had rested the arches.

Macedonia became a Roman province 146 years before the birth of Christ. Sygynes, Tshingians, were taken prisoners to Rome; others fled in small groups, and dispersed everywhere. Some hid in the mountains, others remained to serve the new masters. The Romans pressed on. They colonized Macedonia with retired soldiers. When Emperor Marcus Ulpius Trajan conquered the countries along the Danube and distributed the land among his legionaries, the Gypsies were already there, having broken away from the main stem in Macedonia.

There are over seven hundred thousand Gypsies in the Balkan Peninsula, and only a hundred and fifty thousand in the rest of Europe. It is unimaginable that they should have multiplied themselves from the few hundred that appeared in occidental Europe five hundred years ago. It is improbable that they should have grown into such numbers from the supposed group that was driven out of India by Tamerlane in the fourteenth century, or the prisoners taken by the Byzantians at Ainzarba according to Arab documents. The stem out of which issued the fighters against Walid I may have been the same that gave forth the race Alexander brought to Macedonia, only of a later growth, another group, a subsequent migration of people that fled from Macedonia at the approach of the Romans.

India, where the other castes treated them as impure slaves, was not a pleasant memory to cherish. Had the Gypsies been treated worse in Macedonia than in their homeland, they would have remembered India, just as the Jews remembered the flesh-pots of Egypt when suffering hunger in the Syrian desert. The Gypsies had no reason to be proud of their origin, and no desire to speak to others, or even amongst themselves, of the "good old times." They had no written records to keep alive beyond the individual human life, but they kept their language as untainted as their bodies.

The Jews in Spain, during the golden age in which they lived unmolested amongst both Christians and Moors, spoke the purest Hebrew, while the Jews living in countries where they were persecuted lost their original tongue little by little and adopted a jargon from the language of a people anything but friendly to them. Yiddish, the language spoken by millions of Jews, is derived from German. No people have willingly adopted the language of a friendly nation or race. Foreign languages are imposed, not adopted; it was so thousands of years ago, and is the same today.

Macedonia should therefore be regarded as the home of the Gypsies. It is in Macedonia that they have developed their independence and character, that they have developed their arts and crafts; there they have worked and sung, free men, in a freedom they had not enjoyed in India. *Ubi bene, ibi patria.*

To this day, the people of Thessalian towns and villages do not regard the Gypsy as an inferior being, and there has never been any attempt to compel him to change his mode of life or his manner of dress. There is no Macedonian youth in love who would not walk a hundred miles over mountains to hear a "pharon" sing the song of "the girl who was changed into a flower," and have the Gypsy women *draber* his future.

"San tu Rom?" ("Are you a Gypsy?")

No answer.

"San tu Macedonsky Rom?" ("Are you a Mace-

donian Gypsy?") And the tall brown man looks gaily
into your eyes, as he says:

"*Da tchte san, pralo.* [Yes, I am that, brother.]
Lente. [Of them.] *Piavta.* [Let's drink to our
health.]"

There is no Macedonian who would not drink with
a Gypsy when invited to do so. And if it happens before the tent of the Tzigane, the *Daia* will have a bite
for the men to eat before the first glass is emptied.

The legend of the fourth nail, which I heard in
Macedonia, shows that the Gypsies were traveling back
and forth from Macedonia to Egypt and Palestina long
before the beginning of the Christian era.

"When the Roman jailers were given the person of
Yeshua ben Miriam, whom the world later called
Jesus, that they should crucify him, because he had
talked ill of the Emperor of Rome, two soldiers were
sent out to get four stout nails.

"For every man to be crucified, the soldiers were
given eighty kreutzer to buy nails from some blacksmith. And so when these soldiers were given their
eighty kreutzer with which to buy nails, they first tar-
ried at an inn and spent half of the coppers drinking
the sweet-sour wine the Greeks then sold in Jerusalem.
It was late in the afternoon when they remembered the
nails again, and they had to be back in the barracks
by nightfall; for early the following morning they were
to crucify Yeshua ben Miriam, the Jew who had talked
ill of the Emperor of Rome.

"Soon they stumbled out of the inn hastily, not altogether sober, and coming to the first blacksmith, they
said to him loudly, so as to frighten him into doing the

work even if there was not enough money to pay for the iron and the labor:

" 'Man, we want four big nails made right away, to crucify Yeshua ben Miriam with; Yeshua ben Miriam, who has talked ill of our emperor.'

"The blacksmith was an old Jew who had seen the long pale face and the light brown eyes of Yeshua ben Miriam, when he had once looked into his shop. So the man stepped out from behind the forge at which he had been working, and said:

" 'I will not forge nails to crucify Yeshua ben Miriam.'

"Then one of the soldiers put down the forty kreutzer and yelled loudly:

" 'Here is money to pay for them. We speak in the name of the emperor!' And they held their lances close to the man. The Jew looked the soldiers straight in the eyes, and said:

" 'I will not make the nails to crucify Yeshua ben Miriam.'

"Then the soldiers ran him through with their lances after setting his beard on fire.

"The next blacksmith was a little farther away. It was getting on in the afternoon when they arrived there, so they told the man:

" 'Make us four stout nails and we shall pay you forty kreutzer for them.'

" 'I can forge only four small nails for that price,' the man said.

"But the soldiers showed him how large they wanted the nails. The man shook his head and said:

" 'I cannot make them for that price. I have a wife and children.'

" 'Jew,' the soldiers bellowed, 'make us the nails and stop talking!' Then, they set his beard on fire.

"Frightened out of his wits, the Jew went to the forge and began to work on the nails. One of the soldiers, who tried to help at the forge, leaned forward and said:

" 'Make them good and strong, Jew; for at dawn we crucify Yeshua ben Miriam.'

"When that name was mentioned, the hand of the Jew remained poised high with the hammer. The voice of the man whom the soldiers had killed, because of his unwillingness to forge nails to crucify Jesus with, called out faintly, as if it were only the shadow of a voice:

" 'Aria, do not make the nails. They are for one of our people, an innocent man.'

"Aria dropped the hammer beside the forge.

" 'I will not make the nails,' he said.

" 'Make them!' the soldiers ordered, though they were frightened themselves, for they too had heard the faint voice of the man they had killed. Night was falling and they had drunk forty kreutzer of the eighty they had been given.

" 'I will not make them,' Aria answered stubbornly.

" 'Jew, you said you had a wife and children,' one of the soldiers pressed, coming nearer to him with his lance.

" 'I cannot forge the nails you want to crucify Yeshua ben Miriam with,' the Jew cried out, and stretched himself to his full height. 'I cannot. I cannot.'

"Both soldiers, furiously, drunkenly, ran him through with their lances again and again.

"The sun was low behind the hills and the soldiers were in great haste. They ran to a third blacksmith, a Syrian. They entered his shop while he was getting ready to leave off work for the day. Their lances were still dripping blood when they called to that man:

" 'Khalil, make us four stout nails, and here are forty kreutzer to pay for them. And be quick about it!'

"The Syrian looked at the bloody lances and returned to his bellows. But he had no sooner begun to forge the first piece of iron when the voices of the two blacksmiths who had been killed by the soldiers called to him not to make the nails. . . . The man cast his hammer aside. And he, too, was run through with the lances.

"Had the soldiers not drunk forty of the eighty kreutzer, they might have returned to the barracks and told what had happened, and thus saved Yeshua's life. But they were short of forty kreutzer, so they ran out of the gates of Jerusalem, where they met a Gypsy who had just pitched his tent and set up his anvil. The Romans ordered him to forge four stout nails, and put the forty kreutzer down.

"The Gypsy put the money in his pocket first, and then set to work. When the first nail was finished, the soldiers put it in a bag. When the Gypsy had made another nail, they put it in the bag. And when the Gypsy had made the third nail, they put it in the bag. When the Gypsy began to forge the fourth nail, one of the soldiers said:

" 'Thank you, Gypsy. With these nails we will crucify Yeshua ben Miriam.'

"He had hardly finished speaking, when the trembling voices of the three blacksmiths who had been killed began to plead with the Gypsy not to make the nails. Night was falling. The soldiers were so scared that they ran away before the Gypsy had finished forging the last nail.

"The Gypsy, glad that he had put the forty pieces of copper in his pocket before he had started work, finished the fourth nail. Having finished the nail, he waited for it to grow cold. He poured water upon the hot iron but the water sizzled off, and the iron remained as hot and red as it had been when held between the tongs in the fire. So he poured some more water upon it, but the nail was glowing as if the iron was a living, bleeding body, and the blood was spurting fire. So he threw still more water on it. The water sizzled off, and the nail glowed and glowed.

"A wide stretch of the night-darkened desert was illumined by the glow of that nail. Terrified, trembling, the Gypsy packed his tent upon his donkey and fled.

"At midnight, between two high waves of sand, tired, harassed, the lone traveler pitched his tent again. But there, at his feet, was the glowing nail, although he had left it at the gates of Jerusalem. Being close to a water-well, the Gypsy carried water the rest of the night, trying to extinguish the fire of the nail. When the last drop had been drawn out of that well, he threw sand on the hot iron, but it never ceased sizzling and glowing. Crazed with fear, the Gypsy ran farther into the desert.

"Arriving at an Arab village, the blacksmith set up his tent the following morning. But the glowing nail had followed him.

"And then something happened. An Arab came and

asked him to join and patch the iron hoop of a wheel. Quickly the Gypsy took the glowing nail and patched with it the broken joint of the iron hoop. Then he saw with his own eyes how the Arab drove off.

"The Arab gone, the Gypsy drove away without daring to look around. After many days, still not daring to look around, afraid to open his eyes when night fell, the Gypsy reached the city of Damascus, where he set up his forge again.

"Months later, a man brought him the hilt of a sword to repair. The Gypsy lighted his forge. The hilt began to glow, made from the iron of the nail upon the hilt. The Gypsy packed, and ran away again.

"And that nail always appears in the tents of the descendants of the man who forged the nails for the crucifixion of Yeshua ben Miriam. And when the nail appears, the Gypsies run. It is why they move from one place to another. It is why Yeshua ben Miriam was crucified with only three nails, his two feet being drawn together and one nail piercing both of them. The fourth nail wanders about from one end of the earth to the other."

It is difficult to write the history of any people . . . even when there are records establishing important facts of crucial points in the development of that nation. It is considerably more difficult to write the history of a race not confined within limiting borders, nor submitted to the same climatic, economic, and political conditions. The story of each group of Gypsies is different from that of another. The frame for the picture is larger than the image itself. One should write the history of every nation with which the Gypsies have lived, before attempting to give even a faint portrayal of what happened to the Black Brothers.

Sharing the vicissitudes of every nation and the joys of none, tolerated in one place and tracked like wild beasts in another, driven off the roads into the forests and back again from hiding-places into the open villages, compelled to live a nomadic life in one country and forced in another to domestic occupations . . . the wonder is not that the Gypsies have maintained themselves as a unit as they have, but that they have not totally disappeared.

What happened to the Gypsies of Macedonia during centuries can be surmised only by delving into the history of the Macedonians. If the Gypsies were there since the time of Alexander, they undoubtedly mixed with the Phœnician and Egyptian slaves which the great conqueror had driven like cattle to the capital of his country and distributed over his homeland. Undoubtedly, a number of Gypsies had been sent to work in the arsenals of some of Alexander's allies, and it is in that direction that one may find the solution of the problem that so many philologists, historians, and scientists have sought to unravel. Living in Macedonia with the Egyptian and Phœnician slaves, the best artizans of their time, it is reasonable to suppose that the three races mixed freely. This might be the explanation for the frequently recurring Egyptian type among the Gypsies—a type we see on the bas-reliefs of Egyptian monuments.

In the lower Balkan Peninsula, in Bulgaria, Hungaria, and Roumania as well, the Gypsies are called Pharons by the people.

It is possible that the Gypsies who appeared in the

fifteenth century, in western Europe, claiming to be Egyptians, believed themselves to be so. They had been called Pharons for centuries. When they lived among Phœnicians and Egyptians, intermarriage among these three peoples of more or less similar tendencies and abilities must have been so frequent the native population grouped them in one name. As the memory of the life of the Jats in India had not been worthy of being cherished, the ancestors of the Gypsies willingly accepted the new name that blotted out so well the memory of their original state in India. Pharons they were called; so be it, Pharons. Yes, we are Pharons!

The people of the Lower Balkans are a mixture of all races . . . the remnants and stragglers of the invaders of Europe mixed with the blood of slaves brought there by kings who had sought glory in Asia. The Gypsies are a crystallization of the original stock, mixed with Phœnicians and Egyptians. From Macedonia the Gypsies spread over the rest of the world. The reservoir from which they overflowed into occidental Europe is in Macedonia.

"I have seen you where you never were and never will be.
And yet in that very place you can be seen by me.
For to tell what they do not know is the art of the Romany."

IV—The Gypsies in Roumania

HE GYPSIES WERE ALREADY ON THE BANKS OF the Danube when the Roman legions appeared to dislodge the Daci who inhabited the country. Official frontiers, however, were no obstacles to Gypsies who knew there were people living on the other side of the Danube with whom one could trade. Groups of Gypsies infiltrated amongst them. Larger numbers followed. The Roman legionaires allowed the Gypsies to live as they had always lived without any interference. It was only after the original Roman stock had become diluted with people of other races and nationalities that these principles of autonomy were discarded and the government began to interfere with the daily life of the different populations living within its confines.

Slav, Greek, Turkish, and Levantine blood poured in broad streams into what is now known as Roumania. There are references to Gypsies in Wallachian and Moldavian documents of the ninth, tenth, eleventh, and twelfth centuries. The ancestors of the Gypsies brought to the Danube the original stock of the enormous herds of domesticated buffaloes, *bivols,* now grazing in the marshes when not yoked to the plows or the two-wheeled peasant carts. The *bivolars* along the Danube are a race apart, and may be of the same stock that fought Walid I for the rights to graze their herds.

Some years ago, while living with these Gypsy cattle-breeders, I witnessed a scene that gave me a taste of what these bivolars must have been like when on the war-path.

The Gypsies, about two hundred of them, had arrived on the marshes, driving some six hundred head of black water-buffaloes before them. Fifty-two wheeled carts, each pulled by four of these cattle, had preceded the main body by about two hours. The tents were pitched, and the kettles were on the triangles over hastily built fires, when the enormous black horde, mooing and bellowing, appeared in the distance. The dogs kept them in a compact mass. The grazing was still good though it was rather late in the fall. I judged that the grass would last no longer than a couple of days. There were, all in all, over a thousand head of cattle. The bulls were driven behind a transportable fence; the cows were driven off with stocks by the naked boys and girls who shouted their loudest.

Before nightfall, the black buffaloes roamed slowly and peacefully everywhere, rolling themselves in every bog and hole. The odor exhaled by these animals is so strong even Gypsies burn powder upon wood to avoid suffocation.

Noticing one tent that was pitched quite apart from the others, I knew something extraordinary had happened, or was about to happen. I knew also that the decision to leave the former grazing place for this one had been made very suddenly. More than that I did not know.

The tents fixed for the night and the food eaten, the developments were not slow. Mira, one of their own, was called to account for having abducted the daughter of a high military officer, who was in love with him. His action had put them all in great danger. They had fled their former camp to give themselves a few hours ahead of the authorities sure to come after them. Mira, a tall, broad-shouldered, long-haired, dark devil stood before his elders and listened, with lowered head, to the incrimination of his behavior.

"Did you know what was going to happen?"

"I love her."

"You put the whole tribe and its wealth in danger."

"I love her."

"If they lay their hands on you, they will kill you."

"I love her."

Then, the accusers rose, embraced him and pressed him to their hearts. A man who loved a woman so much that he did not hesitate to endanger his tribe, his wealth, and his life was worthy of his tribe, its wealth, and his own life.

As they were still talking, scouts came running to tell that a "whole army was coming upon them."

In less time than it takes to tell the story, the penned bulls were set free, and they and the dogs drove the great herd into a compact black mass forward toward the two hundred or more cavalrymen. . . . The Gypsies remained to drive the cattle ahead. The long-necked buffaloes rushed madly at the cavalrymen. The horses reared, unseated many and, caught off balance by the herd, were pressed back. The soldiers hacked away with their swords, but their weapons did not seem to make any serious impression upon the thick black hides.

The fire of battle was in the eyes of big and little, of old and young Gypsies.

"Tarro . . . Tarro . . . Tarraho!" they called to their cattle, driving them at top speed. Some of the young girls and boys climbed stark naked on the necks of the animals, and sped them on. Meanwhile, the tents were folded and the carts were made ready.

"Tarro . . . Tarraho!"

A gun was fired by a soldier.

"Tarr . . . Tarr . . . Tarraho!"

No one was hit. But the report of the gun had awakened all the dormant, savage devils, asleep for centuries in the breasts of these men.

"Tarr . . . Tarr . . . Tarraho!"

The Gypsies began to lash the buffaloes with their heavy leather-plaited whips, and stampeded them. Nothing could now resist the forward-running, monstrous mass of black bellowing flesh.

"The army" turned heels, and ran.

The chief of the bivolars shouted an order to the dogs and the youngsters. The herd veered and ran in a straight line toward the Danube. The ones who had been yoked to the carts, however, stopped, each near his own, and bent their long necks. The main herd swam across the Danube into Bulgaria. The carts drove off in different directions. Mira, holding a swooning woman with one hand, was clinging to the neck of a buffalo with the other.

In less than a half-hour, except for a few crippled military horses and broken swords, there was no sign of what had taken place. The herd had disappeared in the wooded shore of the Bulgarian side of the Danube. Thus did the bivolars defend the happiness of one of their own.

An hour later, when a "whole army" came riding top

speed, shooting as it rode, all that was left was the pungent odor that hung about for miles and miles and hours and hours.

When the persecutions against the Gypsies of occidental Europe reached an unbearable point, they flocked back to Roumania in such numbers that they became a real problem, and the authorities had to take protective measures and legislate against them.

There are 300,000 Gypsies living today in Roumania. The old civil code of Moldavia declares that although slavery was against the natural rights of man, it has nevertheless been practiced from time immemorial, without, however, the master having any rights over the life of the slave. Thereafter, the civil code regulated the life of the Gypsies, stating that they should be considered not as things, but as individuals, that a Gypsy should have the right to ask the protection of the law against too cruel a master.

Before these laws had been enacted, the Moldavian Gypsies, having foreseen what was to come, crossed into Wallachia, which was then a separate country. But the Wallachian prince was not long in following the example of his Moldavian brother. The greater number of Gypsies became slaves of the reigning houses.

Each boyar, each landowner, acquired a number of Gypsy slaves who were housed and quartered much in the manner of Negroes in America, and practically subjected to the same treatment. The Gypsy women became wet-nurses, cooks, and housemaids. The men attended to the horses in the stables, were coach-drivers, blacksmiths, shoemakers, and musicians. Some of the boyars, living like feudal barons in castles, organized small armies of Gypsies. Slaves were bought and sold in the open market on a block, and passed from owner to owner together with land, houses, cattle, and goods.

Still, as the Gypsies perished when compelled to stay long in one place, the kinder of the boyars allowed one member of each family to roam freely over the country, while the rest of the clan remained as pawns in the court of the boyar to insure the return of the absent ones. Gypsy gold prospectors of Moldavia and Wallachia paid a yearly contribution to the treasury of the landowner. The contributions they paid took out so much of the little they received for the gold found by them that the average earning capacity of an *aurari,* a gold prospector, was never higher than ten cents a day. But he owned the roads, the fields, the forest, and was his own master.

Another class of wandering Gypsies were the *ursari,* the bear-tamers. There were neither theaters nor concert-halls in those days, and the people as well as the boyars were clamoring for amusement. The Gypsies furnished entertainment. They formed wandering circuses of jugglers, acrobats, athletes, tight-rope walkers, ball-tossers, and sleight-of-hand men, with performing goats, donkeys, and horses. They were also snake-charmers and wrestlers.

To this day, Gypsies leading huge Carpathian bears, followed by women warming a half-dozen snakes in their bosoms, can be seen pacing the roads and side-paths from one end of Roumania to another. Most of these *ursari* travel in single families and not in tribes. The patteran indicates among them the road by which they have traveled, and the direction they have taken. While the head of the family is dancing the bear in

front of an inn, the wife is busy elsewhere telling fortunes or working charms for some peasant women, or
telling the wife of the boyar how to retain the love
of her husband.

The children, ranging from three to thirteen years of
age, are already foraging for themselves. As soon as
a Gypsy mother has allowed her child to climb out of
the bag in which it has been carried on her back, it is
supposed to shift for itself; and it does. It frequently
happens that night overtakes the husband five or six
miles away from his wife, who has remained behind
somewhere for some reason or other. The bear-tamer
lies down to sleep beside his bear, while the wife makes
her bed where sleep overtakes her. The children, too,
may be separated from one another by two or three
miles. Each of them will crawl to sleep into some hole
beside a barn or chicken-coop.

However, before the village awakens, the family
celebrates a noisy reunion, for they never start the day
before they have found one another again. The patteran, two twigs or leaves placed in a certain way on
the road every few hundred feet, has served as road-
post. The manner in which the patteran is placed
tells a Gypsy more than the most explicit letter could.
A four-year-old child knows a patteran. The patteran
is indeed a language in itself, understood only by
people of the blood.

The youngest of the family, probably not older than
four or five, supplies the breakfast for all . . . a fat
chicken or two. Begging or stealing, he may even have
collected more money than any of the others. It is
interesting to watch such a little brown rascal fish for
ducks. Lying flat on the stomach, he floats a wormed

hook on the duck pond or river. When the fowl has swallowed the bait and the hook, it is gently pulled to the shore. Chicken and geese are caught on the road in the same manner.

On the outskirts of the large towns of Roumania— Bucharest, Braila, Galatz, Jassy, and Craiova—are whole streets occupied by more or less sedentary Gypsy families. These Gypsies are mostly musicians, who have long since mixed with the poorer population that lives upon the fringes of the cities. Though the Gypsy type prevails, they are, in a sense, half-breeds. The children of the sedentary Gypsies go to school and mingle with the children of the native population, though neither teacher nor schoolmate ever forgets to put the Gypsy in his place by reminding him of the fact that he is a Pharon. Sedentary Gypsies are like caged sparrows; like pheasants in a chicken-coop. Every epidemic hits them first.

The sale of newspapers on the streets of Bucharest is entirely in the hands of Gypsy girls. The flower women in the cafés and gardens are magnificent specimens of Gypsy women. The men sell fruit and vegetables, which they carry in two baskets that hang from a flexible yoke over their shoulders. There is no music but Gypsy music in Roumania. Even the songs of the peasants are Gypsy songs. All melodic life, not only of Roumanians but of all the peoples of the Balkan Peninsula and probably beyond its borders, is of Gypsy origin.

Had it not been for the Gypsies, the Roumanian folk-lore would have perished before anyone had thought of fixing it upon paper. Some years ago, a folk-lore collector took down from the mouth of one single old

Gypsy in Braila—Pop-Ratazan—over five thousand verses. Braila, a Danube town, has contributed the best musicians of the country. The earning capacity of some of the Gypsy violinists of that town, who are much sought after, compares favorably with that of the best-paid concert performers in Europe and even America. Figures like Barbu Lautaru, Coshma and Barleaza, have become as legendary as the country's heroes.

Some years ago, Dinicu, a famous violinist and cellist, became director of the Conservatory of Bucharest, and were it not for the fact that some of my Roumanian friends would object to my "telling tales out of school" I could name at least a dozen of the most famous musicians and poets who are of Gypsy origin.

Yet little by little, a certain Gypsy element loses its identity and originality, and is absorbed by the lower strata of the population.

There are many villages in Moldavia and Wallachia composed of a mixture of peasants and Gypsies. Before slavery was abolished in Roumania, the Gypsies were not the only serfs, for most of the peasants were also considered as such by their boyars. Land was distributed among the former slaves. The Gypsies born within the slave enclosures of the boyars claimed their share of land, and many of them obtained it and settled upon it. But the law which had liberated them also forbade them to travel from one place to another.

Thousands of Gypsies abandoned their land-holdings, infested the roads and held them against travelers, robbing and compelling merchants to pay them tribute. The Roumanian government acted against the nomads with such severity that many of those who had

left their original homes returned quickly to their
claims, or begged the boyar to retain them in his employ. Thus, for example, upon the domain of Prince
Bibesco, there are several hundred families who persist in living there and demand that they be provided
for. They refuse to take into consideration the Act
of Liberation.

"You are our boyar, prince. You must take care
of us."

Among the Gypsy musicians in Braila, there was
none better known, more esteemed and respected than
Barleaza. He was already an old man when it was
thought proper that he should teach me to play the
fiddle. At his house I met youngsters of my age from
the "better" families of the town. This Barleaza was
a massively built, broad-shouldered man, whose very
dark face looked priestly, crowned and framed in a
shock of snow-white hair. Loved and sought after as
he was by all the boyars and wealthy merchants of the
surrounding country, he had amassed a huge fortune.

There were only two kinds of families within a
radius of a hundred miles . . . those at whose weddings Barleaza *had* played, and those at whose weddings he *had not* played. To have Barleaza play at two
successive weddings proved even more; it proved that
he had been royally paid for the first one. Barleaza
never took money in his hands. He appeared at a
wedding only on condition that another band play the
dance music. He and the five men of his band im-
provised for the assembled guests and connoisseurs,
who retired with him to a separate room. His violin
playing could make people so gay that they forgot
worries and sorrows and became young again. He

could make the gayest of men and women cry out in pain and weep on his shoulders. His violin laughed and cried; grinned and sobbed.

Having played, Barleaza laid his fiddle on the table, and allowed the fortunate ones to throw gold coins through the slits of the fiddle. If the number of gold pieces was to his liking, Barleaza would come again at a later festival. If it was not, he would answer the people who called him that there were other musicians in Braila, as good as he, who needed bread and clothes for their children. He was the Gold Violinist. Never yet had a silver piece desecrated his violin.

At the death of a rich boyar, his heir came from Paris to take possession of his father's domain. The mourning period over, the other boyars decided to entertain their neighbor, and show him what a joyous time there could be in the homeland. There were about twenty guests. The party was held in the castle of Boyar K——. Barleaza was called upon to furnish the music. The young boyar, who had never heard of Barleaza, marveled at first at the Gypsy's playing, but was annoyed by the familiarity between the Gypsy and the guests.

"You are spoiling that Tzigane," the young Parisian told his friends. The strong wine was mounting to his head. Paris had not blotted out the prejudice against the erstwhile slaves of his deceased father.

His friends tried to quiet him, telling him of the greatness of Barleaza, of his marvelous playing, of the pleasure and joy he had given them. But the young man protested that they were too friendly with the Tzigane. When Barleaza had placed his violin on

the table, the boyars began to drop gold pieces into it.
The young man from Paris questioned:

"What is that? Why don't you give him the money
in his hand? And why only gold?"

"But Barleaza never receives money in his hand.
He is our Gold Violinist. His violin has never been
polluted by the baser metals."

"Nonsense! He'll take money in his hands when I
offer it to him. Here, Tzigane!" And he laid on the
table a handful of copper and silver pieces. "Take
it!"

Barleaza shook his snow-white head and smiled into
the face of the young man. "Your father would not
have done such a thing. Do let me play for you a
melody your father loved."

But the young boyar was drunk, furious and stubborn.

"First take in your hand the money I have put on
the table!"

The other boyars were too drunk to interfere. Barleaza turned around and looked at them pleadingly.
Why did they not explain? Before anyone had said a
word, the young man from Paris had pressed his re-
volver against the Gypsy's breast, and, pointing to the
pile of copper and silver coins on the table, demanded
for the last time that he take it. Barleaza merely
smiled and shook his head. The trigger was pulled.
Barleaza fell back dead.

Splinters of Barleaza's violin are inlaid in violins
of Gypsies playing in Paris, London, Berlin, and New
York . . . everywhere. Among Gypsy musicians,
fragments of Barleaza's violin are carried like relics,
framed in gold and set with precious stones.

There is one Gypsy element which, though very dangerous, is the most interesting, because it has remained the purest. The Laeshi have remained untainted, independent, and have preferred death to slavery or domesticity. Darker than the other Gypsies, almost as black as full-blooded Negroes, taller, broader, lighter on their feet, with long glossy wavy hair hanging over their shoulders, eyes as black as coal, and teeth as white as pearls, with arched noses coming straight down from the foreheads, full-lipped and long-necked, they are the handsomest specimens of Europe.

They are of so independent a nature that they do not submit even to their own chiefs and never travel in large groups. They do not camp in open spaces. One finds them only in ravines, in the mountains, and in the forests. They have never sought any relation with white people, and avoid intercourse with the other Gypsies, whom they consider traitors to the race. They so hate the white people that they never attempt to amuse them, and they despise the Gypsy musicians because they have condescended to sing songs and play at the weddings and festivals of the *Gajo,* and because they have outwardly accepted the faith of their neighbors.

A Laeshi comes out of the forest or the ravines of the mountains only when it is absolutely necessary. They are seen at horse-fairs, where they exchange a doctored donkey against a milch-goat, a glandered horse against a cow, and where they always get the better of a bargain with Jew, Greek, or Gypsy. The fascination of their eyes is so strong they induce people to buy or sell things which they have never wanted to buy or sell. They literally hold one in a spell by the fixity of their glance. Their voices are so hypnotizing, one is mesmerized into doing their will.

The Laeshi are a very handy people with tools. Each of them is a skilled mason, a skilled blacksmith, a skilled carpenter, a skilled mechanic; there is no trade in which he can be surpassed. But Laeshi work for white men only long enough to supply their immediate wants. None of them ever possesses anything reserved for the morrow.

Prince Cuza, the first ruler of the United Principalities of Moldavia and Wallachia, who had known these Gypsies very closely, ruled that a white man should be punished with five years' imprisonment for the theft of a horse, but a Laeshi Gypsy only three months for the same offense. The legislator said that three months of imprisonment for a Laeshi was equivalent to five years for a white man.

And Cuza knew, for he himself was of Gypsy origin. Very few Laeshi Gypsies survive three months of jail. There is not a lock they cannot pick; there is not a key they cannot duplicate. They can mix metals and repair copper vessels. They can forge steel and iron; they can make even needles with the most primitive tools. With these same tools they make earrings, rings, and bracelets, which they sell to the peasants. A hammer, a pair of tongs, a file, and a small home-made bellows are carried on the back of every Laeshi. His shop is wherever he happens to be. He uses the same tools for every kind of work. With these same tools he can repair watches, musical instruments, and shoes.

Their women seldom go out fortune-telling, but possess a fine knowledge of medicinal herbs. The

Gypsy women are the doctors of the country. They are called upon to set broken bones and to cure diseases of cattle.

To this day, in the small villages and towns of Roumania, the medicinal knowledge of Gypsy women is held in far greater esteem than that of the village doctor. But they never perform any service for a white man willingly. Not a crime is committed in any locality where Laeshi have been seen but it is put to their account.

In the old days it was from the ranks of the Laeshi that the executioners were engaged. The Laeshi so hated the white men they were only too willing to accept the office of executioner. This was the only work they did willingly.

There are also Gypsies wandering in large caravans under the leadership of a *bulubasha*. At the death of one bulubasha, his successor is elected by vote from the rank and file of the tribe. The authority of this bulubasha was formerly confirmed by the boyar, who invested him with power over his own people. The bulubasha used to act also as go-between for the boyar and his people, and received payment from both sides for his services. The bulubasha was law and judge, and the Gypsies were generally in far greater fear of him than they were of the state authorities. To distinguish themselves from the other Gypsies, the bulubasha dressed in gaudy fashion, wearing heavy gold rings in their ears and gold buttons on their long coats, rode on horseback and carried gilt-handled whips inside their knee-length boots. They were the only ones allowed to wear a beard and an astrakhan cap.

Today the bulubasha is no longer invested with official power, but every tribe still has its bulubasha, who, though no longer as feared as he used to be, is nevertheless as respected, and his decisions are law.

The tribe has no sooner settled on the outskirts of a town than the women and children scatter themselves, knocking at every door, selling little knicknacks and offering to explain dreams and work charms for a thousand different things. Nothing intimidates them; no door can remain closed before them. Within a few minutes, a skilful Gypsy woman has "psyched" and analyzed the woman she has been talking to, and knows exactly what she wishes, desires, or suffers, and is ready to fulfil these wishes and desires, and to alleviate any suffering. She can read the eyes and the movements of the young peasant girl whose lover is away doing military services. The boyar's wife is childless. She longs for a son. The shopkeeper's wife worries over the faithlessness of her husband. The Gypsy woman knows. For a gold piece or two, she takes it upon herself to bring the faithless one back to his wife. For a gold piece or two, the boyar's wife will give birth to a boy in a year's time. The soldier will be guarded against the evil that threatens to come upon him.

The Gypsy throws molten lead into a cupful of cold water and shows the superstitious women what is happening a hundred miles away to the husband or the son. That piece of fantastically shaped metal is the head and the body of the man. There are his hands, and there in the back of him stands the enemy ready to destroy him. "And there stands the woman who wants him for herself!" The mesmerized, superstitious peasant sees everything the Gypsy woman wants her to see in the fantastic forms of the cooled lead; and the

Gypsy pronounces words which the white woman does not understand, incantations brought down from her ancestors in Egypt.

What the Gypsy really says is: "Pig-headed fool! That you may not live to see the sun again. That your eyes should become as cold as the lead in the water!"

Watch the Gypsy woman leave the courtyard of the peasant or boyar. She has a few chickens hidden between the folds of her enormous skirt. Her left hand is closed upon coins of gold and silver. She walks swiftly to her camp, singing on the way. When her friends return to the camp-fire, they will compare earnings, not because they want the money, but because of the competition amongst them. Tonight the husband of the woman who has made the biggest haul will be king. The children will be proud of their mother. There will be a protracted feast till the wee hours of the morning. There won't be much drinking—only a little wine—but there will be singing and dancing and story-telling, and the youngsters will wrestle in the center of a circle of beautiful and excited women.

In the good old days, the boyars had a special penal code for Gypsies. Beating on the soles of the feet until the flesh hung in shreds was only one of the forms of punishment replaced by the whipping-post in 1870.

When a runaway serf was caught, his neck was placed in an iron band, lined with sharp points, so that he could neither move his head nor lie down to rest. The boyars had no right to kill their slaves, but there was nothing said against torturing them slowly to death. No law forbade the boyar to take the most beautiful girls as his mistresses, or to separate wives from husbands, and children from parents.

Yet, to this day, one drop of Gypsy blood is enough to exclude a man socially, although men of the race have held dignified posts in the kingdom. Social etiquette is law in itself, outside the pale of the laws of a country, and ignores all biological laws. In my own home town, Braila, one of my friends committed suicide, upon discovering that the grandfather of his beloved was a Gypsy.

Rasvan, one of the former princes of Moldavia, was a full-blooded Tzigane. As far as nobility of race was concerned, Rasvan had older titles than the Greeks from the Fanar of Constantinople, who were made princes by the Turks and sent to rule and exploit the countries on the Danube. This voivode Rasvan had a saintly passion for liberty, and worked and legislated to give freedom not only to the Gypsies but to the peasants as well. He had great dreams of freeing the country from the yoke of the boyars. Unfortunately, his dreams ended—like most dreams of the kind—in a horrible red reality that swept over him and those he had wanted to make happy.

Though Rasvan occupied the throne of the country, crowned and sceptered in daytime, at night he would cast off his royal accouterments and go to his own tribe encamped near by, to sleep on the bare, hard ground like the other Gypsies. When some of his relatives asked for government positions, he answered that they could have whatever they desired, but that he would behead them for the slightest deviation from what was right and just, and would hang them if they proved incompetent.

There is a tribe of Gypsies roaming in Moldavia who claim to be descendants of Rasvan. The old men tell that Rasvan, disgusted with the ways of the white world and the court intrigues, abandoned the throne, and roamed happily over the country, mending kettles and repairing scissors and shears. He told his people not to change their mode of life; for they, alone, of all people were really happy.

The grandfather of my suicide's friend's beloved was a descendant of the voivode Rasvan.

Of the wandering tribes of Gypsies, there are five or six hundred in Roumania, and not all live on amicable terms. Each tribe counts as many friendly tribes as hostile ones. When two unfriendly tribes meet in a forest or a mountain-pass, bloodshed is almost inevitable. A pitched battle, with whip, knife, stick, and pistol is begun before the horses have stopped in their tracks. Men, women, and children jump out of their wagons and rush at one another. The women brandish their small children over their heads and use them as cudgels. Even the dogs participate in such a battle.

The fight generally lasts only half an hour, but the carnage and the noise, the cries of pain and rage, are hair-raising. Suddenly, everything stops. The dead are buried. The wounded are taken care of. The wagons of the two tribes move on in different directions. The police will never know what has happened.

Occasionally such a battle ends the enmity between two tribes. The older men get together. There is much palaver. The origin of the enmity is gone into. The women, the ones whose sons have fallen in the fight and those who have lost their husbands, are allowed to sit in the council, and they chant, like a *mélopée,* their love for the lost ones and their great sorrow. When these chants have reached an almost unbearable pitch, the erstwhile enemies fall into one another's arms, screaming and yelling.

Meanwhile, the people outside the council tent have also grown friendly, and sit around fires, exchanging impressions and opinions. The "Great Cry" of the elders is the signal for those outside to embrace and hug one another. "Those who cry together, melt together."

The festivities usually last three days. Then the two tribes go their different ways—friends forever, if the two chiefs have become "blood brothers" by a scratch made on the wrist of each man, allowing a drop of blood from one to fall upon the open cut of the other. There will be no wedding tie between these two tribes for at least ten years, as long as lasts the memory of the dead. An act of unfriendliness by any member of one of these two tribes toward any member of the other is considered the worst crime, and is severely punished. The man committing such an offense is outlawed by all Gypsies, and his whole tribe is wiped out completely; without the *Gajos* ever knowing where, how and when. Such is *Leis Prala,* the law of the brotherhood.

These nomadic tribes have been accused of cannibalism, though it has never been proved, and many Tziganes have been killed with ax and pitchfork by peasants and villagers, when a child strayed from home upon the passing of a caravan.

The accusation of cannibalism was brought against the Tziganes in Hungary in the year 1782. Scores of men and women, against whom the crime had never been proved, perished in one day on the gallows. The echo of the long-drawn-out trial against the Gypsies found willing ears in Roumania; villagers and peasants remembered and imagined stories of children who were supposed to have disappeared. The slaughter, known and unknown, was terrific.

The Tziganes hid in holes dug in mountainsides, and in thick forests, living on horse-flesh and dog-flesh. When that was gone, they held the roads, robbing travelers and taking by assault the barns, fowl-yards and corrals of isolated farmers. The reprisal of the government and the people was swift and terrible. Forests were surrounded by armed men, and set fire to.

That the surviving Gypsies avenged their brothers goes without saying. For vengeance is one of the Gypsy's greatest passions, and, also, his virtue. Christian charity cannot be preached to a people who know too well those who preach it. Under the conditions in which the Gypsies lived, nothing was more reasonable than hatred, nothing more justifiable than vengeance.

As late as 1870, the first Gypsy met on the road was compelled to exercise the function of executioner. One day a Gypsy who was condemned to death was being led to his gibbet by two armed soldiers with fixed bayonets, escorted by a number of villagers. For hours and hours they walked the road, without meeting a Gypsy to execute his brother.

Finally they met an old, weak Tzigane, hardly able to stand on his feet, and charged him with the office of hanging the powerfully built culprit. The procession halted underneath a tree. The little old man was mounted upon a table to attach a rope to the limb of the tree. He then passed the noose around the neck of the condemned man, and began to fumble awkwardly as he went through the rest of the necessary operation. The old man had no experience in such matters.

The condemned Gypsy became furious at his inefficiency, broke his bands, slapped the old man in the face, and made such a racket that the two armed soldiers and the people fled. Then the condemned Tzigane quieted down, and, knowing that he had to die, calmly prepared the noose himself, and, kicking the table from underneath his feet, he finished the bungled job of the old man in proper fashion.

The town of Braila has the largest Gypsy quarters of Roumania, and is one of the oldest Gypsy settlements in the country. It has furnished the greater number of musicians, many of whom have won distinction the world over. It is true that amongst those who have gained fame, some have followed schools of music in the Occident; yet the original school was in the deep yards back of the gaily painted houses which line the long streets of the *Tzigania*—the Gypsy quarters. One finds pupils of these old teachers in Paris, Berlin, Moscow, London, and New York, as well as in Rome, Florence, and Madrid.

Along with playing the violin and other instruments, the Gypsy boys are also trained to speak several languages. It is not unusual to hear a ten- or twelve-year-old boy speak five or six tongues fluently, without knowing how to read or write any of them. The use of French is so common on the Calea Rahove it has replaced the Calo as the secret language among the Gypsies. Some of the Calo words have been Frenchified, and a number of French words have been given Calo endings.

Education being compulsory in Roumania, the

young Gypsies must go to school; and though a few have gone very far, and there are a number of school teachers, university professors, writers, and newspaper men of Gypsy origin, the majority of the people are so anxious to save their children from the school benches that they pay bribes to spare their offspring the tortures of academic learning.

Tanasi, today known as the greatest violinist of Roumania, my neighbor and playmate when we were children, pitied me greatly because my father was not rich enough to bribe my way out of school. He did not believe that I actually liked learning geography and history. He thought that my infernal pride made me accept the torture smilingly. That young Gypsy had a great affection for me. Coming to fetch me home from school every evening, he tried to amuse me.

His violin playing already earned him considerable money, part of which he lavished on pocket-knives, pocket-books and other things, which he showered on me. Unable to convince him that school was no torture for me, I ceased talking about it.

Suddenly Tanasi disappeared from his home and the street. His family did not worry, but I felt lost without his company; I had become so accustomed to his soft velvet voice and to his pity that the school hours seemed impossibly long. Every night and every morning I inquired at his home:

"Is Tanasi back?"

"No, Danaiu, but why do you worry so? I can see you don't eat or sleep. Stay with us today. Don't go to school. Poor, poor boy. And we thought your father so very rich!" And Tanasi's mother would press me to her bosom.

Finally, two weeks later, Tanasi, jubilant, happy, came to my home. It was Sunday.

"Here . . . here is money . . . I went away to earn it . . . to Bucharest. Here, one, two, three, four . . . ten gold pieces. You won't have to go to school any more!" And he hugged and kissed me and danced for joy.

He had gone away, and earned, or stolen, the money with which to save me from the torture of school benches.

When, however, Tanasi became convinced that I really liked school, he cried bitterly. I was his greatest disappointment. Though he was only twelve years old, he went to the inn and drank for three days and three nights, until his money gave out. His family did not interfere. They understood his great sorrow. When he sobered up, he refused to speak to me, left town and disappeared.

I saw him again thirty years later in Paris. He had not forgotten me, but he had not forgiven me either. . . .

Tziganes of an entirely different type are to be found in the Dodrudja, in the marshes between the Danube and the Black Sea.

There are large colonies of Tziganes in Kustendje. They have been there for centuries. They are most certainly of those who crossed from Macedonia when the Dobrudja was inhabited by nomadic Huns and Tartar tribes. The Dobrudja Gypsy has no resemblance to Gypsies anywhere else. Attracted to one another by the same mode of living, Tartar and Gypsy had mingled in the long ago, and intermarried. The Gypsies of Kustendje have Mongolian blood. Their heads are shaped like bullets; the small eyes are sunk

deep in their sockets. There are amongst them men
endowed with great wisdom of life—chiefly people
from tribes that have kept themselves pure from any
Tartar or Tcherkez taint.

The marshes of the Dobrudja hold to this day remnants of all the barbaric tribes that have invaded
Europe: Goths, Visigoths, Huns . . . remnants of the
Indo-Slav migrations. Nowhere else in Europe has
there been such a mixture of peoples as in the Dobrudja. The Calo of these half-Tartars is almost un-
intelligible to other gypsies. The men are nearly all
horsemen. There has never been a musician amongst
them, but many bayaderes, dancers of the East in Constantinople as well as in Cairo and Alexandria, have
been recruited from amongst their women. They also
affect to be faithful Mohammedans, though they are
addicted to strong drink, which is forbidden to the
faithful of Mohammed. The older women, flashing
violent reds and yellows, turbaned with green kerchiefs, and skirted with colored, baggy pantaloons,
their fingers full of rings of all shapes and forms, and
earrings dangling over their bare breasts, leave their
homes early in the morning, and never return empty-
handed. The Tzigania of Kustendje looks like a row
of dung-heaps crawled over by huge colored insects.

A number of Calo words have gone into the current
Roumanian language, and a great number of words of
Roumanian origin stud the tongue spoken by the Gypsies the world over. It is true that only in Roumania
has the Gypsy been enslaved. Yet, the rest of the world
has been so much more cruel to them that Tziganes
have considered Roumania a paradise to live in.

That the Tziganes have not been completely absorbed by the population is due to sporadic outbreaks of hatred against them, and to the aversion of natives against former slaves. Still, Gypsy blood does flow in the veins of many peasants, and there are villages where Calo is spoken fluently by the whole population.

Tziganes have risen to great fame in the country. I have already mentioned Dinicu, Ciollacu, Barleaza, Pop-Ratazan, Barbu Lautaru and the voivode Rasvan. There are a number of Gypsies in the clerical world, priests of high rank, and professors at unversities. There are a number of actors and singers of Gypsy origin at the National Theater and in the Opera at Bucharest. The younger element of the town Gypsies have lately become very conscious and proud of their old race. There have been projects for a weekly magazine, edited and published by the Gypsies in their own tongue.

Roumania without the Gypsies is as inconceivable as the rainbow without its colors, or a forest without birds.

The musical aptitude of the Roumanian Gypsies is such that they need listen only once to the most complicated concert selection to reproduce it immediately with the most delicate tone-shades. The usual instruments of the Tziganes are the violin, the *cobza* (an instrument resembling the mandolin, which is used by singers to accompany themselves), the *naiu* (a sort of Pan's Pipes), the *moscalu* (an instrument which defies description) and the *cembalo* (a primitive portable piano, played upon the open strings with two curved sticks).

At the birth of a child, the relatives of the Gypsy mother dig a hole in the ground, fill it with cold water, and bathe the new-born babe while they sing incantations. Wrapped in rags, the child is then immediately put to sleep on the bare ground; the baptism of water and earth. "Fear no water; it is thy good friend. Love the earth; it is thy best friend."

Among the wandering tribes, the mother will begin to teach the child to dance before it is a year old. At the age of two, the child will know how to steal and cheat. Before the age of five, a girl child will know how to dance the *tanana*—the racial dance consisting of leaps and lascivious poses. A Gypsy girl is a mother before she is eleven years old, though the father of the child may be three or four times older.

Some tribes are monogamous and some are not. The marriage ceremonies depend on the imagination of the parents of the bride. They are sometimes very simple, but sometimes reach such barbaric fantasies that one wonders what mind has invented them. The bride is bought and paid for. She can be divorced any time at the will of the husband, but she has the same privilege. Women and men are generally faithful to each other, yet it is not considered sinful for a woman to give herself to a white man for money. But she is killed by her husband if she as much as looks tenderly at another Gypsy. Only when she gives herself for money she does not commit adultery.

Gypsy children are never ill-treated by their parents. It is considered a greater crime to beat one's child than to beat one's parents. Children of a caravan are the most tyrannical rulers Gypsies ever endure.

At the death of a man, all his clothes are burned. A dead woman is buried with her clothes as a pillow under her head.

HE GYPSIES HAD SPREAD THEIR TENTS OVER the flats of the Pusto of Hungary long before the Magyars, led by Arpád, had taken possession of the land: such is the contention of Gypsies, and the belief of scholars like Vaillant and Bataillard. Bataillard goes so far as to maintain that the Gypsies were in Europe in the Bronze Age, and that they introduced the metal on the Continent.

The origin of the Magyars is still as nebulous as was that of the Gypsies until not long ago. The followers of Arpád accepted a culture that was not theirs, and have grown with it, but certain of their traits point them out as kin to the Gypsies. The Magyar language, in spite of a thousand years' contact with different peoples, has remained pure.

The similar intensity of hates and loves, is an indication of the common parenthood of the two races, and, like the Gypsies, the Magyars change from exuberant gaiety to deep melancholy so rapidly the moods seem to merge one into another. Like the Gypsies, the Magyars are capable of great tenderness and inhuman cruelty. It is only because they have not been persecuted as the Gypsies have been, and came to Europe as a domineering, terror-spreading horde under the leadership of a man who knew how to hold them together, and who had a conqueror's national dreams, that the Magyars have not continued to spread their tents all over the world as the Gypsies have done.

The Magyars came to Europe as a horde of nomads. They metamorphosed into a settled people on the green aprons of the Carpathians and the banks of the Theiss. Love for their horses, which grazed upon those plains, is responsible for the settling of these nomads.

It is the unconscious memory of the days when they themselves were a migratory people from the east, moving on foot and on horse westward and southward, when they themselves were feared, hunted, as the Tziganes were and are to this day—that has made the Magyars tolerate and understand the Tzigane. But the Tziganes have had to tread lightly, for their very presence was a reproach . . . like that of poor relations.

The Gypsy has never been ostracized in Hungary as he has been in other countries. Tolerated, received, the Gypsies fraternized with the people of Hungary they believed to be their kin. The Gypsies living within the confines of Hungary considered the land their own country as well as that of the settled population, and they did not attempt to evade the duties and obligations of citizens as they have in other countries. Feeling themselves Hungarians, they have served in the army, and have even espoused the hatred of the Hungarians toward their neighbors. Because the Hungarians have been, from time immemorial, enemies of the Roumanians, the Hungarian Gypsies feel the same hatred toward the Roumanian Gypsies. Because the Hungarians have always felt enmity toward the Poles, many a pitched battle has followed the meeting of Polish and Hungarian Gypsies when one or the other has crossed the border. Hungarians and Poles have never had truer frontier guards than the Tziganes.

For centuries the Gypsies have there been allowed to live their own lives, so long as they kept themselves more or less within the limits of the laws of the country. Having recognized the fact that the Gypsies were a wandering race, the Hungarians let them be, accepting them as they were, and taking advantage of their abilities as master-craftsmen and musicians.

Gypsies live in agricultural countries because they are needed there. No agricultural country in Eastern Europe has been able to get along without Gypsy blacksmiths and wagon-makers. Roumania, Hungary, Bulgaria, and Russia owe the Gypsies a large measure of thanks for the development of their agriculture in the last thousand years or so.

Not a Hungarian village but has its Gypsy blacksmith. Not a Hungarian wine-house or inn that has not its Gypsy musicians. And if it were not for the noise of the street-cars and automobiles in Budapest, the Hungarian capital would seem to be wrapped in thick layers of Gypsy music, played day and night upon the terraces of the cafés and hotels, along the shores of the Danube.

Undoubtedly, the climate, the rapid change from summer to winter and from winter to spring, without modulation, has influenced the Gypsies' choice of the Hungarian plain. The Tzigane's desire for sharp changes, his aptitude for extreme emotions, found in Hungary a climate which agreed with him perfectly. Always at the extreme poles, always treading on the thin line between security and danger, between absolute freedom and imprisonment, sudden climatic changes, from heat to cold, they find much to their liking. Those unable to adjust themselves to such a climate have perished long ago; those who have remained are immune to it.

I have seen Gypsy children, barefooted, and barelegged, playing up to their knees in snow while I, myself, shivered under my fur coat. I have seen mothers sitting upon blocks of snow outside their tents, their nude babes suckling exposed breasts, without either mother or child feeling the cold. While a terrific snow-storm was shrieking and howling, I have sat within a Gypsy tent, wrapped in everything that could be folded about me, and have listened to fiddlers. Their fingers were as nimble and dextrous as if playing in a comfortably warmed concert-hall or beside a lively wood-fire on a mild spring day somewhere in the occident of Europe.

At other times, because of the contrariness in the nature of the Gypsy, in midsummer, in the boiling sun of midday, when even the Magyar peasant was unable to stand the heat in the open field at harvest time, the Gypsy harvesters were dressed in warmer clothes than they were wont to wear on the coldest winter days, and continued to play about, as if the intense heat were just the thing they had been waiting for, as if that temperature were the one they liked best.

Like the Gypsies of Roumania, the Hungarian Gypsies are not all of the same kind. There are such who wander in single families, with only a tent or two, who never stay longer in one place than overnight, who seldom, if ever, appear in the larger towns, who are as shy as deer, holding themselves aloof even from other Gypsies.

There are horse-trading Tziganes who travel in large tribes, ruled over by a voivode. There are town

Gypsies, especially musicians, who cannot be considered nomads at all, though they do displace themselves often. These town Gypsies, like their brothers in Roumania, live on the outskirts of cities and have intermarried with the poorer population.

It is strange that, though living under such favorable conditions, among people who received them well, the Gypsy musicians should never have had the intention to express the sentiments of their neighbors for whom they played. Caring for no one but themselves, appreciating no one's feeling and no one's sentiments, the Gypsy musician has expressed only his own sentiments, and expressed them so often and with such force that he has succeeded in imposing them upon his audiences.

The character of the Hungarian was largely formed by the Tzigane musician. The Magyars have listened so often to Gypsy music, it has transformed them into Gypsies. Gypsy melodies have had an even greater penetrating power than intermarriage on a large scale would have had. And because, in some nebulous long ago, the two races once were one, the Gypsies have succeeded in awakening such of the Magyars' dormant feelings as corresponded to their own.

There is a sensible difference between the music of the Hungarian Gypsies and that of the Roumanian Gypsies.

Unable to make themselves understood and appreciated with their own music, the Roumanian Gypsies made concessions to the spirit of the people for whom they played, rhyming their own melodies to the conventional dance-figures of the Roumanians, and to the pastoral spirit of their songs. The rhythmical movement of the music of Roumanian Gypsies is totally different from that of Hungarian Gypsy music. In Hungary, the Gypsies have not found it necessary to adopt other rhythms; they have sung their own Iliads just as the *rhapsodos* of Greece once sang poems of Homer.

Hungary is the only European nation which has not, except for short intervals, separated the Gypsies from the rest of humanity and denounced them. In a country like Hungary, where there is so much distinction of class, the Gypsies have had their own internal divisions of class and society; but as a body they have not been considered inferiors by the native population.

As early as 1383—forty-four years before they appeared in Western Europe—the Gypsies were empowered by a decree of King Sigismund to choose their own magistrate from amongst themselves, this officer to be recognized and respected by their tribes throughout the country. It was recognition that the Gypsies were a separate entity, a people who had as much right to live in accordance with their own traditions as other peoples living under Hungarian laws, a recognition of the rights of minorities. Had the Hungarians themselves, together with other Balkanites, persevered on the same path, the world would have been spared many wars that were, and probably many more to come.

Before Gypsies had settled in the towns and cities, and while they were still wandering in small groups from one place to another, they were welcome guests, at the homes of peasants and the castles of barons, at the inns of villages as well as at the festivities of kings and princes. The splendor of a wedding was reckoned by the number of Gypsy musicians playing at it. At the balls of the barons and princes, the most famous Gypsies led orchestras as large as those playing today in the great symphony halls of the capitals of the world.

Speaking of Gypsy music, I have already mentioned the particular kind contributed by the Hungarian Gypsies. Liszt, Sarasate, Brahms, Schubert, and other great composers have popularized Gypsy music under their own signatures. Liszt's Hungarian Rhapsodies are but transcriptions of Gypsy melodies that he had heard on the Hungarian and Roumanian plains.

Some years ago, a Gypsy band was playing at the Ambassador Hotel in New York. I went there one night with a group of friends. The men played beautifully, and my guests were very enthusiastic. Mr. Horace Liveright, the publisher, leaned over and said to me:

"What they play is very beautiful and very touching. But, to enable me to judge of their quality as players, I should like to hear them play something I know. Would they play Liszt's Rhapsody?"

I called the leader, and repeated to him my friend's wish. The eyes of the Tzigane gleamed with pleasure. He spoke to his band, five of whom were his own brothers. When the first chord was struck, the walls of the hall seemed to disappear. The ceiling was transformed into a blue sky sprinkled with silver. The music took us down into the very depths of the Gypsy race. Our own veneer of civilization cracked. We were then lifted out of the depths by one powerful swing, and brought to such heights our dizzy heads pierced the skies to float above ethereal dream gardens. Never before, and seldom since, have I been so moved or shaken by anything I have heard or seen.

When the music stopped, the last chord dumping us back onto this world, Horace Liveright, always a critic, remarked:

"It was beautiful, marvelous! But it was not as Liszt wrote it."

I repeated these words to the leader. He raised himself to his full height, and said with great passion:

"Is it my fault that Liszt was not able to put down the music on paper as he had heard it played by my fathers?"

Known in Hungary until the eleventh century by the name of Ishmaelites, the Gypsies were ordered by Ladislaus I to be converted to Christianity and settle down as agriculturists. The Gypsies had pretended they were Mohammedans to evade church obligations. But they ate pork. And as the Magyars learned to know that neither Jew nor Moslem eats pork, and did not know the existence of other religions, pork-eating became the test of the Gypsies' religion. When in doubt as to the religion of an individual, he was offered pork. If he ate it, he was a Christian; if not, a heathen of some sort.

In 1092, Ladislaus concluded that the Ishmaelites were neither of one nor of the other religion. He ordered that they be baptized en masse, that they build churches at their own expense. The injunctions of Coloman were that if an Ishmaelite was caught eating meat during fast, even though it be pork, or carrying out other Ishmaelite usages, he was to be sent to the king, and the informer was to get his reward from the property of the accused. Like other legislation that runs counter to current usage, this also served blackmailers, who, under the guise of honest citizens, became informers when the bribe offered by the Gypsies was not superior to what they could obtain otherwise.

The occupations of these Ishmaelites, wandering merchants and blacksmiths, leaves no doubt that they were Gypsies. Still, the government was so anxious that they be absorbed by the rest of the population that according to Humphrey's "Ethnography" the law explicitly said that "an Ishmaelite must not marry his daughter to a member of his tribe, but only to a member of a Maghiar tribe."

This proves that, far from considering the Ishmaelites of inferior blood, the Magyars were anxious to better their own stock by marrying into the Ishmaelite tribes. That the Gypsies were the ones who held such mixture in abhorrence is evident by the law which imposed it upon them. That the *heathen* still sought to avoid intermarriage is shown by subsequent legislation, increased severity, and by the tale of the Arabian author and traveler of those days, Jakut, who met a group of these Ishmaelites in Aleppo. They told him that they came from a country beyond Constantinople, Hungary, where they lived in about thirty villages, of which each was the size of a small town. "But," said they, "we are persecuted by the Christians, though we cut our beards, dress in Frankish manner, bear arms and fight with the Magyars against their enemies."

The Mohammedans gave these good faithful unto Allah a great reception, and the brotherhood was satisfied.

In Aleppo, the Gypsies pretended to be persecuted Moslems who had come there to fortify themselves in their faith, and repent the sins they had committed.

Four centuries later, however, they came to Western Europe, pretending to be Christians who were persecuted by Mohammedans. What the Gypsies wanted then, as now, was to live free of any outside interference. They really did not care whether they were made Christians or not, but they fled, before the shackles of civilization were clamped on their feet. The freest bird would survive in a cage longer than a Gypsy. My own nurse, a Gypsy who was very much attached to me, once became so ill that my mother allowed her to take me to her people.

To this day, the term "Ungar" is applied by the French, Spanish, Russian, or Arab Gypsies to any of their race who arrive from another country. It is synonymous with "stranger."

The first Gypsy band appearing in Germany did not deny that they came from Hungary where they had resided. The letters from King Sigismund they carried, whether authentic or not, could not have been in the hands of people who had merely crossed a country as rapidly as Gypsies do. Many of the Ishmaelites submitted to Ladislaus' law, settled in villages, built churches and married their daughters to Magyars. There are two villages in the district of Zemplin, called Magy-Czigand, whose original founders were of these Ishmaelites. There is another such village, Cziganyocs, in the Ung Comitat, and another one, Cziganasti, in Bihar (now under Roumanian rule). There are any number of villages in Transylvania that were originally settled by Gypsies. The Gypsies in Aleppo did not lie when they spoke of thirty villages. They had understated rather than exaggerated.

But how many refused to submit to the Christian

zeal of the king! The few existing records tell horrible tales. That so many fled from a land in which they had lived well, which was favorable to their temperament, tells more than any description of cruelty could tell. Those who remained and accepted baptism and everything else were no better off than those who fled. "Informing the king" was too well rewarded, and the Ishmaelites, or the Saracens, as they were later on called by the Magyars, were reputed to be wealthy. Their polished copper pots glistened like gold in the sun. Their women wore jewels and heavy silver and gold necklaces. Each caravan had herds of cattle and horses. The wealth of the Gypsies incited the Magyars to good citizenship.

Whatever friendship had originally existed between Magyar and Gypsy was destroyed by the laws which aroused the cupidity of peasants and villagers. The "New Christians" were the prey of every blackmailing blackguard, who brought information against them whenever he coveted what they possessed. Thus the cloak of Christianity served to disguise rapacity, and gave the "New Christians" a well-founded horror of churches and priests.

And still the Gypsies were the happiest people in Magyar land. They knew how to bathe in the sun; and to sleep looking at the moon was better than to lie down with the thought of the shining button of a copper pot. While informers' scratching voices were denouncing them, the Gypsies, instead of crying, listened to one more song, one more melody in praise of the sky and the stars.

"Your last wish?" a Gypsy was once asked, before he was to be hanged.

"I want to hear the cuckoo call once more."

The story goes that the Gypsy's wish was allowed; but no cuckoo called that evening, nor the following, nor the third. The condemned man's friends knew how to silence him . . . and the fourth day the Gypsy was far, far away.

In the year 1232, King Andrew took a vow in the forest of Bereg to forbid a Saracen to employ a Christian servant or to have a Christian wife. He also charged the bishops to make inquests amongst the Saracens and carry away the Christian wives they already had, confiscate their property, and take as slaves the Saracens found guilty of having Christian servants or wives. This order came a century after the selfsame Gypsies had been forbidden to marry amongst themselves by an order of King Ladislaus.

Good Christians settled upon fields the heathens had tilled, and occupied homes the "ungodly" men had built, as the "Ground Books" of Hungary reveal. Many of the "guilty" Gypsies fled to Roumania, to Wallachia and Moldavia, to be taken as slaves and presented as gifts to monasteries, to princes and boyars. Hasdeu, the Roumanian philologist and historian, tells that Mircea the Great presented forty families of Transylvanian Tziganes to the Monastery of Tisman in 1387, and three hundred Tzigane families to the Monastery of Cosia.

The Magyars were unable to destroy the race which they compelled—by Draconic laws meant to accomplish the opposite—to wander from place to place, to steal, and to practice sorcery. It must not be forgotten that in the eleventh century the Magyars themselves had not yet fully abandoned the nomadic life which had led them from somewhere in Asia to the center of Europe; and that the Magyars had fought against, and later side by side with, the Petshenegs, the Tartars, the Kumans, and the Khazars, and later had allied themselves with their former enemies to fight against the Christian world.

They themselves were very new Christians, and had been much more humane before they accepted the word and the blood of the Meek One who died on the cross for humanity. It is sad to remember that most peoples have accepted the teaching of Christ two thousand years too soon . . . or too late. Those who have received Christianity at the point of the sword have tried to impose it by the length of the whole blade.

The first accusations of cannibalism against the Tziganes of Hungary date from the end of the fourteenth century. The Magyars had themselves been accused of the same thing by the rest of the world when they first appeared in Europe. How, when, and why this accusation was first brought against the Tziganes is now difficult to establish. The toll of Gypsy life must have been awful. The peasants and the scum of the cities were willing to believe the accusation. It was not absolutely necessary to give to the king the confiscated property. Dead men told no tales; gold bore no private seal; and the horses and cattle could not speak. The *Tziganias,* the quarters of Gypsies in the larger towns of the country, swelled; for the accusation of cannibalism had been brought only against nomads and agricultural Gypsies. The Gypsies who appeared in Germany in 1417, claiming that they had come from Egypt through Hungary, had good reason

not to tell how long their stay had been in Magyar-
land.

Hungary changed rulers, and her dominions passed
into the hands of new conquerors, but still the Tziganes
hid in the mountains and dense forests in the daytime,
and traveled rapidly at night, crossing their own tracks
like wild beasts pursued by implacable enemies. It is
said that the wild Laeshi are the offspring of the children born to Gypsy women of those days; children
raised in terror, with wolves and foxes.

Soon the Hungarians became too occupied with
themselves to continue the persecution of a people
within their borders. The Tziganes reappeared timidly in the villages. By making themselves useful,
they knew how to win back the tolerance of the peasantry. Yet they never again settled in great numbers
for long periods anywhere in Hungary.

The thirty villages of which the men at Aleppo
spoke to Jakut were no longer theirs.

Instead of posing as Mohammedans, they accepted
Christianity, and the religious zeal of the Hungarians
having lost in intensity, the Tziganes alone frequented
the churches, and took part in all religious processions.
They were willing to make every concession but one:
the renunciation of their nomadic mode of life. It
was better not to live in too close contact with people
who looked with jealous eyes upon the wealth of others.

Never has a people sacrificed so much for its conception of life. Never has a people suffered so much
because it has refused to submerge its will to that of
another.

The Hungarian Gypsy loaded his wife heavy with
golden crosses, silver bracelets of small crosses, neck-

laces of coins stamped with crosses. The harness of his horses was studded with crosses. There was a cross on every wagon, and when a caravan halted somewhere, the tents were disposed so as to form crosses. They left nothing half-way, did nothing in a half-hearted manner. The whole world could see how Christian they were. They crossed themselves so often and so fervently their fingers stamped the sign of the cross on their bodies . . . hollowed it out as are hollowed the marble steps at the tomb of the Savior by the countless millions of the faithful who have pressed their foreheads against the hard stone.

Years later, well-intentioned but stupid reformers advised Maria Theresa, Empress of Austria and Queen of Hungary, that she could gain everlasting glory and fame by compelling the Tziganes to settle down. In 1768 she forbade them to live in tents and huts, and ordered that they must build houses, register themselves, carry means of identification, and no longer speak their own tongue. It was a crime to call oneself, or be called by others, "Tzigane." The Gypsies were to be known as "*Uj Magyar*—New Magyars," and were ordered to wear the national costume. The younger Gypsies were drafted into the army and incorporated into regiments stationed far away from their homes. No Uj Magyar was permitted to marry before proving that he had means to support wife and children. The officers of the law were charged to watch the morality of the newly made Hungarians. Maria Theresa, decreed that the Tziganes had allowed themselves to be too happy; therefore, they were immoral.

When these laws had not worked out to her satisfaction, and she had not succeeded in making the Gypsies miserable enough to suit her gloom, other laws regulating the every-day life of the Tziganes were promulgated. The empress in her misguided charity went even so far as to build settlements for her subjects. It pained her to see them the happiest people of her realm.

The Tziganes fought shy of her gifts. The settlements were so many prisons. Like deer in a fenced forest, the Gypsies pined away within the confines of their villages when compelled to live in them. Their race memory was even stronger than their nomadic instinct. Even those who had formerly lived in villages now took to the road. Thousands crossed the Carpathians into Wallachia; others spread into Poland, and from there to Russia. The end of the eighteenth century saw a new Gypsy migration into Germany and Italy, into Sweden and Norway, into Spain and France. Isolated groups even crossed the ocean, and are to this day roaming over the fields of Louisiana and Illinois. Still others went to Brazil, to mingle there with the Gypsies who had been deported from Spain by a similarly misguided queen.

Reformers are as persistent as they are stupid. The mania of legislation is so strong in some rulers, they imagine they can change the course of a river by a law upon paper. Maria Theresa trudged long and stubbornly in her course, blind to the misery she caused and the utter futility of her efforts.

"The waddling duck clucked to the canary to come down to him in the bog, though the canary had never asked the duck to join him at the tip end of the oak." This Gypsy song sums up Maria Theresa's efforts.

Joseph II, to do no less than Maria Theresa, issued another law in 1782, and his henchmen succeeded in gathering enough Gypsies into colonies to give their ruler the satisfaction of apparent success. There are still a few villages of the anemic "Uj Magyars," scratching the soil for a miserable living . . . pheasants compelled to live in a fowl-yard of a narrow-minded would-be benefactor. But the rest roamed freely . . . danced and sang and slept and loved in the open.

It was in this year—1782—that the charge of cannibalism was brought against Tziganes. There were no proofs. The charges were brought against them to still their happy laughter. The emperor and his court hated all signs of happiness. Though the accusation was only against one tribe, the echo spread over the whole living race of the world. The charge was never proved. The Tziganes who had confessed their guilt recanted, explaining that their confessions had been wrung under duress in the torture chambers. Yet only their confessions were believed. Their recanting found deaf ears. People always believe what they want to believe. Proof . . . bah! There are no proofs. Willing ears, that is important. Only deaf people could be really just. The eyes of men have never been trained well enough to check our hearing. The ears are the fake news-gatherers of humanity.

The trial of the Gypsies lasted two months. There were thousands of witnesses. No one dared to witness in favor of the accused. To defend any of the accused was equivalent to suicide. All witnesses not bringing additional proof of guilt against the Tziganes were suspected of being themselves guilty of cannibalism.

The vehemency with which one accused the victims and denounced cannibalism was the measure of his own innocence. Thousands of Gypsies were denounced by whosoever considered their existence an obstacle to his own plans and desires—or just for sport. Two hundred and twenty Gypsies were found guilty of cannibalism and condemned to swing on gibbets. Public opinion, like Moloch at Carthage, demanded victims. The dust of the road to civilization had to be sprinkled with blood.

The whole Gypsy race had been judged and found guilty. Gypsies fled from settled farms and village shops to hide in the mountains. The poor souls behaved little less savagely than wild beasts, because they had been treated as such. The character of persecuted peoples changes to resemble the picture drawn of them by the oppressors. Now those who were responsible for the Gypsies' plight, those who were responsible for what had happened to them, pointed out that the Gypsies had gone back to savagery, and that nothing could be done to civilize them.

The echoes of these trials were not slow in crossing the border between Hungary and Roumania, and thence into Bulgaria and Russia, France, England, and Spain. The whole world resounded with charges of cannibalism against the Tziganes. These charges came at a time when the western world had almost become accustomed to the wandering tribes in its midst. The world had been amused by their antics, by their strangeness, by the romantic atmosphere about them, and the mystic powers these strange people were supposed to possess.

They had vicariously satisfied the wanderlust of

sedentary populations. What the Gypsies did, the way they lived, was what everyone desired to do but did not find the strength of will to carry out. Prisons, monasteries, nunneries, circuses, like bull-fights and boxing matches, are so many means of satisfying or giving expression to suppressed desires of unreligious, unromantically living people.

And suddenly the race was accused of something terrible! So, after all, people argued, shopkeepers and farmers were superior beings. The reason the Gypsies lived such care-free lives was not because of a philosophy of life that disregarded the comforts of settled life, but because they were savages and cannibals! Every Gypsy camp at night, every camp-fire around which sat brown-faced men and half-clad women, was a criminal place. These camp-fires were so many criminal meetings at which the flesh of some human being was bargained for, then distributed. Stories were circulated how the chief always demanded the heart, and his wife the liver; the rest was distributed according to rank, or gambled away on the turn of a card. Stupidity springs eternal in the human breast!

Those of lighter color faded away, mingling with foreigners of other nationalities. In towns where they had already lived a more or less settled life, the Gypsies themselves denounced the wandering tribes, disassociating themselves from them, claiming to be of a different race altogether. This denial of kinship lasted until the accused generation died out . . . until the generation that had accused them had disappeared. The effect of the accusation of cannibalism was for many years so strong that no Gypsy in Hungary dared to cook any food indoors. The Gypsy women would call peasant women to witness what kind of meat was put into the pot before cooking it. Still, only last year, in 1927, a group of Gypsies living in Hungary were convicted of cannibalism.

During the short life of Bihari, the Gypsy fiddler and improviser, connoisseurs and Gypsies walked and rode great distances to hear him play. Bihari never played one and the same thing twice. He was forever improvising new melodies on his violin. Once Bihari had been induced to listen to another Gypsy violinist whose reputation was growing very rapidly. Suddenly Bihari began to cry, and kissing the player's hands, he begged him to play again the piece he had just finished, so that he, Bihari, might learn it. "I have found my master in you!"

"But," the player cried out, "I have been playing one of your own pieces, master . . . one which I heard you play a few months ago!"

In 1825, Bihari was called to Vienna to appear before the emperor. The vivacity of the Gypsy's eye, and the great charm of the man were such the noblest ladies of the court strove to gain his favor. One day, when Bihari had played for the emperor, the emperor asked him to express some desire. "Whatever you wish will be given you . . . even a title of nobility. Do you want letters of nobility?"

But Bihari, a true Gypsy, generous, and with no idea of limitation, asked for letters of nobility for his whole band. No Gypsy could own something which the others did not have. Bihari smiled at the emperor's confusion.

Marie Louise, Princess of Naples, and the Czarina

of Russia were among the women whom Bihari had fascinated by his playing. The amorous intrigues of her daughter compelled the empress to ask Bihari to present his wife to her. She then begged him not to look with such insistence into the eyes of princesses, for his own wife was more beautiful than any other woman.

As generous with his money as he was with his heart, distributing what he earned to his people in need, Bihari died in great poverty.

He never looked at notes; did not know how to read music; still he played the works of Lavatta, Csermack, and other composers. One hearing was enough for him to play what he had heard, and to play it better and with richer color.

Csermack, another great violinist and composer, suddenly disappeared from the tables of the wealthy and powerful at the height of his fame. In rags, barefoot, with haggard eyes, and long disheveled hair, this most loved of Gypsy musicians wandered through villages and towns, playing at inns and at street-corners for a piece of bread and a glass of wine. No one knew that the Gypsy was the famous Csermack.

Count Etienne Fai, a great admirer of Gypsy music, who had known Csermack when the Gypsy was at the height of his fame, told the following story.

"Some time ago I listened with several musicians to a mass ordered by Count François Deszofy, who was himself a very fine organist. In the midst of the solemnity there appeared a man in rags. With burning eye and wild gesticulation, he tore the violin out of the hands of the orchestra leader, and, to the stupefaction of all present, played the rest of the music as if it were an inspiration of his own. At the end of the mass, when the stranger had put down the instrument of which he had possessed himself, and was asked who he was, he answered with great pride, 'Csermack!' We threw ourselves at his feet, begging him to come back to us.

"Count Deszofy took him to his home and gave him garb more befitting such a man than the rags he was wearing. Far from being grateful, Csermack looked at us with disdain, and refused to play. It was only after we had got him half drunk with Tokay wine that he again took the violin in his hands. Paganini had never impressed me as much as Csermack did that day. The agility of his fingers and the perfection of his tone, the somber despair of his melodies sung more than the despair of a single man, more even than the despair of his race. It contained the despair of the whole world!"

Yet Count Deszofy could not hold the violinist long. An unfortunate love-affair had wounded the Gypsy's heart. Csermack, with his violin under his arm, continued to beg from house to house. When people were hospitable he paid them with the divine tunes of his bow. When the hospitality of a home was more generous, he stopped for as long as they would have him, even doing menial services in the kitchen or the stable. But he seldom stopped longer than a few days, and never consented to sleep indoors. Nothing in the world could make him return to civilized life and end his wandering. A lady of the nobility had spurned his love after she had encouraged him. "What have you to give me to compensate for the world you ask me to leave behind?" the lady had asked. Csermack had

shown his violin and laid his hand on his heart: "This."
The lady had laughed aloud, and turned her back on
the Gypsy. So he took himself away from the civilized
world that had hurt him.

He died in a village inn. A few hours before his
death he composed the melody known to this day in
Hungary as "Csermack Halala" or "Csermack's
Death."

Unable to finish the writing of the melody, Csermack
wrote at the bottom of the page that Bihari should end
it. Bihari refused, saying that he would willingly
share Csermack's grave but not his honor.

Another Hungarian violinist who astounded the
world at Hamburg, London, Paris, and in America
with his playing was Reményi. Reményi played Bach
as well as Vieuxtemps and other famous composers of
his day. But at the end of every concert, as if to show
that the art of his people was not inferior to the art of
the others, nay, as if to show how much more beautiful
Gypsy music was, he would always play *lassans* and
csárdáses. After a concert tour, Reményi would return
to his tribe in the Pusto of Hungary, to bathe himself
clean of the impurities of Europe.

One of the most famous Hungarian Gypsy musicians,
Michel Barnu, was in the employ of Cardinal Csaky.
So confident in his unsurpassable skill on the violin was
this Michel Barnu, that he arranged a contest at the
residence of his master, inviting the best violinists of
that time to take part—a contest analogous to that of
the famous Minnesingers at Eisenach in Germany.
Twelve of the very best were chosen to wrest the palm
of honor from Barnu. These artists were in the service
of great lords. Each of these lords was desirous of

showing that he had a musician at least the equal of him who served his Eminence the Cardinal.

Barnu so decisively outclassed his rivals that the result of the contest was to enhance his already widespread renown. The cardinal then ordered the finest painter to do a life-size portrait of Barnu in court dress, with the coat of arms and colors of the house of the cardinal. At the bottom of the portrait his Eminence had the painter inscribe in Latin, "The Orpheus of Hungary." This painting hangs in the great room of Radkan Castle, where it can be seen to this day.

A Gypsy woman of the middle of the eighteenth century, Csinka Panna, also won renown as a violinist. Married to a Gypsy musician at the age of fourteen, she organized, with her two brothers, a family orchestra that became known far and wide.

As elsewhere, the Gypsies of Hungary have contributed a large share of the happiness and the joy of the people among whom they lived. Their contribution rises as high as the depths into which they have plunged are deep.

The Hungarian Gypsy considers Hungary as his home. The reforming propensities over, the blood which has been shed sucked in by the earth, Gypsies and Hungarians now live side by side with great understanding of one another. The Hungarian prides himself on the quality of his Gypsies, and includes their contributions to music as part of his own contribution to the world.

Undaunted, the Gypsies have continued to be what they have always been. Even those who have settled in towns and villages continue to lead a seminomadic life. Mountains and valleys are still echoing the songs of traveling Gypsy caravans, of wandering minstrels, holding their violins under the coats.

True, a good many Tziganes are to be found in occupations which seem to demand a sedentary life . . . in factories and as longshoremen on the Danube, bricklayers and masons. But the Gypsy knows how to combine even such occupations with a nomadic life. They are a floating industrial population. And those who live in large towns frequently join some cousins' tent caravan, to fill their lungs with the sharp air of the mountains, and to commune again with their own kind.

FFICIALLY, IN A MANNER OF SPEAKING, THE Gypsies first appeared in Paris on August 17, 1427. They had, however, been in France long before that. In the north of France, in Abbeville, in the year 1388, there were a number of Gypsies holding official positions with the State Department. In old French documents we find a Bertremieu "Tinguery" as Inspector of Bread and Herring, and in charge of the artillery defending the burg. Pierre "Tinguery" was Inspector of Wines. Another Tinguery was the Corporation Blacksmith. Règne "Tinguery" was the Carpenter of the City, etc., etc. Now, all these Tinguerys of Abbeville were none else but our friends the Gypsies. Gypsies had come trickling into France probably a century before that.

In the early Middle Ages, the city of Abbeville manufactured copper pots and kitchen utensils. In his book of "Proverbs and Popular Sayings," Crapelet tells that the Polish Kingdom sent copper and gold and silver, wax and peltry in bullion to Abbeville to be manufactured into copper and kitchen-ware. From the Carpathian Mountains, where metal was mined by Gypsies, there must have been a steady, long procession of the brotherhood into France. That the workers in this metal were not Frenchmen is proven by the fact that the *Calderari,* copper-pot workers, and tinsmiths in general, were exempt from all duties and were considered as "detached from the soil." They were not included among the purchasable peasants when villages passed from the hands of one baron to another. The "duke" and his followers who arrived in France in 1427 had been thoroughly informed and styled by their *pralos,* brothers, who had traveled back and forth between the north of France and their home in the Carpathian Mountains, as to the habits and the psychology of the French people. These "dukes" knew how to imitate the grand manner of the French feudal barons and noblemen. To emphasize the genuineness of their own nobility, the "dukes" assumed the manners of French noblemen, rode on horseback, while the rabble went on foot, and kept hounds on the leash and falcons chained to their wrists.

As long as the "duke" was alone in Paris with his twelve followers, things went well. But the mass of Gypsies could not keep the pose long, and returned to their tricks; stealing and fortune-telling and pocketbook-snatching. Posing is against the grain of the Gypsy. A Gypsy woman can weep easily enough about her dying children when she appeals to the heart of a pitying lady; but if the coin does not come fast enough, she breaks her monologue and says something else.

Spreading from Paris into the outlying districts, the Gypsies terrorized, with their sorcery and incantations, the superstitious Frenchmen. But they attacked the property of French peasants. Peasants, the world over, are more attached to what they possess than city people are; for they have had to work harder for everything they own. The avarice of the French peasant is too well known to need expatiation.

Compared to the French, even the Scotch peasants are lavish spendthrifts. The crooked, crablike fingers of the French peasant bury whatever comes between them in the hard flesh of the palm, and close over it forever. Even death cannot release that hold. A French peasant dies with closed fists.

Forgetting that the Gypsies were a people on pilgrimage, forgetting they held letters from the pope which forbade anybody to touch them, forgetting even their powers of sorcery, the peasant defended his property with pitchfork and cudgel. Mayors of villages and towns promulgated laws reading that whosoever's property had been taken by Gypsies had the right to enter a Gypsy camp and take by force the equivalent of the stolen property. Needless to say that the French peasants obeyed that law, and needless to say that they paid themselves back many times over what had been taken from them.

The world's peasantry was given a reputation of honesty by interested and biased demagogues. The peasant only demands, but never gives, honesty of weight and measure. He is neither kind-hearted nor honest. Moreover, he could not live if he were honest. The "ennobling" work of the soil depoetizes the earth and the sky of the charms of love and the mystery of death.

So, when peasants came to "take back" their property, demanding ten mules for every strayed donkey, there were pitched battles ending in a number of deaths on both sides, and in the flight of the "Egyptians." Those caught, met with scant justice. The thrifty French peasants saved the ropes with which they had hanged one Gypsy for further use when other tribes should pass. Fleeing tribes joined their brothers in the north of France; others returned whence they had come, while still others crossed into Spain. Newcomers from Hungary, Macedonia, and Roumania entered France quietly and kept to themselves as much as possible. Yet an edict issued by Louis XII in 1504 ordered all officers of the kingdom to rid the land of Gypsies, and to send to the gallows those who lingered. Harassed, driven from pillar to post, the Gypsies committed acts of savagery and vandalism. Their only answer to oppression was greater recklessness. They did not turn the other cheek.

Another edict in 1561 put a premium on the head of every Gypsy; yet people wondered why Gypsies were thieves, and questioned why they did not settle down to honest work. And everybody envied them their free and wild lives in the open, and cursed them when they heard them singing in the forests and mountain passes after a day of untold misery!

Still another edict, issued by Louis XIV in 1675, ordered that the Gypsies be "exterminated by fire and sword." Bands of peasants went on Gypsy-hunts with hounds and hunting horns. Daily, men, women, and children were thrown into cisterns or hung from the limbs of trees, and then were fed to the dogs.

Gypsy-hunting lasted four years, when at last the game became rare and the country was thought purged of Gypsies. Humorously, a writer proposed that there be closed and open seasons for hunting Gypsies to preserve so good a sport. When the rigorous measures were abandoned, the Gypsies gradually reappeared timidly out of hiding places, went back into frontier cities and villages, to ply their trades as horse-dealers, horse-clippers, and basket-makers, while their wives told fortunes, begged, or practiced medicine.

The Gypsies were needed. They were good blacksmiths and better wagon-makers than other people. Though peasants still kept a watchful eye over stables and households when Gypsies were around, the piece of hempen rope owned by every farmer was no longer used.

A decree of 1538 forbade the people to give any Gypsy refuge or to buy anything from him. Every contravention to this law was punished with a hundred livres fine. An ordinance of 1641 recalled these ancient dispositions, and held responsible for the thefts and damage committed by Gypsies those who had offered refuge or charity to them. Charity! Charity of French peasants!

Yet it was impossible to exterminate the Gypsies. They moved on from one place to another. Somehow, the Gypsies always knew when and where their pursuers were, and the time they were supposed to pass by one place or appear at another. The patteran was a swifter messenger than men on horseback. The Gypsies also had smoke signals long before civilized Europe became aware of this method of communication. Slinking along the roadsides, passing from tree to tree like monkeys when pursued, they tired out their enemies. The great solidarity of Gypsies, the danger of one being the danger of all, increased their alertness to a higher degree than had risen the zeal of their pursuers. When the Gypsies had finally reached the Basque Country, in the lower Pyrenees, they were almost out of danger, their enemies were so far behind. We shall see later why they return to countries where they are most persecuted. It will be one of the keys to the secret of their wanderings.

The Basque Country is a very mountainous region,

thickly wooded, and was then only sparsely populated. Horses and mules were roaming freely in the forests, and pigs and fowl were everywhere on the mud roads. The boundary line between the Basque Country and Spain is only a short distance away, and there were Gypsies on the other side also. A stolen mule from the Basque Country was exchanged for a stolen horse from Spain. Both animals were sold on the next market-day . . . the donkey in Spain, the horse in France.

As the farms were far apart from one another, the peasants overlooked small depredations on the part of the wanderers, and tried to live with them in amity. The audacity of the Gypsies in the Basque Country increased with the impunity they enjoyed. Large bands took possession of empty granaries and abandoned stables, and settled their women and children in them, while the men went out for booty. The scum of the cities, those pursued by justice, joined the Gypsies, bringing with them the vices and sicknesses of jails and slums. Because of some strange similarity of character between Basque and Gypsy, and because of Basque hatred of everything French, even laws, the native population was not inclined to help the government, in spite of threats on the one side and depredations on the other.

Wherever the Gypsies have intermarried with white people, Gypsy characteristics are evident even after the fifth and sixth generations. In the Basque Country, however, these characteristics have disappeared after the second or third generations; and in places where such intermarriages have been more frequent than in others—in the lower Pyrenees—such offspring is hardly to be distinguished from the native population. The number of Sanskrit words in the Basque language tends to indicate that the Basques may be of the same origin as the Gypsies. Though the Basque language is very difficult for strangers to learn, the Gypsies mastered it with surprising facility, and spoke it fluently only a few years after their appearance in the Basque Country; spoke it so fluently and so convincingly that they were frequently taken for Basques. Basques who joined the Gypsies for reasons of their own acquired the Calo so well that they could pass for Gypsies and escape being detected even by the sharpest eye or ear. This riffraff of the cities frequently served as police informers against the Gypsies, and it was due to this betrayal that the Gypsies in France and in Spain are known to be so shy in speaking their language in the hearing of strangers. But speaking it rarely, they have themselves forgotten their language, and the younger Gypsies today know it only very imperfectly—so imperfectly that other Gypsies refuse to believe they are of the blood.

In the lower Pyrenees, across Saint-Jean-de-Luz, on the Gulf of Biscay, is a little fishing village that rises on the slope of the hills—the village of Cibour. Now that Saint-Jean-de-Luz has won such fame, the world over, and has attracted people from everywhere to its sandy shore, to the greenness of its hills and to its Casino, new and magnificent villas are rising every day also in Cibour, overlooking the bay and the blue sea beyond.

Cibour is fifteen miles from Biarritz, and only twenty-five miles from the Spanish border. To the ordinary, unadvised eye, the inhabitants of Cibour are little different from the inhabitants of Saint-Jean-de-

Luz. On Thursday and Sunday evenings, at the fandango dance in the market-place, the youth of Saint-
Jean-de-Luz dances with the youth of Cibour. I had,
however, been mystified when maids we employed denied that they were born or lived in Cibour. I had also
wondered why at the Feast of St. John, the native population burned the effigy of a huge ox in front of the
church, and carried the burning form through the
lower part of the city, while several trees, soaked in
petroleum, were burned at the entrance to the church.
No one seemed to be able to give me any plausible explanation for these strange local customs. No one was
able to give me even the approximate date when this
custom originated. Watching the dancers night after
night, I observed that the precision of their rhythm had
no parallel either in France or in Spain. Five hundred
people snapped their fingers to the movements of their
bodies. The tempo was so exact, the attack so precise,
one would never have thought that a thousand separate
hands produced it. It was more as though a drum were
being beaten by one single hand.

One evening, an elderly man and his wife stepped to
the center of the ring and danced solo to the music of
the fandango. But they danced the *tanana;* the Gypsy
dance which only few outsiders have ever seen performed, and which I have been privileged to see a few
times. There was no mistake; it was the tanana. I
caught the stare, the side glance, in the eyes of the
dancers. And I knew then and there why our maids
denied they lived in Cibour. Yet—when, where, why?

During the war between France and Spain in 1635,
and during the sack of the city of Saint-Jean-de-Luz
by the Spaniards, the Gypsies who happened to be then

in the Basque Country took possession of the houses deserted by the fleeing native population. When, after the Treaty of Utrecht, the original townsfolk returned, the Groundbook, or official real property register, had been destroyed, and few proprietors could prove their claim to the houses inhabited by the Gypsies. Those who possessed proofs of ownership were only too glad to pass their rights over to the Gypsies for negligible prices, unwilling and unable to live with or amongst them.

At the end of the war in 1713, Louis XIV turned over to England the colonies now called Newfoundland and Nova Scotia, which in turn took over the sea trade with Labrador. This resulted in the decline of the prosperity of Saint-Jean-de-Luz and Cibour. The majority of the male native population migrated to the new world, but the Gypsies remained. The nearness of the Spanish border line was too advantageous to abandon Cibour and a part of Saint-Jean-de-Luz which they had so thoroughly settled. They had learned the language of the people; they had mingled and intermarried with them. There were as many half-bloods as there were full-bloods. The rest of France was dangerous. The bands that still roamed in the north and in the south were being harassed and pestered. Though summary execution was no longer as frequent as it had been, Gypsies were forcibly expelled from the country or transported across the seas to Louisiana, in North America.

The Gypsies of Cibour manned the fishing vessels. This adventurous life was better adapted to their temperament than tilling the soil, for which they had never shown any aptitude. They developed into skilful fish-

ermen, boatmen, and daring seamen, who went out with
their nets farther than others had ever gone before.
Acquiring wealth, they settled down, and became outwardly as meticulous sticklers for property rights as
the Basques had ever been, and thus entered into the
good graces of the merchants and the native population.
One can win a peasant's heart by being more avaricious
than he is. The Gypsies learned to know that, and
practiced what they had learned, much to the disadvan-
tage of their teachers. Cheating cheaters was a noble
game; great sport and profitable.

At the beginning, the Church held aloof from the
Gypsies, who were treated more or less the same as
the Cagots—a people in the south of France, in the
Pyrenees, with which the other natives have refused to
mingle, and who have suffered as much from unjust
laws as have the Gypsies.

The Cagots, descendants of the Merovingians, were
in that part of France long before the present inhabitants had come to settle upon it. In France, the Cagots
duplicated the lot of the Gypsies who had been in India
long before the present inhabitants had invaded the
Ganges. Even after the Gypsies had accepted the
Church, the priests never forgot to mention upon bap-
tismal and marriage documents that the celebrant was
a *Cascarot,* or a Gypsy. Still, by acquiring more and
more wealth, the Cibour Gypsies succeeded in also acquiring equal rights with the French and Basques, and
finally obtained permission to enter church by the same
door as the other Christians long before the Cagots
had obtained similar privileges.

Most of the inhabitants of Cibour are sailors and
fishermen, and their wives are fish-peddlers. At the

market-place of Cibour, upon the bridge connecting the town with Saint-Jean-de-Luz, I became aware of the origin of the merchants. The language of both buyers and sellers is as colorful as is their dress. Without understanding what is spoken, one can feel the Homeric quality in a dispute between two fishermen.

That smuggling still furnishes a large part of the livelihood of the inhabitants of Cibour is clearly seen, and even the original trade of coppersmith has never been totally abandoned. The finest kettles in the Basque Country are made by the inhabitants of this fisher village, who also excel in other handicrafts, the products of which are peddled to tourists as well as to inhabitants of distant towns.

Yet, though the Cibour people are more or less settled, the other Gypsies in the Basque Country have not ceased their wanderings. One meets their caravans on every road. Their songs echo through all the hills.

In 1708 the Vice-Seneschal of Béarn received the order to go with his archers into Navarre, to arrest the Gypsies he could find, and to kill on the spot those who resisted. But the Gypsies got the breeze in their sails before the expedition against them was under way, and the Seneschal of Béarn fought against non-existing windmills.

Later in the eighteenth century a price was set on the head of every Gypsy man or woman. A few years afterward, either because the Gypsies had come to the conclusion that their strength lay in traveling in larger groups, or because they were emboldened by the impotence of the gendarmes, they stormed the markets of Saint-Jean-Pied-de-Port and of Helette, and took away, as booty, cattle, goods, fruit, and grain. This exploit was followed by acts of equal violence and daring. There was open warfare between the Gypsies and the authorities. Led by Basque robbers, Gypsy bands of preying highwaymen dominated the country. No road was safe. No man, no home, no farm, no village, was safe. At bay, the French government sent an army corps against them. Thousands of Gypsies were caught, and imprisoned in the citadels of Saint-Jean-Pied-de-Port and Bayonne. A few isolated Gypsy families succeeded in crossing the Spanish border, but the Spanish authorities extradited them to the French. The Gypsies who did not perish in the prisons or on the gallows were thrown pellmell, with their women and children, into the holds of ships about to sail to the French colonies across the seas.

The war between France and England, however, intervened. The French government had no time to waste on the extermination of Gypsies. Many of the brotherhood succeeded in extricating themselves from the meshes of the law, and helped others to escape from the prisons. Gypsy women had won the hearts of governors, of prison-guards, and even of hangmen. A great number of "these impossible roving scoundrels" obtained their liberty by joining the army. Free again to escape from the ever-pursuing laws, the Gypsies of the Basque Country understood that they had to give themselves a civil status to avoid being arrested as vagabonds. Each one acquired a small piece of land, or an abandoned hut, and procured for himself the appearance of a property-holder. Yet the next generation forgot what the previous one had suffered, and wanted personal experience.

In the year 1825, the Gypsies felt they had been quiet for too long a time. They could not live without risking danger—an experience as necessary to them as the emotions of love and hatred. "Life without danger is emptier than life without love," says a Gypsy proverb. Under the leadership of Biedart, a notorious robber, they spread terror far and wide for over ten years. Another band, formed by another leader across the Spanish border, worked in cooperation with Biedart's band. They crossed the frontier at will. The guardsmen were terrorized. No wall was too high. No lock was too strong. Villages offered them monthly tribute in exchange for peace and security. Biedart, like the robber barons in the Middle Ages, dividing his band under leaders who were responsible to him for everything they did, ordered marches and countermarches. Peasants and villagers refused to give information to the authorities, and shielded the captain of the band when he was surrounded by soldiers. They provided him with food and means of escape, and frequently joined him in battles against his pursuers.

Under the leadership of a Gypsy named Ardaix (*Ardaix* means *pepper* in Roumanian Calo), another band enlisted all the native riffraff from Bayonne to Bordeaux. This Ardaix claimed to be a descendant of Rasvan, Voivode of Moldavia, and behaved as though he wanted to establish himself as king over southern France. The end of these robber bands came in 1829, when the leaders were betrayed to the gendarmes by neglected sweethearts.

Basque Gypsy tales, embroidered with local legends, made of Ardaix a popular romantic hero, who labored to free the poor from the yoke of the wealthy. When a merchant had cheated a poor widow of half of her silver, Ardaix ordered that the bag of money be brought to him, and breaking between his fingers every coin, he returned one-half to the widow and one-half to the merchant.

In one night he and his band had plowed the field of an old peasant, whose three sons had been taken as soldiers:

"And we shall be back in time to harvest your wheat!"

At harvest time, half of Ardaix's men worked in the old man's field, while the other half fought the gendarmes who had surrounded them; the Gypsies having been betrayed to the authorities by the old man's daughter, whose love Ardaix had refused.

Nowhere have Gypsies been able to mix their breed so easily with that of a native population as in the Basque Country. In the eighteenth century, the state of Navarre issued a decree forbidding any intercourse with Gypsy women that might make them pregnant.

The story of the adventures of Adam, Abbot of Baigorry, begins like the story of a robber, and ends like the legend of a saint. This Adam, Abbot of Baigorry, prompted by his great love for earthly things, joined a Gypsy band, of which he soon became leader. However, his chief desire being sensual pleasure, he never caused bloodshed, but was, throughout his days, a doer of good deeds and kindly services. One winter night, when the storm raged in the mountains, Adam came upon a lonely peasant dwelling, occupied by a young widow and her three children. Talking with the woman, he learned that she not only had lost her husband, but was on the verge of being dispossessed by the landlord, because she was unable to redeem a bill left unpaid by her deceased husband. Adam placed the money in the woman's lap, and took leave without waiting to hear thanks. The woman paid the bill the following morning. But during the night, Adam stole into the farmer's house and robbed him. Once again in possession of his money, the robber abbot brought food for the widow and her children. This extraordinary kindness seemed to render the young widow suspicious of his further intentions regarding her. But the wily abbot reassured her, saying: "Do not fear, my good woman. Adam knows how to respect virtue wherever he finds it."

For fully ten years this man continued his criminal career. When he was finally caught and thrown into the prison of Pamplona, he showed such signs of repentance he was regarded as a model of virtue by his fellow prisoners, and by the authorities as well. At the expiration of his prison sentence, Adam begged leave to stay where he was, and was later appointed chaplain. Twenty years later, when it was announced to the inhabitants of Pamplona that the "Good Rogue" had died, everybody cried: "The saint is dead, the saint is dead!"

The Gypsies of the lower Pyrenees speak Basque. Most of the women can speak no other language. But most of the men have learned French in the army or in prison. Now that the youngsters are compelled to go to school, the new generation will soon speak only French.

The Calo has degenerated until it has dwindled to an argot or slang which they sometimes use. It consists of corrupted Basque words, mixed with other words of Gypsy origin or borrowed from words used in the prisons. In 1858, Baudrimont and Michel could collect no more than 352 pure Gypsy words in the whole Saint-Palais region. All the rest were merely variations of Basque, French, or Spanish words. One can hardly consider as Gypsy words such as: *orena*, hour; *animalia*, animal; *bilouac*, horse; *ceria*, sky; *eria*, finger; *hamia*, fishing-line; *ithsasca*, sea; *mirailla*, looking-glass; *oulia*, fly; *soudoura*, nose; *sortcia*, to be born; *lanoua*, cloud; *shouria*, bird; *azaskouria*, finger-nail; *beharia*, ear; *aria*, rock; *gueka*, snake; *arreba*, sister; *atala*, drum; *lura*, earth; *pishia*, urine; *orga*, carriage; as well as all those words, which, according to Baudrimont, are the same as in the Basque language.

In February, 1836, there appeared an article in the "Mémorial des Pyrénées," calling attention to the prevalence of highway robbery and murder on the roads, especially on market-days. The writer went on to say that his best remedy was deportation of Gypsies *en masse*, inasmuch as ordinary lawful measures were ineffective, since the Gypsies could so easily cross the border.

A Parisian paper, the National, undertook to defend the Gypsies, saying: "Their misdemeanors are the result of the situation society places them in; they are given no opportunity to sow or reap, and yet they are blamed for stealing. One might just as well blame them for the crime of wanting to live."

To this the Pyrenees press retorted, contending that the Gypsies had full freedom to acquire property, to work, to attend the markets, etc., but that they were too indolent. The mayor of Saint-Palais, a district infested with Gypsies, published in 1842 the most vehement accusations against them, saying that the Gypsies were absolutely immune to civilization or religion. He advocated deportation as the only means of ridding the Basque Country of the pests, to put an end to the bad example they set for the native criminal element. "The Gypsy is fit for nothing else but stealing, begging, drinking, and vagabondage. He has as much fear of work as a mad dog has of water."

And another government official attributed no less than thirty-two cases of first-degree crimes to Gypsies for the period 1849 to 1860, in his district. He also demanded that wholesale deportation be resorted to, pointing out that in the last two years twenty-five Gypsies had been deported, and that the whole Basque Country felt a considerable and material relief as a result of this riddance.

The Gypsies of the Basque Country who have intermarried with the natives have lost their good qualities and acquired all the vices. They have lost the feeling of solidarity with the rest of the race, and have become police-informers, double-dealers, owners of houses of prostitution, and harbor every form of moral depravity in their homes.

Once, while a large band of Gypsies was being surrounded by a company of soldiers who closed upon them, cautiously stealing through the pine forests of the Landes, Bratu Voicu, a young Gypsy in love with the chief's daughter, came to talk to the old man:

"They won't be here before midnight."

"No. I don't think they will be."

"It is the day Tinka has promised to marry me."

The old chief gasped. They were hounded like wolves, driven, speared, shot at; and this young man thought of marriage. Yet . . . who knew what might happen to any of them within a few hours! And life was life. He looked at Bratu.

"You speak like a real Gypsy. Call Tinka. Call all of them."

As·if the great danger were not within arm's length, the Gypsies assembled before their chief. Fires were lit. The women began to prepare the wedding meal. Rugs were piled high for the bridal couple to sit upon during the ceremony. And then Stan and Marga decided to marry also, and Jorgan and Maria changed their plans. Why should they wait? Tonight was as good as any other night. The enemy was drawing nearer. Who knew what would happen in a few hours? Life was life. They began to sing, sitting around the fire. Then Radu began to sing. His voice was beautiful. There were still a few drops of brandy in a bottle. The youngsters began to dance the tanana. It might be the last time any of them would dance. Nicolai, the fiddler of the camp, began to play an old melody which they all knew. They sang along as he played.

From time to time, the echo of a shot was heard through the low-lying forest. The shots came nearer. So they danced faster, sang louder, embraced one another with greater passion. Life was life. Who knew what would happen in another hour? Not one but eight marriages were being celebrated. It was a rare evening. The joy of it was greater than the danger. Eight couples were being united. If they should all remain alive, there would be eight Gypsy children before the year was over.

Shots were coming nearer. Yet . . . the tanana had awakened in them all a desire to dance, to live. Their guns were empty. They had no ammunition to fight back. They knew they were surrounded. They could not flee.

"Play another tune, Nicolai. Throw some more wood on the fire. Sing . . . Sing! Dance!"

They could now hear the voices of the enemies; from the right, from the left, from everywhere.

"Dance, dance, dance! Sing, sing, sing!"

The Gypsies forgot the soldiers, forgot death, and knew only that they were alive. Their eyes and ears, all their senses, were drunk with life.

Shots were now falling into the fire, amongst the dancers. One shot landed between a bridal couple; between Bratu Voicu and Tinka. They did not move. The bullet had not disturbed them from the long kiss.

Then the soldiers began to appear from behind trees. What did the Gypsies mean by dancing in such moments. They did not shoot back. They made no attempt to flee. What did the Gypsies mean? The soldiers approached nearer.

"Dance, dance! Sing, sing!" boomed the chief's voice.

Astounded, the tired soldiers came nearer. The Gypsies were in their power. It did not matter. But they refused to take the slightest notice of them. When two soldiers had come near enough to a large group dancing round and round in a wide circle, one of the girls took a soldier into the dance and whirled him around. Another Gypsy did the same. Soon all the soldiers were dancing in the hora. The Gypsies called them brothers.

Life was life. Who knew what would happen in a few hours?

At dawn, when soldiers and Gypsies were too tired to dance and the bridal couples had disappeared, the soldiers noticed that their guns were gone and that their scabbards were empty of swords. But what did that matter? They were soldiers sent to fight an enemy. They could not fight a group of joyous people who were dancing and singing. They could not go back to their barracks. The sergeant spoke:

"I stay with them."

"So do I."

"And I."

"And I."

"And I—I would sooner dance with them than shoot them."

And so the Nestor band of Gypsies wooed to destruction a few hours previous was four times as strong before the sun had caressed the top of the trees. Because they knew that life was life. . . .

The Gypsies who came to France were most probably of the "Zingari," of the kettle-maker type, called there by the Tinguery who worked at Abbeville in the north of France.

The name "Tzigane" is a corruption of the word "Zincar," worker in tin, zinc, copper and bronze plate. "Tingar" was also their name in Roumania, a name also derived from their occupation. All metal-plate, be it of copper or iron, the Roumanian calls tin. The ending *ar* is a Roumanian ending, as in *macelar,* butcher, *cizmar,* shoemaker, and *tamplar,* carpenter. *Tshingian* in Greece, *Zincan* in Macedonia, *Zingari* in Italy. *Czigany* in Hungary, *Tincar* in Roumania; *Dengelaer,* coppersmiths, in High German; *Tinkler* (*Tinker*) in Scotland, and *Tingheri* in France—all these names by which the Gypsies have been known, have one origin, the trade they plied. At one time, all the Calabreze living in Spain were called Calderari, because many Calabreze were kettle-workers.

To this day in Germany, all second-hand clothing dealers are called "Juden," whether they be Jews or not.

"What is his occupation?"

"He is Jude." And the "Jude" is frequently a good Catholic, or the son of a Baptist minister.

In France, church servants are called "Suisses."

In the United States, all hirelings were once called "Hessians."

The Basque Gypsies are not musical—no more musical than the Basques are. Gypsy coppersmiths prefer drink to song, and danger to passion. They dance with great abandon and with lascivious poses.

Frequently, after the fandango dance in the marketplace at Cibour, Saint-Jean-de-Luz, or Bayonne, small groups still continue to dance to the rhythm made by the snapping of fingers. They have no need of music, preferring to dance to a monotone rhythm. The other folk know who these late night-dancers are, though they never call them by name. When a young boy or girl shows a predilection for these late parties, parents and strangers wink knowingly at one another, and know that it is a *sangre* or one of the blood.

A policeman of Saint-Jean-de-Luz with whom I had long conversations on the subject of the people of

Cibour and the neighborhood, and whose information and knowledge made me suspect him of closer ties than he claimed to have with the Roms, told me of a large party of Gypsies camped just outside of Bayonne.

There were twenty large tents. The men were working at their trade, kettle-making. Some of them were unusually handsome, and looked very different from the others. The camp literally swarmed with children of all ages, most of them only half dressed. Most of the younger women were beautiful, very well dressed, with enough colored sashes and kerchiefs about their hips, necks, and heads to drown the background in a veritable flood of color.

A woman of about thirty years, tall, well-built, with beautiful clear white skin and black glossy hair, lost her shyness after she had emptied my cigarette-case and tried on my wide-brimmed hat, which became her very well.

The children crowded about me, begging, turning somersaults, and pulling one another's hair.

"Throw them a handful of pennies," the young woman advised, "and I shall ask them to let you alone."

"*Crute tu, kantchiuk*" (Run away, kids), I called. The children, hearing their own tongue, backed away.

The woman was anxious to be alone with me. Though her husband was calling to her repeatedly, she answered him nastily that she had more important business on hand than to come and talk to him.

"Why don't you come and stay with us?" she asked me. "You are a 'burbat' man to find a woman here."

I had one look at her husband, and answered: "Because I hate to be knifed in the back."

"I wish," she answered, smiling, "somebody were

faster than he is with the knife—or something else . . ."

Looking around, I said to her, "You are not all of one and the same tribe. Who is the *barossan* among you?"

"Hey, hey," she sighed. "Barossan? There is no barossan here. *Leis prala* is dead."

"And neither are you of the Biscaya Roms," I went on to say.

"No, I am not. I come from the Roms of your country," she answered, and forthwith began to speak Roumanian to me.

"Born where?" I asked.

"In America. But my parents came back instead of staying there, fools. And sold me to that Rom there! Sold a lamb to a wolf."

"But if you hate him so, why do you stay with him? You are no limb-tied lamb."

"It is because you don't know Stan that you talk so. He is a wolf, a real wolf, even if I am not a lamb."

Stan, a terrible-looking, pockmarked villain, abandoned his anvil, which was standing in a group of fifteen other anvils at which Gypsies were working furiously, and came toward us with swinging long arms that almost reached his knees.

"Meet me later in town under the arcades," the Gypsy woman whispered quickly to me, and then burst into peals of laughter as if to drown the echo of her whispers.

"It is a man from my country—from America," she said, "but his parents were also born where mine were; and I can't *dukker* him. You can't *dukker* a Brailian."

Stan narrowed his eye-slits, enveloped us both in one

penetrating glance, and asked me for a cigarette. I told him his wife had already taken all I had. I pleased him immensely. Without asking her to give him one, he turned his broad back on us and went back to his anvil, certain that his wife was following him.

I met the Gypsy woman later in the day under the arcades, and there she told me that her husband had literally enslaved several Gypsy families to him, and was the owner of an open-air factory of kettles. The Gypsies labored for him on a piece-work basis. He kept his men at work ten and twelve hours a day, under threat to have them arrested as vagabonds. They were recently arrived "Ungars," Gypsies from the Balkans who knew nothing of the language and the laws of the country, while Stan knew everything there was to be known, and was friendly with the police. He had also attached to himself several of the young women from among these "Ungars," without marrying them, according to custom, and without paying their fathers for them. Still he was very jealous of his wife. He sent her out *dukkering* in the city, but searched her every night when she returned, lest she hold some money from him.

"Then why don't you leave him, and run away?" I questioned again.

"Because he would kill my young brother if I should leave," she answered.

"Then why don't you report him to the police?" I suggested, timidly.

"Because I am no gorgio. These are our affairs, and have nothing to do with the police."

"You talked to me about your affairs," I said.

"To you it is different. You are twice from my country—the country where my parents came from, and the country where I was born."

"What can I do?"

"I just wanted you to know—if anything happens. . . ." And then she left me.

At the end of that summer, I learned of a large Gypsy camp near Bordeaux, over which reigned a beautiful woman—a queen, whose power over the people of the camp was absolute, and who was supposed to possess such supernatural powers that the wealthiest bourgeois of Bordeaux craved her advice and paid heavily for the magic she worked.

She met me with a broad smile, and she said, "The Ungars ate him."

"What do you mean—'ate him'?"

"Just so!" she said, gaily. "One day he was not at his anvil. Nobody had ever missed him. And one of these Ungars is my Rom now. He ate him."

The tribe was twice as large as it had been, considerably cleaner, and some of the younger girls, of twelve and thirteen, were even tastefully dressed. The queen had the intention of pitching her tent at the *Foire* of Bordeaux, and wanted information about a possible migration to America. She was born there; therefore, she was entitled to return any time she wanted. That she knew. But was not a queen entitled to take her subjects with her?

Now that the danger of strenuous persecution in France is over, year after year there arrive more Gypsies from everywhere, and the roads are as crowded with them as those of Hungary. A motley crowd, all kinds—acrobats and tight-rope walkers from Syria and Arabia, basket-makers from Slavonia, bear-tamers from Roumania, kettle-makers from Hungary—they travel in very small caravans, generally of one family each, and camp outside the gates of cities and towns.

The native *Roms* consider themselves superior, and refuse to have anything to do with these newcomers, who are classed under one depreciatory name: *Ungars*.

In June, 1927, Ignacio Zuloaga, the Spanish painter, very much interested in Gypsies and their affairs, told me that a friend of his had reported a large camp of Tziganes in Montreuil at the gates of Paris, on an open field beyond the fortifications of the city.

I went there. There were at least a hundred tents, camp-wagons and barracks, some of them exceptionally clean, and others indescribably filthy. The children tumbled over one another with the dogs and pigs in the mud and muck in front of every tent and shack.

The foremost wagon, raised high on piles, had white curtains on the windows and red hangings on the door, and was inhabited by the chief, a handsome dark man wearing a pointed black beard. The immediately adjoining tents belonged to the "females" of his family, as he explained it—his wife and his wife's sisters and their children. Wives of Gypsy chiefs have many sisters in monogamic countries.

At the far end of the camp were a dozen tents containing about a hundred souls, of blond, short, large-faced, broad-nosed, narrow-eyed, and thick-lipped people, who lived in such filth and squalor it made even the dirtiest Gypsy tents look like models of cleanliness.

Not one individual was whole-limbed. Each had

some physical defect. There were so many one-eyed ones, the camp looked like the last specimens of a degenerate nation of Cyclops. Pigs and geese and dogs and mangy donkeys were all under one tent together with women and children. The stench was abhorrent. But though these people lived so close to the Gypsies— practically in one camp—there was no trace of blondness in any of the Gypsies living in the other tents.

An imaginary line divided the two peoples. Even the Gypsy dogs seemed to respect this imaginary line.

When I asked the Gypsies about the blond people, I was told they were Cagots. "We never mingle with them. We never have anything to do with them, though we travel together occasionally."

The Cagots fulfilled the same function for the Gypsies as the Gypsies themselves had once upon a time fulfilled in India for the other castes. These Cagots were considered as impure and as detestable by the Gypsies, as the latter had been, and still are, by most people. The Gypsies spoke fluent French after a fashion, yet even the children spoke Calo amongst themselves, the chief refusing to listen to any other language when spoken to by his people.

This Gypsy camp has been at the gates of Paris for twenty-five years. The *barossan* and his family owned all the tents and shacks, which he rented to Gypsy people visiting the capital of France. It was a sort of camping hotel for Gypsy tourists.

"And the Cagots?" I asked.

"They have been here long before us. We found them here."

What a curious repetition, on a small scale, of what

had once happened to the Jats in India, when another race had conquered them. At the very gates of Paris, and how few people knew of their existence!

At that camp I heard an interesting Gypsy proverb: "When you cut a Gypsy in ten pieces, you have not killed him; you have merely made ten Gypsies."

"Explain," I asked.

"If you don't know that, you know nothing of our people. Go far and wide and return to see me in twenty years," the old Gypsy counseled.

VII—THE GYPSIES IN SPAIN

NOTHING IS MORE DISAPPOINTING THAN TO AR-
rive at Seville on an early summer morning.
One's eye is prepared to receive the shock
of a thousand intermingling colors, folding
and refolding upon themselves, rising in the air in
spirals and coming down in a rain of a thousand violent
hues, shed by a luminous sky; and one meets a quiet,
flat, gray, dusty waste, so barren of color one despairs
of ever seeing anything but grays and dirty whites,
blacks and deep ashen strips which seem never to have
had any contact with color.

The Sevillan men and women are no more colorful
than the inanimate things on the streets; they merge
with the cobblestone of the pavement. The women are
dressed in black; the men in gray. If anything breaks
the monotony of the first half-hour, it is an occasional
beggar in rags, rags beyond description—so tattered
one wonders how they hold together the body of a
human being. But as one advances into the slightly
billowing city, violent red bits of color, like poppies,
seem to shoot out and disappear from everywhere.
Poppies, daisies, bluebells seem to dance before you,
and merge just as rapidly into the grayness and the
blackness of the background. It is as though these
flowers were lying low in a barren field, and were only
shyly peeping over their shoulders at the newcomers.
And suddenly one realizes that the poppies and the
daisies and the bluebells are heads of human beings,

of swarthy, bronze, gracefully swaying Gypsies who appear from behind whitewashed walls, from deep courtyards, street-corners, from behind straw-covered peasant wagons whose horses have turned around in their harness to nibble at the straw and the grass of the driver's seat.

As the first impression of colorlessness vanishes, the vision one has expected in Seville realizes itself as fast as a stage play whose subject matter we know. Nay, faster than that!

Then one walks down the streets of Seville with the feeling that all earthly ties have snapped; that all physical laws have been ordered dismissed. There is neither weight nor form to one's body, and the ears perceive ethereal sounds one has never perceived before. The air whispers, the rustling of the trees becomes a mystical language which one understands for the first time, and the bending and the swaying of the top branches are so many graceful dances to which one is invited. Splashing against its stony shore, the Guadalquivir furnishes the rhythm of the precision of castanets played by master fingers. From afar, piercing through this music, comes the muffled sound of church-bells, unlike any real church-bells, but so much more like the imagined sound of church-bells; as though one had been deaf and had only imagined what such sounds should be before the faculty of hearing had been discovered.

If it were possible for a newborn child to realize all about him with the intelligence and experience of an adult, the suddenness and the strangeness would not be more complete than a first visit to Seville. But try to approach and come nearer to see and touch these beautiful shy flowers, and they disappear. They vanish as by the wave of a magic wand, until your own rhythm and your blood has adjusted itself to the new sensations. Then they not only do not disappear, but come toward you smiling, laughing, their deep eyes provoking and defying you, their glistening white teeth so set as to tempt you to feel the sharpness of their bite, and to kiss the lips that enclose them.

I have come in contact with Gypsies almost everywhere in the world:

The rustics in England, at fairs and on the roads, in inns and at racetracks—saucy, full-mouthed, gay and a bit vulgar, like good-natured traders who think more of the sport of bargaining than the gain therefrom— more like Scotchmen become articulate than like Gypsies; the Gypsies of Hungary, whose eyes reflect wild melancholy, whose faces always give you the impression that they are about to break out into loud cries, hysterical happiness alternating with fits of depression so intense and gripping one cannot resist the current set in motion by them.

I know the Gypsies of Roumania, former slaves, humble and arrogant, edging the paths of forests, or filling loudly the streets of crowded cities—beautiful specimens, magnificent in their bearing, clear-voiced and clear-eyed, women whose anger is more to be feared than that of tigers.

I have heard the singing Gypsies of Moscow, the Tartar Gypsy showmen of Asia, the heavy mulelike Gypsies of Bulgaria. I have slept in the tents of the quiet, intense, world-wise and all-knowing Gypsies of Macedonia, who make one think immediately of the American Indian, whom they resemble so much facially and in character; one thinks of a camp of Sioux Indians upon seeing the pointed pitched tents of the Tzicanis on the place that was once Pella, the capital of Macedonia.

I have broken bread with Basque Gypsies—dexterous, grinning, handy, and broad-shouldered smugglers and fishermen whose eyes pierce and envelop at the same time, whose knives are as readily buried in the bodies of human beings as they are placed in their sheaths, as though there were no difference between the flesh of a *gajo* and the emptiness to which the knife returns.

I have seen the French Gypsies of the north and the south, of the east and the west, who made me think of convicts released from long jail terms, trying to rehabilitate themselves by an excess of apparent honesty; standing at the gate of a peasant's dwelling, yelling their lungs out to offer their baskets. I have seen them everywhere.

But I have never seen Gypsies as handsome, as graceful, as vibrant, as fine, as mysterious and as self-sufficient as the Gypsies of Andalusia. Everything else may be claimed for the Gypsies of other countries; the Gypsies of Spain are the nobility and the aristocracy of the road. Could I have my wish when I shall be born again, I should want to be born a Spanish Gypsy.

A thousand people walk down the narrow trottoirs of Calle Serpe in Seville. The windows of the shops are hung with violently colored shirts, red shawls, blue velvets, and green capes. Over the doors of merchants glitter heavily brocaded bull-fighters' costumes. Beautiful women of all nationalities glide up and down, powdered and painted. Yet when the little Gypsy girl passes the middle of the street, her presence throws everybody aside in a meaningless heap. The glitter and the colorfulness of the shop windows is dulled. The whole street is outcolored, outclassed, and neutralized by a pair of nervous brown little feet, moving rhythmically, nonchalantly, and by the poise of a head that looks as though carved out of copper and bronze by the delicate chisel of Benvenuto Cellini.

There are hardly more than three thousand Gypsies in Seville, all herded in Triana, across the bridge of the Guadalquivir, the great river, so called by the ancient Moors. Hardly more than thirty or forty Gypsies ever venture out of their district into the center of the town. And yet their plasticity is so distinguishable from that of the rest of the population, their gait and their voices so different from those of any others, one sees nothing but Gypsies after seeing a member of the race; the rest of the Sevillans, including the tourists, serve no other purpose than to give them the necessary neutral background.

After the heat of the day, you sit quietly sipping your syrups at the terrace of a café, and a lone Gypsy girl asks for your hand to read your past, present, and future. And though no other Gypsies approach you that day, she has created the impression that your hand has been asked for by all the Gypsies in the world.

Every Gypsy has about him the atmosphere of the whole race. The Gypsy girl will laugh provokingly, and lean so close to you that you can feel her breath and hear her heartbeats. She holds your hand, and you feel her pulse as though you held a fluttering little bird between your fingers. She is shy, and yet you fear her. When your fear has left you, and you answer her timid

smile with a more provoking one, she only looks at you
—looks at you as no human being has ever looked at
you, and a thousand invisible sharp knives come nearer,
and the rustling of leaves and the splashing of the
Guadalquivir warns you not to move, not to make one
step if you value your life. Your hand, that has
divulged your past and present, falls limp at your side
before your future has been told. Never look at a
Gypsy girl of Seville like that, stranger. People have
died for less than that.

You go to a bull-fight. Twelve thousand people are
seated around the arena. The Spanish women have
come wearing their high combs. Their white man-
tillas are hanging down over their shoulders, and their
graceful, plump bodies are wrapped in colored shawls.
The sun beats down upon the balustrades hung with
swaying red and green silks, a rising slope of violently
colored human flowers.

High in a corner of the grand stand is a group of
three Gypsies. One of them has a lone red rose stuck
in her jet-black hair. Another one holds a white carnation between her teeth. A third one wears a little
yellow strip of cloth around her neck. A bareheaded,
clean-shaven man stands near them, apparently no different from the thousands of swarthy men eagerly waiting for the appearance of the *cuadrilla;* yet one sees
nothing but Gitanos, and hears only their clear laughter. Their staccato articulation of words pierces
through the noise made by the whole throng. The
Gitanas are here. Three women against fifteen thousand, and you see only them!

The big black door of the arena opens. The bull-
fighters and their assistants appear, twenty in all,

marching to the toreador music from "Carmen." A few minutes later the big door is swung open again, and an infuriated bull stops short in the glare of the sun. Six bulls are to be killed that afternoon by three matadors—each one killing two. The movements of one of the three matadors are so different from those of the others! Instead of fighting the bull, he dances with him. He taunts and teases and plays with the bull until the animal becomes a playful kitten that withdraws its claws as soon as it has stretched out its paw. The bull looked so immense upon its entrance into the arena, and the matador so small! The picture reverses itself. It had seemed unfair that the little man should face an infuriated bull whose sharp horns are a hundred times more dangerous than the thin blade in the hand of the matador. And now it seems unfair that so helpless a little animal should stand before an armed giant, to be played with before it is slaughtered.

The Gitanillo, the little Gypsy matador, the idol of Spain, makes a pass with his hand in front of the bull. The bull recovers his fury and immensity—appears now twice as big as he really is, and a thousand times more dangerous. The Gitanillo has again become like a pigmy before a giant. The hearts of the crowd are beating for the matador. The arena is hushed and metamorphosed into an open-air cathedral where a holy rite is carried out. The Gitanillo kills the bull with the same reverence as if he were a priest offering sacrifices to a god.

Can you understand what has happened? You will have no such sensations when the other matadors do their work. It will appear what it really is—killing for sport.

You go to the theater. The evening performance begins at eleven o'clock. Half a dozen singers and dancers follow one after another. The last number is that of Dora la Cordobezita—the Gitana from Cordoba. She is short and stout. I wondered why she was there at all! I did not understand why the posters in front of the theater gave her so much prominence. Her voice! Ridiculous! There was a great disparity between her and the accompanist. They fought one another. They were never in time, nor in tune. Suddenly, Dora faced her audience squarely. She raised her eyelids and lowered them again, and held me captive between her eyelashes. She stretched out her arms and embraced us all. Her raucous voice told rather than sang the tale of an abandoned woman and the revenge she planned to take. Each word was thrown at the audience. She gave to each word a portentous meaning. We men thought of women we had neglected, and the revenge sung by Dora became the revenge sung by all womanhood.

Dora glided from this song to another one—a gay one, a saucy one. A court of justice was instantly transformed into a house of mirth. I chuckled at first and then laughed, and then held my splitting sides—laughter so loud I could not hear what Dora was saying—hypnotized by her: I, who had been so near to crying just a minute before.

Dora stopped, waited until the last echo of laughter had died, then snapped her fingers, and the pianist stopped his tinkling. She bent a little forward, and looked into the eyes of the audience, melting them together into a thousand-headed monster. When we were quiet again, Dora began to beat out strange rhythms

with the heel of her shoe upon the floor. When the
rhythm had permeated us, taken possession of us, she
embroidered upon it a song, of which every fourth
line was "My Mother Was a Gitana."

I am attempting to write a story of the Gypsies.
Yet for those who have heard that song sung by Dora
la Cordobezita, dates and facts, descriptions and evo-
cations are so feeble I cannot hope to explain in a
thousand years what Dora accomplishes in but a few
minutes. Dora and the Gitanillo, the bull-fighter, tell
the history of the Gypsies not only of a thousand uncertain years, but of all the years past and all the years
to come. Can anyone understand what I mean?

At the fair-place, the *Feria,* are thousands of people
on foot and on horseback. At the far end of the fair-
ground are a half-dozen tents and as many wagons
drawn by mangy donkeys and half-starved horses. To
one wagon a donkey is harnessed beside a horse, to another one a young heifer near a decrepit mule. People
are buying and selling, disputing vociferously, discus-
sing prices, bargaining, shaking hands, drinking to the
health of an ox or a cow they have bought or sold,
calling to one another, laughing and shouting. Why
are the Gypsies so unconcerned at everything happening around them? They don't seem to have anything
for sale—anything anyone may want. Have they come
to the fair to see people? To greet friends?

Imperceptibly, the isolated Gypsy camp gains life,
first by other Gypsies who greet their acquaintances,
then by peasants who are attracted despite themselves
nearer and nearer to the Gypsy camp-fires. The Gitanos ignore the existence even of the peasants. When

the fair has come to an end for the day, and buyers have withdrawn somewhere to the shade, the Gitano crowd has increased, from the original twenty, to a hundred. In a half-hour, however, tight-fisted peasants, short-necked, thick-necked, and stubborn, depart, one with a mangy mule he did not want to buy, and another one with a few silver pieces but minus the cow he did not want to sell. They walk a few paces, stop, hesitate, want to return, to get back the money or the cow. They have been convinced by the Gitanos that they have made the best bargain on earth—the one by buying the mule, and the other by separating himself from his cow. Yet when they are alone, they begin to realize that the contrary is true. The Gypsies have cheated them. But a bargain is a bargain. They are men. They are proud. They are Spaniards.

The Gitanos have already vanished. The tents have collapsed. The wagons have disappeared in different directions; to meet again on the outside of the town where the men will stretch on the ground, face skyward, until the blue of the heavens densifies itself and the stars glitter against the velvety background.

In Granada we are warned not to go up to the Albaicin—the Gypsy quarter—unless we are accompanied by someone who knows the district.

The Albaicin nestles upon the hill that faces the Alhambra. Leaning over the walls of the Alhambra, the last retreat of the Moor, one can see the holes dug out in the rock of the Albaicin. At dawn the people swarming out of these holes look like wolves coming out of caves. The whole side of the Albaicin is combed ten rows high with these holes in which the Gypsies

live with their families. The faint sound of a guitar
is thrown upon the early morning breeze that blows
toward the snow-covered Sierra Nevada. High-
pitched tones of angry women harmonize with the
clinking of the bells dangling from the necks of mules.
As the morning advances, the noise from the Albaicin
increases: the mingling of a dozen orchestras playing
contra-rhythms against a single time.

I walked down the hill across the little brook hon-
ored with the name of "river," and was warned again
by a friend who happened to be with me not to go
alone up the Albaicin. This warning was given me by
people who knew me and by those who did not.

Before I had made a dozen steps up the hill, an old
Gitana offered to sell me flowers, read my palm, dance,
sing, and tell me the place where a doña is waiting for
me. I shook the old witch off, and continued my way.
The doña she had been talking about in glowing terms
appeared before me from behind a tree. Bowing ever
so politely, she asked for a cigarette in exchange for the
red carnation she carried behind her ears.

"You are an *extranjero,* are you not? I would adore
being your guide. There is an old mill not far off,
the history of which I know thoroughly. It has been
a castle once—a Moorish castle. There are still broken
columns in the yard with Moorish inscriptions upon
them. And if you want to hear Gypsy music, I know
the only place. Why, the best Gitana guitarist is my
closest friend. There is an old woman who still knows
flamence songs that have been otherwise forgotten."

If you don't show any interest in what the Gypsy
girl has to say, she whispers in your ear that a friend
of hers, just out of jail, would like to sell the treasure

he buried somewhere before being taken to his cell. It could not be sold to a local man, but an *extranjero* would get it for a few pesetas. If you are still not interested, the young Gitana will raise herself to her full height, look at you, turn you around by your shoulders so as to face you squarely, and ask: "Well, are you a hundred years old? I have been waiting for you. I have been longing for you."

You are almost inclined to believe her, her voice rings so true, when you remember the warnings given you by friends. If you keep on walking, she will leave you abruptly. The domain of her activity has definite bounds. A few steps farther on, you will be met by others who will offer to guide you, allow you to take group photographs, introduce you to the king of the Gitanos, organize choruses for you, dances, parties, sell you antique copper pots, rugs, statues in silver and ivory which have been handed down to the Gypsies by their ancestors, the Egyptians and Phœnicians. No? Perhaps you are interested in the people that another *boro ray,* another great man, once came to meet! Yet whatever was told that *boro ray* is not true. He came from America (or was it England?) to ask them what they knew about their ancestors. The Roms lied to him. One would like to tell *you* the truth about the Gitanos.

Before you have said yes or no to him, the Gitano tells you all he knows. If you have allowed him to go on for a few minutes, he considers himself hired by you to do everything—procure songsters, women, dancers, copper kettles, ivory statues, a guitarist; you are in his hands. He is your master. With a wink of an eye and a whirl, he drives away whosoever attempts to approach you. To the hundreds of half-naked children who buzz around like flies, he cries out that they cast a bad light upon the whole race by begging from a señor who has come to them with his heart full of friendship. . . . "Señor, throw them a handful of copper pieces. Rid us of this vermin! Here, scoundrel!"

The whole thing is a mad, wild dream—a nightmare. The beggars look more like real kings in make-believe costumes. It seems impossible that a man so handsome and imposing, so proud in demeanor and gait, should have talked the way he has; impossible that these beautiful women should stretch begging hands for a piece of silver to buy their children a crust of bread; impossible that such a people should live like wolves and foxes in dark holes dug out in the mountains, and wallow in the filth and dirt of the narrow road passing in front of their homes. Two women dressed in colored rags stepped out from a mountain hole. Two villainous-looking men, their heads covered by wide-brimmed hats worn over colored handkerchiefs, snapped their fingers. The women began to dance and sing. Other women joined them. Now there were six, ten, twenty women dancing. A blind guitarist strummed an indefinable tune upon his wires. Wine appeared—Muscatel, Tío Pepe, Val de Peñas. They drank, sang, danced, and shouted. Fifteen minutes later, they disappeared as suddenly as they had come. Was it real? Was it a dream? A Fata Morgana? I was left alone on the road.

The Gitanerias of Seville, Granada, Cordoba, and Madrid are the reservoirs of the Gypsydom of Spain. Each Gypsy or family of Gypsies belongs to a Gitane-

ria. They may even cross the border into another country; still they belong to the clan, are subject to the customs, traditions, and laws of the clan. The old authority
of the Gypsy chief still holds sway over the members of
his tribe, the laws of the country notwithstanding. The
racial memory of an organization keeps Gypsies together as a body. Though a Gypsy knows that he cannot depend, when in trouble with the civil or criminal
authorities, upon the whole Gypsydom of Spain, he
knows that the Triana or the Albaicin will come to his
rescue—will indeed impoverish itself to save him from
a prison sentence, or rescue him from the gallows.
Gypsy influence is so powerful, the pressure a clan can
exert upon the dispensers of justice, upon the lowest-
rank policeman or the highest civil official, is so strong,
that it has become proverbial. The Spaniards say:
"It is easier to hold an eel than a Gitano."

I saw something of this influence some years ago in
Pamplona, two hours from San Sebastian, the summer residence of the King of Spain. I had come there
for the midsummer fair and the bull-fights. One-third
of the fair-grounds was occupied by garlic, a chain of
mountains of garlic twenty feet high and sixty feet
wide. The odor was so strong I was literally drunk
when I emerged from the alley between the two rows
of garlic mountains.

Upon the advice of Señor Zuloaga, I went to the
grounds reserved for the horse-fair. Here were horses,
donkeys, and cattle of all kinds, watched over carefully by solid and powerful mountaineers who still
wore the costume their ancestors had worn hundreds
of years ago; velvet knee-breeches, sleeveless jackets,
embroidered lace collars.

At the edge of the fair-grounds were a dozen Gypsy
tents. A few mangy mules and glandered horses were
tethered to the tent pegs. No one seemed to watch
them. A hundred feet away across the road Gypsy women were boiling food for the clan, while the men
squatted or lay stretched out upon the sparse grass,
face upward, totally indifferent as to what was happening to their families and beasts, indifferent as to
what was going on in the market. Behind scattered
trees, young Gypsy lovers were holding hands and
looking into one another's eyes. I wondered why the
Gypsies were not more active—why they were not in
the thick of the fair, as I had seen them at fairs in other
countries. Even the old women made no attempt at
dukkering (telling fortune) the *gajos*. They had merely come there for a holiday. About eleven o'clock in
the morning, the Gypsies sat down to their first meal.
It was unbearably hot at noon. The visitors at the
fair began to thin out. In half an hour there were
hardly any strangers. Only the peasants and mountaineers who had brought their cattle for sale remained;
but after eating large slices of bread and drinking
deeply from the wine carried in leather pouches slung
over shoulders, they began a search for shady places.

The Gypsies became more and more active, in the
measure that the others became less so. They folded
their tents, and attracted the attention of two policemen to the fact that they were going away, and that
they were taking only what belonged to them.

The policemen looked on half asleep. It was the
hour of the siesta. A few of the younger Gypsies left
on foot across the field. The caravan split to go in
different directions, leaving off a few old men and wo-

men about a third of a mile from the fair-grounds. Toward four o'clock, when the peasants and mountaineers arose from their drowsiness and half-drunkenness, there were loud cries. Three horses and four donkeys had disappeared. No one doubted the Gitanos had stolen them. The policemen were called.

They came upon what remained of the Gypsy caravan—a few old men and women—and conducted them, amidst a great hullabaloo and with threatening gestures, to the "Gendarmeria." There the old Gitanos were asked where the others had gone. One of the old men, who walked doubled up like a jack-knife, suddenly straightened himself out to his full height, and began to tell, in fluent and forceful Spanish, what was going to happen to the policemen who had arrested him—him, an innocent man. He dragged in the names of several of the most important people of Pamplona, claiming they would immediately come to his aid; and, pointing his finger at the policemen who had arrested him, he cried out: "And you, you and you will be thrown out upon the street, and your wives will go a-begging and your children will go a-stealing, hungry! I shall tell my protectors how you have arrested me unjustly, threatened me, beaten me, upon the request of stupid *busnes,* who have put a few pesetas in your hands! You have been bribed by them. I know. Wait and see!"

The *rurales,* who had until then been on the side of the claimants, turned against the peasants at the mention of the names of the personages, and began to curse them out roundly for accusing innocent men of theft. One uniformed man, with a more dialectic turn of mind than the others, asked the principal claimant:

"And if you are asked to prove that you really had the two horses you claim have been stolen from you, how could you prove that? Eh? And if you did not have them, how could anybody have stolen them from you? You are a drunkard. You sold your caballos last week. You don't remember. You have not had them today at the fair. Can anybody here witness the fact that you had two horses at the fair, eh? No?

"Well, and if you have had them, perhaps the man who bought them from you has left the horses with you until he returns from the Corrida. But you, *you* have meanwhile sold them again to somebody else, and now you claim they have been stolen from you! You saw a few old honest Gitanos, and that gave you the idea. You are a thief and a liar and a cheat, and deserve twenty years' penal servitude. Gitanos are better Spaniards than you are! I know you.

"Am I to lose my means of livelihood and have my wife go begging from door to door because of the likes of you?" the policeman shouted. Tears streamed from his eyes. His voice trembled. His face was purple-red. The other claimants left the police station before the *rurales* turned upon them; the last ones to go were "booted" out.

The old Gypsies bowed themselves out, and left by a road which branched out in a half-dozen directions.

A little later in the afternoon, I talked to one of the *rurales.*

"What could I do?" he said to me over a glass of wine. "I know that the Gitanos have stolen the horses. But Don Ignacio is an *aficionado* of the Gitanos. His children have had Gitano wet-nurses, and there is more to be said that everybody knows and nobody speaks about. And if it had not been Don Ignacio, it would have been some other man—a higher official who is also *aficionado*. They are slippery people, these Gitanos. And it is better to look away when they do something. I tell my children: look elsewhere when Gitanos pass the road!"

Stolen horses and cattle quickly find their way across the border into France, where the Basque Gypsies take them in exchange for cattle that have come into their hands during the week.

It was early morning in the *rastro,* the thieves' market of Madrid. Around in narrow alleys, upon a wide square, were little heaps containing all imaginable things which men and women offered for sale to the passers-by, of whom we were among the first. Soon, however, came hundreds of people from every angle. In one heap there were pocket-books, revolvers, knives, paintings, clothes of all descriptions, and ivory canes. In another heap, watched over by a tall Gypsy, were watches, rings, shoes, and swords.

Beside a huge pile of old toreador clothes stood a man in the fifties, his eyes shaded by a battered old sombrero, the rest of his face almost buried under his coat. My friend, Don Pedro, reached for my hand. A tremor passed through his sensitive body. He closed his eyes as if he were ready to faint, as though fascinated by the pile of old colored velvets and the man who stood behind it. He dragged me aside.

"Come quickly from here. This is an old toreador selling his things—the things in which he won glory and thousands of pesetas."

When we had walked away, Don Pedro turned

around again. Two lithe Gypsies were bargaining with the man for his clothes.

Everything that is stolen or begged in Spain during the week finds its way to the *rastro* every Sunday. Not a thing is too cheap or too costly to be there. It is brought in pockets, in bundles, on the backs of donkeys, in hay-carts, in battered automobiles. An unwritten law protects stolen property after the week is up. You can go and buy it back at the *rastro,* telling the man behind the heap of rags that it was yours once. But if you do so, you may have to pay a higher price: pay for the sentimental value it must have for a former owner; a value which it has not to the ordinary passer-by.

I suddenly reached for my pocket-book, and placed it inside my coat. Don Pedro explained to me that nothing is ever stolen at the *rastro.* You can leave your belongings in the middle of the street and no one will touch them. It is a tradition, and Spanish traditions are never broken. We stopped before several piles to buy knicknacks here and there.

At the Bretaña, where we stopped for breakfast, a troupe of four Gypsies and their wives were dancing and singing Flamenco songs to a crowd of revelers so fresh and so untired I did not know whether they were late revelers of the previous night or whether they had started their morning early.

And suddenly I discovered that my watch had been stolen. Don Pedro refused to believe that the century-old tradition about the *rastro* had been broken. In his eyes, the traditions of the whole of Spain, the traditions of centuries, were involved. Spain's glory and literature, Spain's art and religion, the honor of all

Spain was involved in the stealing of my watch in the *rastro*. He turned savagely upon me:

"And how do you know that I have not taken it? Yes, what makes you so certain I have not taken your watch?" When I refused to understand, he said: "That is why foreigners will never understand Spain. And that is why we will never become the country of tourists like France. You will never understand the depth of our traditions. Your watch was not stolen at the *rastro,* señor. It is against its traditions!"

Don Pedro was so angry I made believe I believed.

The Gitanos of Spain believe that they are of Egyptian origin. They disclaim any community of origin with the Gypsies of Hungary, with the Ungars, and only reluctantly admit kinship with the Basque Gypsies, their neighbors. When I pointed out the similarity of their Calo with the Calo of the Ungars, they refused to acknowledge that this was proof of a common origin. A Gitano of the Albaicin, in Granada, who had a little book-learning, drew my attention to the fact that the Gypsies of Spain did not look like the Gypsies of other countries, and that they resembled rather the profiles on the bas-reliefs of Egyptian monuments. When that did not convince me, he rose to his full height, and, pointing to a number of Gypsy women going down the hill, he cried: "Look at the bearing of our people, and compare their proud gait to the crawling of the Ungars! Ungars behave like the lowest kind of animals before a white man. I have heard it said that they were and still are slaves in their countries. They have always been slaves. And *boro rays,* great men, from the country of the Ingloses and from the country of the Alemanos, have proven now that the Ungars came from India, where they have, since time immemorial, been the slaves of the people there."

And then he repeated to me an old legend:

"Once there was a great Egyptian king whose name was Pharaoh, who, when he had conquered the whole world, became despondent because, loving war as he did, there was nothing left for him to do. At last he challenged God to come down with his host of angels and match his strength against the might of Pharaoh.

"God said: 'I shall not match my strength against that of a man.' Nevertheless, God was angry at Pharaoh, and, to punish him, opened a huge cavern in the side of a mountain and caused a strong wind to blow Pharaoh and his army into the cavern. Then the mountain closed after them. To this day, whoever goes to the mountain on the Eve of St. John can hear Pharaoh and his armies singing and carrying on in the depths of the earth.

"When Pharaoh and his armies had disappeared, the kings of the nations who had been vassals to Egypt revolted against her. Inasmuch as Egypt, having lost her king and soldiers, was without defense, her enemies easily triumphed, and drove the Egyptians out of the land, scattering them to the four winds over the earth That is how we came to Spain."

Indeed, the Gitanos of Spain *are* of a nobler type than the Gypsies elsewhere. Taken as a whole, the men are handsomer and the women are more beautiful than the Gypsies of Roumania or Hungary. While they are fully as dark as the Ungars, there is an entirely different pigment in their darkness, as though some green had been mixed in the copper-bronze of their skin. The hair of the Gitana is darker than that of her sisters of other countries, and though not smoother, it is more lustrous. The flexibility and sleekness of a Gitano body are such as are not possessed by any other people on earth, Gypsies or non-Gypsies. Gitanas do not walk, but glide like a young tigress. The leaps of their dances are absolutely tigrish.

The Gypsies of other countries fear the white people among whom they live, but the Gitano disdains white men, considers himself so superior to the Spaniard, he looks upon mixed marriages as royalty looks upon mis-alliances.

A Gypsy woman who has married a Spaniard is treated by her people as is a white woman in the South of the United States who has married a Negro. A case in point is that of a beautiful Gitana dancer living in Paris who married a celebrated French actor. Not only has she herself become an outcast of her clan, but her family, living in the Albaicin at Granada, was ostracized and had to leave town, despite the fact that the "crime" had been committed in Paris. That young Gitana is so afraid of the wrath of her people that, though she pines for her dear Andalusia, she dares not cross the borders of France, and hides her face when she sees one of her people. "You mark my words," she told me, "one day I shall be stabbed or strangled. I have betrayed my people."

The rules for the maintenance of the purity of the race are and have been so strict for the last hundred or hundred and fifty years that there has been very little admixture of foreign blood. Yet, as a matter of

fact, it has not always been so. The Gypsies came
to Spain at the beginning of the fifteenth century.
Official documents prove that they were already in
Castile in 1490. They had been in Portugal long before, and probably had lived in Barcelona before the
celebrated group had entered Paris under the leadership of their "counts" and "dukes."

In those days, wandering from place to place, and
driven from pillar to post, because of their strangeness,
because of their reputed paganism and their depredations, they joined the wandering *calabrezos* living in
Spain, who may or may not have been calabrezos, but
were kettle-makers, iron-workers, and nomads. These
various groups of calabrezos and Gypsies intermingled
so that the Gypsies lost their identity, and were also
called "calabrezos" by the people, and referred to as
such in various documents. The edicts and laws of the
time speak of them as the "calabrezos and caldareros."
Some called them "Alemanos" (Germans), Greeks, or
"people who pretend that they are Egyptians and speak
all languages."

When the Church and the civil authorities noted that
the Gypsies, through their sorcery, had gained an as-
cendency which superseded their own authority over
the superstitious Spaniards, the "Egyptians, calabrezos,
and caldareros" were accused of being enemies of the
country and of Christendom, and of being in the pay
of the Moors, with whom the Spaniards were then at
war.

Other accusations followed. The Gitanos were accused of desecrating holy images, and of selling stolen
children into slavery in Africa. Every known and
unknown crime committed in the whole of Spain was

laid at the feet of the Gitanos. But the Gitanos loved Spain: a country which suited them so well because of its climate and because of its topographical conditions. The Gypsies who entered Spain had learned from long experience in the west of Europe how to get by in Christian countries. They introduced themselves into the homes of the most prominent families of Spain. Gitana women retained their powers over the sensuous Spaniards by refusing themselves to them. Seville and other Gitanerias were the centers of debaucheries and orgies for the delectation of the *busnes.* But though the Gypsy women danced for the white men, and assumed the most lascivious poses before them, driving the youth of the nobility insane, they withdrew when arms were stretched out for them, as soon as the purity of the race was menaced.

Somehow, the Gitanas of Spain had an almost insurmountable dislike for the Spaniards, though they did not have the same repugnance for the Moors. The Moors were a people of similar temperament; the only difference being that the Moors lived in tents of stone, behind marble lace and columns and gilded canopies. The Moors resembled them in color, and shared with them a taste for dancing and other forms of rhythmical expression. There being no reciprocal aversion between these two peoples, many a Gypsy woman found her couch in the harem of a Moor. Gitanos preferred serving as spies for the Moors against the Spaniards to serving the Spaniards against the Moors.

At the fall of the Alhambra, when Cordoba and the rest of Andalusia became Spanish territory, there was enough Moorish blood in the Gypsies to mold the type of the clans that had remained to live in Christian

Spain. It is this Moorish blood in the Gitanos which makes them look so different from the other Gypsies, and which has in many respects so changed the character of the people.

With the Moorish blood, the Gitanos have also inherited an intense hatred against the Christian oppressor. Gitanos, though rightly claiming that not one of them has ever been destroyed by the Inquisition, only feign to have accepted Catholicism. At bottom, they have no more understanding or love of that religion than they have of any other. The efforts of George Borrow and other well-wishing "Biblers" have been wasteful when they have not been stupid.

The Spanish government has exerted itself in the last five hundred years to solve the Gypsy problem more than any other government. The edict of one Spanish king forbade the Gypsies to call themselves "Gitanos" and threatened to punish with heavy fine and imprisonment any Spaniard who dared to refer to them by that name.

Issuing laws against the Gitanos—one forbidding them to vagabond, the other forbidding them to live in cities and towns, ordering their banishment, compelling them to become agriculturists, forbidding them entrance to churches and ordering them to become good Christians—and laws by which they were forbidden to practice blacksmithing (the one trade in which the Gypsies were and are of all peoples the most skilled) —issuing such laws became the great sport of the Spanish kings at the beginning of the fourteenth century. When a king was tired of idleness, he toyed with laws against the Gitanos. Court flatterers knew how to provide the necessary excitement to make such laws appear the salvation of Spain and the king the savior of his country.

Upon accession to the throne, each Spanish ruler framed a new anti-Gitano law, nullifying the measures taken by his predecessors to rid the country of the unwelcome guests. Each king changed the wording of his own laws at least a dozen times during his reign. To rid Spain of the Gitanos by all means was the main purpose. The mournful Spaniard resented the wild gaiety and happiness of the Gypsy quite as much as he resented the colorfulness of the Moor.

But the Gypsies had nowhere to go. Defeating the Moors, Ferdinand and Isabella closed to the Gitanos their only country of refuge. France did not want them, and had enacted laws as Draconian as those of her neighbor. Germany and Italy hunted them down with the utmost rigor. It must not be forgotten that the Gitanos who first entered Spain were of the same generation with those who had passed through the very Christian countries of Italy, Germany, and France. Beyond Spain was the sea—or Africa. And many were the Gitanos who, having had a taste of Spanish Christianity, preferred to go with the Moors when these unfortunates were driven back to Africa at the beginning of the seventeenth century. But this friendliness of the Moors cost the lives of many Gypsies who remained in Spain.

The Gitanos who crossed secretly into France, fell into the hard hands and against the pitchforks of the most cruel people of Europe: the Navarre peasants. Hundreds of people, men, women, and children, were strangled and impaled in one single night. Those who survived, recrossed secretly and hastily into Spain, to hide there in the wilderness and in the inaccessible mountains.

As all the laws against the Gitanos provided the manner in which they should die, and not a single one a manner in which they might live, the hunted people forged their own laws for that purpose. During three hundred years they preyed upon every non-Gitano in villages, towns, fields, in the mountains, on the highways, and in the forests. Highway robbery, wholesale destruction of fields and villages, sorcery, cattle-poisoning, total disregard for human life and property, became the law of the Gitano—*Leis prala,* the law of the brotherhood. An untamed, lawless people to begin with, the Gitanos now became savage beasts as a result of the laws of Spanish kings. If it is possible to domesticate a wolf by kindness, it is also possible to make a wolf out of a good man by cruelty.

Francisco de Cordova tells the tale of the sack of the city of Logroño during the pestilence of 1618, as an example of the Gitano audacity and cruelty:

"About the middle of the sixteenth century, there resided one Francisco Alvarez in the city of Logroño, the chief town of Rioja, a province which borders on Aragon. He was a man above middle age, sober, reserved, and in general absorbed in thought; he lived near the great church, and obtained a livelihood by selling printed books and manuscripts in a small shop. He was a very learned man, and was continually reading the books which he was in the habit of selling, and some of these books were in foreign tongues and characters, so foreign, indeed, that none but himself and some of his friends, the canons, could understand them.

He was much visited by the clergy, who were his principal customers, and took much pleasure in listening to his discourse.

"He had been a constant traveler in his youth, and had wandered through all Spain, visiting the various provinces and the most remarkable cities. It was likewise said that he had visited Italy and Barbary. He was, however, invariably silent with respect to his travels, and whenever the subject was mentioned to him, the gloom and melancholy which usually clouded his features increased.

"One day, in early autumn, he was visited by a priest with whom he had long been intimate, and for whom he had always displayed a greater respect and liking than for any other acquaintance. The ecclesiastic found him even sadder than usual, and there was a haggard paleness upon his countenance which alarmed his visitor. The good priest made affectionate inquiries respecting the health of his friend, and whether anything had of late occurred to give him uneasiness; adding, at the same time, that he had long suspected that some secret lay heavy upon his mind, which he now conjured him to reveal, as life was uncertain and it was very possible that he might be quickly summoned from earth into the presence of his Maker.

"The bookseller continued for some time in gloomy meditation, till at last he broke silence in these words:

" 'It is true I have a secret which weighs heavy upon my mind, and which I am still loath to reveal; but I have a presentiment that my end is approaching, and that a great misfortune is about to fall upon this city; I will, therefore, unburden myself; for it were now a sin to remain silent.

" 'I am, as you are aware, a native of this town, which I first left when I went to acquire an education at Salamanca. I continued there until I became a licentiate, when I quitted the university and strolled through Spain, supporting myself by touching the guitar, according to the practice of penniless students. My adventures were numerous, and I frequently experienced great poverty. Once, whilst making my way from Toledo to Andalusia through the wild mountains, I fell in with and was made captive by a band of Gitanos, or wandering Egyptians. I should probably have been assassinated by them, but my skill in music saved my life. I continued with them a considerable time, till at last they persuaded me to become one of them, whereupon I was inaugurated into their society with many strange and horrid ceremonies. Having thus become a Gitano, I went with them to plunder and assassinate upon the roads.

" 'The count, or head man, of these Gitanos had an only daughter about my own age. She was very beautiful, but, at the same time, exceedingly strong and robust. This Gitana was given to me as a wife or cadfee, and I lived with her several years, and she bore me children.

" 'My wife was an arrant Gitana, and in her all the wickedness of her race seemed to be concentrated. At last her father was killed in an affray with the troopers of the Hermandad, whereupon my wife and myself succeeded to the authority which he had formerly exercised in the tribe. We had at first loved each other, but the Gitano life, with its accompanying wickedness, becoming hateful to my eyes, my wife, who was not slow in perceiving my altered disposition, conceived for me a deadly hatred. Apprehending that I meditated withdrawing myself from the society and perhaps betraying the secrets of the band, she formed a conspiracy against me, and, at one time being opposite the Moorish coast, I was seized and bound by the other Gitanos, conveyed to the sea and delivered as a slave into the hands of the Moors.

" 'I continued for a long time in slavery in various parts of Morocco and Fez, until I was at length redeemed from my state of bondage by a missionary friar who paid my ransom. With him I shortly after departed for Italy, of which country he was a native. There I remained some years, until a longing to revisit my native land seized me, when I returned to Spain and established myself here where I have since lived by selling books, many of which I brought from the strange lands which I visited. I kept my history, however, a profound secret, being afraid of exposing myself to the laws of force against the Gitanos to which I should instantly become amenable, were it once known that I had at any time been a member of this detestable sect.

" 'My present wretchedness, of which you have demanded the cause, dates from yesterday. I had been on a short journey to the Augustine Convent, on the plain in the direction of Saragossa, carrying with me an Arabian book which a learned monk was desirous of seeing. Night overtook me ere I could return. Losing my way, I wandered about until I came near a dilapidated edifice with which I was acquainted. I was about to leave when I heard voices within the ruined walls. I listened, and recognized the language of the Gitanos; I was about to fly, when a word arrested me. It was "Drao," which in their tongue signifies the horrid poison with which this race are in the habit of destroying cattle. They now said that the men of Logroño should rue the Drao which they had been casting. I heard no more, but fled. What increased my fear was that in the words spoken I thought I recognized the peculiar jargon of my own tribe. I repeat that I believe some horrible misfortune is overhanging this city, and that my own days are numbered.'

"The priest, having conversed with him for some time upon particular points of the history that he had related, took his leave, advising him to compose his spirits as he saw no reason why he should indulge in such gloomy forebodings.

"The very next day a sickness broke out in the town of Logroño. It was one of a peculiar kind; unlike most others. It did not arise by slow and gradual degrees, but at once appeared in full violence in the shape of a terrible epidemic. Dizziness in the head was the first symptom; then, convulsive writhings were followed by a dreadful struggle between life and death, which generally terminated in favor of the grim destroyer. The bodies, after the spirit which animated them had taken flight, were frightfully swollen, and exhibited a dark blue color, checkered with crimson spots. Nothing was heard within the houses or the streets but groans of agony. No remedy was at hand, and the powers of medicine were exhausted in vain upon the terrible pest. Within a few days the greatest part of the inhabitants of Logroño had perished. The bookseller had not been seen since the beginning of this frightful visitation.

"Once, at the dead of night, a knock was heard at the door of the priest, of whom we have already spoken. The priest staggered to the door and opened it—he was the only one who had remained alive in the house, and was himself slowly recovering from the malady which had destroyed all the other inmates. A wild, spectral-looking figure presented itself to his eye. It was his friend Alvarez. Both went into the house, when the bookseller, glancing gloomily on the wasted features of the priest, exclaimed:

" 'You, too, I see, amongst others, have cause to rue the Drao which the Gitanos have cast. Know,' he continued, 'that the fountains of Logroño have been poisoned by emissaries of the roving bands who are now assembled in the neighborhood. On the first appearance of the disorder, from which I happily escaped by drinking the water of a private fountain which I possess in my own house, I instantly recognized the effects of the poison of the Gitanos, brought by their ancestors from the isles of the Indian Sea; and suspecting their intentions, I disguised myself as a Gitano and went forth in the hope of being able to acquaint myself with their designs. They intended, from the first, to sack the town, as soon as it should have been emptied of its defenders.

" 'Midday, tomorrow, is the hour in which they have determined to make the attempt. No time can be lost. Let us, therefore, warn those of our townspeople who still survive that they make preparations for their defense.'

"Whereupon the two friends proceeded to their chief magistrate, who had been but slightly affected by the disorder. He heard the tale of the bookseller with horror and astonishment, and immediately took the best measures possible for frustrating the design of the Gitanos. All the men capable of bearing arms in Logroño were assembled. Weapons of every description were put in their hands. By the advice of the bookseller, all the gates of the town were shut, with the exception of the principal one; and the little band of defenders, which barely amounted to sixty men, was stationed in the great square, to which, he said, it was the intention of the Gitanos to penetrate in the first instance, and then, dividing themselves into various parties, to sack the place. The bookseller was constituted leader of the guardians of the town.

"Later that afternoon, the sky was overcast, and tempest clouds, fraught with lightning and thunder, were hanging black and horrid over the town of Logroño. The little troop of defenders, resting on their arms, stood awaiting the arrival of their enemies. Rage fired their minds as they thought of the deaths of their fathers, their sons, and their dearest relatives, who had perished, not by the hand of God, but, like infected cattle, by the hellish arts of Egyptian sorcerers. They longed for their appearance, determined to wreak upon them a bloody revenge. Not a word was uttered. The profound silence that reigned around was interrupted only by the occasional muttering of the thunder-clouds. Suddenly, Alvarez, who had been intently listening, raised his hand with a significant gesture. Presently, a sound was heard—a rustling like the waving of trees or the rushing of distant water. It gradually increased, and seemed to proceed from the narrow street which led from the principal gate into the square. All eyes were turned in that direction. . . .

"That night there was a *repique,* or ringing of bells, in the towers of Logroño, and the few priests who had escaped the pestilence sang litanies to God and the Virgin for the salvation of the town from the hands of the heathen. The attempt of the Gitanos had been most signally defeated, and the great square and the street were strewn with their corpses. Oh! what frightful objects: there lay grim men blacker than mulattoes, with fury and rage in their stiffened features; wild women in extraordinary dresses, their hair, black and long as the tail of the horse, spread all disheveled upon the ground; and gaunt and naked children grasping knives and daggers in their tiny hands.

"Of the patriotic troop not one appeared to have fallen; and when, after their enemies had retreated with howlings of fiendish despair, they told their numbers, only one man was missing, who was never seen again; and that man was Alvarez.

"In the midst of the combat, the tempest, which had for a long time been gathering, burst over Logroño, in lightning, thunder, darkness, and vehement hail. A man of the town asserted that the last time he had seen Alvarez, the latter was far in advance of his companions, defending himself desperately against three powerful heathens, who seemed to be acting under the direction of a tall woman who stood nigh, covered with barbaric ornaments, and wearing on her head a rude silver crown."

Such is the tale of the bookseller of Logroño, and such is the narrative of the attempt of the Gitanos to sack the town in the time of pestilence, which is alluded to by many Spanish authors, but more particularly by the learned Francisco de Cordova in his *Didascalia,* one of the curious and instructive books within the circle of universal literature.

Yet this is only one-half of the tale. What had the people of Logroño done to the Gypsies that caused such bitter hatred? The Spanish records do not mention anything against themselves. The Gypsies have no written records. The defense of the accused has never been heard, has never been listened to.

In 1619, Philip III ordered the Gitanos under pain of death, to establish themselves in cities and towns of one thousand families and upward. Yet they were forbidden under the same penalty to work as blacksmiths or to have anything to do with the sale of cattle, great or small. It was like forbidding fish to swim.

In 1633, Philip IV ordered the Gitanos to disperse and mingle with the other inhabitants, and decreed that they must not marry among themselves, but with Spaniards—who hated them and whom they hated. Did the Gitanos submit to these laws? No.

I met in Paris not long ago an elderly Gypsy woman who had been famous in her day as a dancer. She lived rather luxuriously in a beautiful apartment that was decorated with the leaves and petals of the dried flowers that had evidently been sent her in the twenty years of her triumphant career. While we were sipping our coffee, the maid brought into the room a huge bouquet of roses.

"From Señor Ramero," the maid mentioned.

The old Gypsy's eyes moistened. Lighting a cigarette, she said:

"Poor Señor Ramero! It is almost twenty-five years that he sends me flowers daily. He is an old man now,

and I am an old woman. I see him once a week. He
takes me out to the Bois in his carriage. When he was
twenty-five, he fell in love with me. And I with him.
But when he gave me the first kiss, it seemed to me
that I smelled the odor of burning flesh. My grandfather, you see, had his cheeks seared by hot irons
by a Spaniard. I remembered his face. The tale of
how it was done was told me a hundred times. That
Spaniard represented all the Spaniards—my grandfather, all the Gitanos. The man who had kissed me
was a Spaniard—I, a Gitana. That is why when he
kissed me I smelled the odor of burning flesh. I loved
him. He loved me. But it could never be. I came
to France. He came to France. Every day he sends
me a bouquet of flowers. I still love him. He stills
loves me. I keep every petal, every leaf of his roses.
Look at them. Only if these flowers should revive by
themselves would I be able to kiss him. Poor Ramero!
Poor Gitana!" And the old Gypsy cried.

Needless to say that the result of these laws was to
make conditions worse among the Gitanos and incite
them to even greater lawlessness. To corrupt the officers of the law was no difficult task, bribery having
always been considered part of the income of a public
officer in Spain.

One of the worst laws against the Gypsies was one
which, after forbidding vagabondage, decreed that
everyone who caught a Gitano in such a state, had the
right to claim that Gitano as his lifelong slave. The
thrifty peasants went out on Gypsy hunts whenever
they needed men to help them with the harvest or for
general agricultural labor, or to replace mules that
had been stolen by the Gitanos. To the Gitanos,

slavery was worse than death. This law resulted in the withdrawal of the Gitanos from small villages into the mountains, and in a greater recklessness and savagery toward their would-be captors. Holding liberty more valuable than life, the Gitanos killed every white man that came their way.

Toward the end of the eighteenth century, Charles III, realizing that the laws of his predecessors against the Gitanos had had no effect, enacted a new law which took into consideration the fact that the other laws had been vicious because too harsh. And, though in the twenty articles of the law of Charles III punishment by death was decreed for recalcitrants, the tone was one of willingness to forgive the wayward ones.

The Gitanos were declared to be Spaniards, and were even asked to call themselves such in order to enjoy all the rights of Spanish subjects.

Treated more humanely, the Gitanos came down from the fastnesses of the mountains—timidly at first —to settle peacefully in villages and towns. Not the Gitanos formed the quarters, the Gitanerias. The other inhabitants moved away from the streets in which Gitanos settled, to avoid neighborhood with a people reputed to be composed of pagan sorcerers, accused of eating human flesh and carcases of animals that had died of disease.

The echo of cannibalism in Hungary had reached Spain. The Gitanerias of Seville, Cordoba, Granada, and Madrid, like the Negro districts in the large cities of America, have not been formed by the Gypsies themselves, but because the other people kept aloof from them, avoided contact with them.

The old antagonism against the Gitanos in Spain

ceased in the measure in which the laws against them became more humane. The recklessness of the Gitanos diminished in proportion as the laws became less severe.

The Spaniards of today are proud of their Gitanos, and claim that "our Gitanos" are physically and artistically so superior to the Gypsies of other countries that it is unjust to class them in the same category with the Ungars. They are Spanish aristocracy today.

Great Spanish composers, like Albeniz, Granados and Manuel de Falla, have collected Gitano music which the world has since learned to know. Every Spanish painter since Goya has attempted to portray the Gitanos. There has not been a Spanish writer, from Cervantes to Blasco Ibañez, who has not put forth his best efforts to tell a Gitano story. The Spanish government is still occupied hunting down the Gypsy *contrabandistas;* but this has been used as material for opera and drama. Spaniards would no longer know what to do without *contrabandistas,* and would miss them as much as they would the castanets on the fingers of a dancer.

Though the Gitano population is hardly forty thousand, it has furnished to Spain most of the country's color and talent. The national music of Spain is Gypsy music; the national songs of Spain are of Gypsy origin. The Spanish dances are Gypsy dances, and most of the best matadors are of Gypsy origin.

To know Calo, the language of the Gypsies, is considered a great accomplishment by every Spaniard. Gypsy words have entered the Spanish language to such an extent that it has alarmed many a Spanish academician.

The number of *aficionados,* or friends of Gypsies, has become so great, the Gitanos themselves are alarmed by it. And one Gypsy in the Albaicin told me that in a short time the Calo would become the language of all Spaniards, and that his people would have to learn Spanish in order to hold secret conversations among themselves.

VIII—THE GYPSIES IN GERMANY

IT WAS IN GERMANY THAT THE GYPSIES MADE their first official appearance in Western Europe in 1417. From there they spread into Italy and France, and thence into Switzerland and Spain, and over the rest of Western Europe. I say the first official appearance because I have no doubt that small bands of Gypsies, perhaps only single families, had already visited the Hanseatic German towns before that; but their visits are not specifically mentioned anywhere. These single families had been sent out to spy the land, and, only upon their reports, a larger group, or larger groups, under the leadership of "dukes" and "counts" followed, bearing letters, purporting to be from the pope and the emperor, which contained different versions of what had caused them to leave Egypt, their supposed country of origin. It is not established whether it was one single group under the head of one "duke" and one "count," or several groups under the leadership of several "dukes" and "counts" possessing duplicates of these important letters, that presented themselves at the different German Hanseatic towns, demanding asylum and sustenance in the name of the pope and the emperor. The only reliable documents are the records of the towns they visited, records of the expense incurred by the communal authorities, and the debates and decisions of the town representatives as to how long they were to harbor the "Heiden," the "Aegypter," in their midst.

Another point which has not yet been cleared is whether these Gypsies who had appeared in Germany were of Hungarian or Russian origin, or were of both. Some learned German of the time, speaking with them, came to the conclusion that they spoke among themselves a "Vedantic" tongue. This would seem to indicate that they had come from Russia. Russia, however, seems hardly possible as the original home of this first group. I am quite certain that they came from a Catholic country. How else would they have known of the power and authority of the pope in Catholic lands?

They would not have known how to avail themselves of either authentic or counterfeit letters from the pope and the emperor. The trades these people plied, and whatever still survives of the admixture of words in their language to this day, indicates that the Gypsies, passing through Germany, were of Hungarian origin. And since this first group, according to all accounts, was not more than a hundred strong, it would be reasonable to suppose that bands of Gypsies followed one another at short intervals and spread everywhere, knowing very well that they could not maintain very long the good impression, the veil of mystery, which they had created. And they had guessed right. Elsewhere they had learned how to mitigate the severity of laws against them with bribes and effrontery.

But such procedure was impossible in the Hanseatic towns, where reigned German rectitude and lawfulness. Laws, rules, and regulations came down upon the poor Gypsies like sledge-hammers, to punish them for every misdemeanor and for every little infringement of the sacrosanct *Gesetzen*. They were thrown pitilessly into dungeons. When they had been ordered out of a town or province, and were found still to be there, they were summarily hanged without even a pretense of a trial. The poor Gypsies learned to know what German *Gesetzlichkeit* meant.

Dispersed, driven into hiding, the horror-stricken *Zigeuner* retreated into the forests from where they emerged only to get enough food barely to sustain themselves. But *Die guten Deutschen* hunted them down like wolves, and burned down whole forests when they could not otherwise capture their human prey. The rigorous climate took a toll equal to that of the law. Within a year the number of Gypsies had been reduced to less than half.

Some time late in the fall of 1418, or probably in the spring of 1419, the Gypsies of Western Europe held a grand gathering in Switzerland. Those who had crossed into Switzerland before had, by some means, communicated with their less fortunate brothers in Germany, and told them that the reception by the Swiss mountaineers had not been as unfriendly as that by the German townsmen. How many attended that rendezvous? Bataillard, who had studied this point very thoroughly, came once to the conclusion that there might have been 1,400 individuals. Later on he modified this figure and thought there were only 600 present. Others who had studied the question spoke of even fewer, and some claimed that only 150 were present.

It is possible that there were two meetings—one in 1418 and one in 1419—to which the scattered remnants of the original band that had come into Germany were also called to Switzerland by Duke Andre

or Duke Michael, or by both of them. What happened
at that rendezvous, what decisions were reached, and
what happened in general to the Gypsies in the few
following years, still remains an unanswered question.
It is quite possible that many of them decided to return
whence they had come, which would account for the
German words that have embedded themselves in the
Calo of the Hungarian Gypsies. It is also possible
that they were advised to efface themselves for the moment until the bad impression they had created should
be forgotten, and were told to live in small groups as
well as they could, subsisting in any way they might
so long as they could keep themselves out of sight of
the Germans—until they should meet again, one section at Forli in Italy in 1422, and the other at the same
time in Bologna.

At this second meeting, they could not have been
more than 150, according to all accounts. They had
been reduced to that number from probably 2,000 who
had trickled into Germany five years before. The
band of Gypsies that entered Paris five years later, in
1427, was the remnant of the band that had come first
to Germany, and counted no more than 150 souls. But
the Gypsies had met somewhere in France before they
appeared officially in Paris, just as they had probably
met somewhere unofficially in Germany also. This
conclusion seems reasonable because no contemporary
in either Germany or France makes mention of the
Gypsies' ignorance of the language of the respective
country. Evidently the leaders spoke German and
French. As it is hardly probable that they had learned
these languages otherwise than from personal contact
with people who spoke them, they could not have

learned them elsewhere than in Germany and in France.

However that may have been, in spite of the terribly severe treatment they received in Germany, in spite of the cruelty they had to expect upon remaining there or coming there, and in spite of all German vigilance, the country has never been purged of Gypsies, and small bands have been continually roaming through the country, relying upon time and the timidity of their own behavior for an amelioration of their status. It is inconceivable that the bands that continued to come from other lands into Germany were ignorant of the treatment that awaited them there.

What, then, attracted them to a country where they had been so badly received, and where punishment awaited them for the slightest infraction of the law, and where they were hunted down like wild beasts? The answer is the Cult of the Dead—stronger in Gypsies than it is in any other people.

Wherever Gypsy life has not been adulterated through contact with other peoples, and where they have had the opportunity to allow their own traditions and their own inclinations to express themselves, this Cult of the Dead has evidenced itself in the strangest manner. To this day, some Gypsies in Spain, after burying their dead, burn everything that belonged to the deceased and, when they do not have too great a fear of police interference, kill his horse and burn the carcass along with the corpse of the deceased.

In the Pustos of Hungary, the peasants and those who have come in close contact with the Gypsies confirm that the Tziganes dig out their dead after they have buried them, and burn them secretly; for they believe that the soul of the deceased never leaves the earth until the body has been so burned. Did the Gypsies learn this from the Hindus, or did they practice cremation before the Hindu invaders had enslaved them? *Qui lo sa!*

In Roumania, Spain, and Bulgaria, Gypsy women of wandering tribes are not permitted to wash themselves—even to touch water until the body of the dead has completely disintegrated in the earth. Yet in some mysterious way, some Gypsy women are allowed to wash themselves only a few months and sometimes a few weeks after the death of the husband. Some relative or friend, possibly some man who is anxious to marry the widow, frees her from the long torture by digging out and burning the body of the dead husband.

In the cemeteries of Roumania, Bulgaria, France, Spain, where Gypsies are buried, the family of the deceased frequently comes to deposit food on the grave. For a full year, and frequently much longer, if the widow has remained faithful or the children still remember the dead one, the grave is fed in that manner; for the man is not considered completely dead. Gypsies have assured me that forgotten grandparents, husbands, or wives have frequently visited people of their families at night, and reproached them for their negligence. Gypsies have told me again and again that dead ones have appeared, flesh and bone, not only in tents and homes but even in inns, and loudly denounced, before all those present, their negligent relatives. An insane Gypsy woman was pointed out to me in Semileanca, near Buzău, two hours from Bucharest, whose throat was horribly burned by the fingers of her dead husband who had come to strangle her.

The more Gypsies were killed in Germany, the greater number came from the original homes—fathers, mothers, sons, brothers—in search of the dead who called them. And when German vigilance destroyed them, it only brought still more Gypsies from everywhere, to roam over roads and villages to find the graves of their dead.

There must have been a continual stream of messengers who took it upon themselves or were ordered by their chiefs to announce to relatives the death of one or another of their dear ones. No power on earth, no severity of law or climate, could hold back the stream of relatives from coming. The more severe a country has been to the Gypsies, the more it has been visited by them.

Now I understand the proverb: "When you cut a Gypsy in ten pieces, you have not killed him; you have only made ten Gypsies." Once a group had started out from a center where Gypsies lived, other groups were bound to follow. When groups had emigrated to America of their own free will, they came in complete families, because of the great distance. This Cult of the Dead would explain why, when England, France, or Spain forcibly transported single individuals across the seas, their families, to the third generation, insisted upon following them, regardless of hardship and danger. It was the Cult of the Dead that brought thousands into Brazil, to Barbados, and to Louisiana, though it had been the intent of the respective European governments to send only a few hundred away.

Yet neither the Germans, the French, the Spanish, nor the English had ever understood this Cult; nor realized that the Cult of the Dead was more powerful

than life itself. The Germans understood this even
less than the others, confirmed in their opinion that
Schrecklichkeit and severity would purge the land of
the unwelcome guests. Germans have never understood the psychology of another people. They expect
everybody to behave under all circumstances as they
themselves would behave. An Englishman is sur-
prized, a Frenchman amused, but a German is always
stupefied by the unexpected behavior of a people. German *Kultur* admits no other culture but its own. Yet,
intolerance is the first proof of lack of culture. It is
German nature to believe that the rest of the world
will eventually recognize the superiority of everything
German. The wars against the world were made by
well-meaning emperors who were anxious to hasten the
processes of time, through sword and fire, to the benefit
of those ignorant of German bliss and culture.

The museum of the ancient Free City of Nördlingen
is rich in material for the history of civilization.
Among other things, it contains two warning placards
for Gypsies, whose meaning is obvious even without the
explanatory inscriptions underneath them. The placards date approximately from the year 1700, and give
a gruesome picture of the short shrift given to the
Gypsies. The first placard portrays a man, the flesh of
whose body has been torn to shreds by whipping, being
driven to the gallows on which another Gypsy is already hanging. The second placard portrays the flogging of a Gypsy man and woman at the foot of the
gallows, on which a companion of theirs has expiated
the crime of not being born a German. Underneath
this second placard is the inscription: "Punishment
meted out to Gypsies and their women found in the

country." These placards had once been nailed to the gates of the castle belonging to the Oettingen-Wallerstein family on the rocky heights bordering the river Wörnitz, southeast of Nördlingen.

There were severe decrees everywhere in the civilized countries of Europe regarding Gypsies. But they were frequently no more than threats. In Germany, however, these threats were always carried out to the letter. According to the mandate of Emperor Charles VI, in the year 1726, Gypsy men caught in Moravia were to be hanged, while the women and children were to have their ears cut off and then be driven by a man continually flogging them, to the border of his territory. When caught again, whether in Moravia or Silesia, their cut-off ears being evidence of their recalcitrance, they were to be put to death summarily. And yet the Gypsies were happier than the Germans. They could sing and dance with their ears cut off. They sang and laughed as they went to the gallows. Nay, because they knew their days to be short, the Gypsies of Germany rioted more than other Gypsies. They became frenetic dancers and singers.

Gypsies found within Prussian jurisdiction were to be executed without delay, regardless of sex or age. And still Gypsies came on and on, and some of them returned though mutilated, courting death, and being considered as already dead, upon leaving, by their friends and relatives who prepared to follow them.

There were Gypsy hunts in Germany until the first third of the nineteenth century. As late as 1826, Freiherr von Lenchen returned from one of these hunts with two valuable trophies: the head of a Gypsy woman and that of her child.

The Germans were deaf to the music the Gypsies brought with them, deaf to the beautiful songs they heard, blind to the rhythmic movements of the Gypsy dancers, without feeling for the deep and melancholy eyes of the women whose bodies they mutilated. What the Germans knew was that they were confronted by a people antagonistic to the roots of their civilization—a people who had no respect for law and order, whose ambition was not to settle down somewhere and build a home near a cemetery, recognizing that things as they are are things to be for all time.

The keystone of German civilization is permanency, stability; frequently mistaken for, or interpreted as, faithfulness—devotion. If it is true, as the Gypsy legends maintain, that all human beings once had wings, the ancestors of the German race must have been the first to lose them.

To settle down in one place and remain there forever is contrary to everything in the Gypsy's nature. His ancestors were of the last of those who lost their wings. The Gypsy is still practically in the bird stage.

Nowhere does one see so many knapsacked pedestrians along the roads and climbing the mountains as in Germany and in Austria. Yet German wanderers and mountain climbers seem glued down to the earth, and to carry, like snails, their homes on their backs. It is true that the wanderlust has taken many a German from place to place; but he has carried Germany everywhere with him, and has retained it no matter how long he has lived in another country. I have no quarrel with that. It is German nature.

But how contrary to the spirit of the Gypsy! How contrary to the Gypsy's conception of life is boundary

and limitation! The German lawgivers were unable
to grasp the grandeur and nobility of a people who
came to pay what they thought was a holy duty to their
dead ones. I shall never forget what I saw in Alsace
some years ago, when a poor beggar was buried with
the pomp of a king. The best clothes, food, and jewelry
were buried alongside the corpse. That night, and for
the three following nights, we danced and sang to keep
merry company to the soul of the departed one. Every
morning the wife of the deceased hung a towel near a
jug of water, that he might wash when he arose.

It was only after 1850 that the Draconian laws in
Germany were replaced by others much milder. The
Gypsies already in Germany, who could prove they
were born there, were allowed to remain on German
territory, provided, of course, they settled down to lawful occupations and traveled only when permission was
given them by municipal authorities. Those who were
merely passing through the country, on their way to
other countries, were to be allowed *Durchgang* provided their passports were in good order. These were
allowed to remain no longer than twenty-four hours,
and then only outside town limits on grounds especially
reserved for them. The Gypsies then living in Germany, as well as others who came from the Netherlands
to claim German citizenship, were so devitalized and
had been so cowed that groups of them formed small
villages on the outskirts of cities, and German law and
order saw to it that they built rows of houses for themselves, and abandoned tent life. Travel was made very
difficult. Under no conditions were they allowed to
live in tents, not even on their own lands; tents, being
un-German, symbolized a return to their old-time life.

Law and order was being enforced. The windows were closed; and if the wings of a bird were caught in the closing, they were allowed to flutter until death.

By that time Grellmann's book had appeared. It traced the origin of the Gypsies to India. This gave the Zigeuner a certain degree of nobility in the eyes of the Germans. If Grellmann's book had accomplished nothing else, it had at least temporarily saved the lives of many Gypsies in Germany and elsewhere. Numerous German philologists began to seek contact with the Zigeuner, trying to prove this, that, or the other theory, to contradict or to add to Grellmann's great discovery. Many of these scholars were happy they no longer had to roam the roads and search the paths for individual Gypsy tribes. Instead of hunting with gun and spear, they now hunted with pencil and paper in their Rucksäcke, glad that the animals had been driven behind walls and fences. It did not occur to them that it was like studying wild-animal life in a zoological garden. What could these poor fools learn about the eagle's power with his wings when the feathers had fallen out because of lack of space to move?

One of the *Gelehrten* described his visit to a Gypsy village. With great horror he witnessed that, though the Gypsies had neat little homes all in a row near one another, they preferred to live on the ground in front of their homes, eating and sleeping outdoors—the children almost in a state of nakedness, burned to a still darker tinge by the sun and hardened by the cold. At a temperature at which this German scholar had to button his fur coat tight about him, the Gypsy children roamed outdoors, tumbling and doing somersaults while their mothers, fathers, and brothers were walking barefooted in the snow. "They have not accepted civilization," the German scholar complained. "They eat most of their food raw."

A few years later, Germany went mad on *Natur* life, and preached to the world nakedness and the raw food diet. But this they learned from books and laboratories and not from people.

As a further remark, the German *Gelehrte* adds that the Zigeuner were all in remarkably good health; that there was not a single sick one among them, and not one physically maimed or crippled. Yet it did not occur to the German *Gelehrte* that the perfect health and fine physical condition of the Zigeuner was due to this devotion to outdoor life. What he saw was that they were still un-German, therefore uncivilized; that the fathers and mothers of these children were inhuman and had no consideration for the well-being of their offspring.

The authorities must have taken the outcry of this gentleman into consideration. For later on, there is a report on the same village by another *Gelehrte*.

Speaking with great pride of what the benevolent severity of German law had accomplished, this *Gelehrte* said that the Zigeuner were now living in their houses, indoors, like other people. The neighboring villages had lost their fear and disrespect for them, and there was evidence of a beginning of friendship leading, as he hoped, to intermarriage. The Gypsy children had been compelled to frequent schools, according to law, and considered their newly acquired superiority so great that, calling themselves *Lalere Sinte* instead of Gypsies, they looked with scorn upon the nomad Gypsies who passed by on their way to other countries or to fairs. This *Gelehrte* added, however, that many of the Gypsies had lost their hardiness and their ruggedness, and that there was a great number of consumptives among them. Wherever Gypsies have settled in houses, their percentage of consumptives is far greater than that of the native population. This is true of Roumania, Hungary, France, Russia, Germany, and very true of the United States. The children of my Gypsy friends in New York perish of tuberculosis after a year or two in the classrooms.

Had the Germans not begun the cruelties which met the Gypsies everywhere, the Occident might have been today comparatively free of Gypsies—the Occident which has never known how much it has benefited by the nearness of its unwelcome guests, with how much beauty the Gypsies have repaid the cruelties of their hosts! Because of the treatment the Gypsies met in Germany, they became shy, or savage and unapproachable when they appeared in other countries. The wonder is not that they hate us so, and have so much contempt for the *busnes,* but that they have not much more hate and contempt. The wonder is not that so many of them have been guilty of highway robbery and murder, but that many more have not sought out, instead of running away from, the office of hangman which was everywhere forced upon them.

There are still a few thousand Gypsy families today in Germany, roaming from one end of the Reich to the other, and crossing occasionally into the Netherlands and Switzerland. They claim to be a people apart and not of the same origin as the Ungars.

But the Lalere Sinte betray their race by their negations. The term Lalere Sinte has its origin in the Hindustani word "Lal," which means "dumb." The Gypsies in Spain call the Portuguese Gypsies *Lalori* and *Lale,* meaning "dumb." Other nations also call foreigners dumb because they cannot understand their language. The Russians call the Germans *Niemtsy,* which is derived from the adjective "niemoy," meaning "dumb." The Hungarians likewise call the Germans *Nienetz,* which means "deaf and dumb."

A close examination of the Calo as spoken by the Lalere Sinte shows them to be of Hungarian and Roumanian origin, no matter how strongly the Black Brothers deny it. *Colombo* for "dove," *shipka* for "cat," *crai* for "emperor," *paputsh* for "shoe," *lantsu* for "chain," *kopatch* for "tree," *lampage* for "lamp," would be enough. But words like *hamo* for "harness," and *lacato* for "lock," *chaska* for "cup," and a number of others betraying the origin of the Lalere Sinte are to be found in their language as spoken today. In western Germany, one can still see whole camps of Gypsies buying and selling cattle, and putting up their small hand-forges in villages where there are no local blacksmiths. These caravans still maintain the old tribal way of living. Women still tell fortunes, and many peasants still place much more confidence in the medical knowledge of the *Heiden* than in that of "Herr Doctor." Peasants go far and wide in search of a Gypsy when their cattle are sick, or when a broken bone has to be reset.

Alsace and Lorraine have become in the last few years the favorite countries of the Lalere Sinte. There are large groups around Strasbourg and Metz, and everywhere in the industrial region where the men can work a few days while the horses rest.

There is very little music among the Lalere Sinte people of today. In its stead, they have an inexhaustible fund of stories they are always ready to tell to whoever is willing to offer a glass of beer. There are so many blond and blue-eyed Gypsies, one is inclined to believe that, in spite of all persecution, there was a considerable mixture of German blood; that occasionally German gendarmes did forget their duties in the arms of a beautiful dark woman. They are also cleaner about their persons than most Gypsies, and much more thrifty and less improvident.

Bernard Gilliat-Smith, telling of a night he had spent with the Gypsies, writes:

"We dined that night with the *Sinte;* we were afraid of depriving them of their frugal meal, and took little, but the chief told us that no meal was so small that it could not be shared among friends. On the morrow, early in the morning, I witnessed a never to be forgotten scene, when some young Gypsy lads made a raid on Brauch's *Mühle.* The miller himself being out, Draga, the giant Gypsy's *romi,* firmly held the miller's fat and screaming wife, while the lads chased and caught and throttled and made off with a couple of splendid young turkeys.

"The whole encampment swore it would not leave until the following morning, but the counsel of the giant chief, whom they called the *Baro-dar,* prevailed, and they realized that it behooved them to fly and travel at breakneck speed. At four o'clock in the afternoon we decided to follow them on bicycles, inquiring in every village as to the direction they had taken. The villagers thought we were afraid of the *Zigeuner,* and explained how we could best avoid them. When they learned that we were pursuing them, they would have it that we had been robbed, and one village offered its policeman and a contingent of plowboys. They obviously did not believe us when we assured them that we merely desired the Gypsies' company above all things in the world. Thus we sped on, stopping once for half an hour at the invitation of some peasants who were picking grapes on a *Weinberg*. Toward sunset we came upon our friends on the outskirts of a village between fifteen and twenty miles from Sponheim. We found the doors of all the houses barred, and were ourselves taken for Gypsies when we banged at the closed shutters of a *kartsima* to get some drink. In our hurry to find our friends, we rushed from the tavern, forgetting to pay for our beer, but were recalled by the irate *kartsimaro*.

"They evinced no surprize at seeing us, beyond their usual excitability. We advanced a mile out of the village, a halt was called, and, sitting in a ditch, we had a weird wild lesson in the *romano kova*. As the dictation proceeded, the *Baro-dar* grew more and more excited. His wife, Draga, sat opposite me on the roadside of the ditch, which was dry, my brother on my right, and the *rom* on the left. Swarms of children buzzed around, snatching our caps from our heads. Upon our pretending not to know the meaning of the word *tsum,* the *Baro-dar* explained by kissing me on the left ear. His beard smelt of beer, burnt wood, pine trees, and the indescribable something—in fact, again the *romano kova*. His mind ran on horse dealing, in the various meanings of the phrase, upon the events of the day, the long flight across country, the miller's fat wife, America, children born in ditches, great gatherings of the *Roma,* conjugal disturbances, and the affairs of every-day life."

In spite of German thoroughness and soul-killing respectability, it is evident that the wandering of the Zigeuner is not yet a thing of the past, that the westward movement of the Gypsies is just as strong as the *Drang nach Osten* is in the Germans themselves. For one settled emaciated tribe which German love for law and order will eventually succeed in destroying, a hundred other families will come in its wake from Hungary, from Russia, from Greece or Turkey, or even from as far away as Persia. The degree of savageness and destructiveness of these newcomers will largely depend upon the treatment they meet at the hands of the Christian countries which have been preaching so assiduously "Peace on earth, good will to all mankind."

IX—The Russian Gypsy

ECENTLY, WHILE IN PARIS, I WAS VISITING
some Gypsy musician friends on the rue
Saint-Georges. The meeting had been arranged by Tanasi, whose playing had caused
a furor at the Ritz. The large furnished apartment
which the Gypsies had rented had partly been transformed into a camp. The tables, chairs, and other
"unnecessary" things had been piled in a corner, not
to be broken by the children; the mattresses had been
taken off the beds and put alongside the walls, which
were decorated with red and yellow cloth and rugs of
weaves from all parts of the world.

This was the first time I met the wives of Tanasi,
Nitza, Aurel, Stan, and Basili. Tanasi's wife was a
Russian Jewess, the daughter of a Moscow rabbi. She
had run away with the Gypsy after hearing him play
at the wedding of her sister. Aurel's wife was a young
French lady from Nantea, a high-school teacher, who
had remained to live with him after a short visit to
Paris on a holiday. Basili's wife was an English lady;
a lady in the strictest sense of the word. Stan was married to a Roumanian woman.

Nitza's wife was the only Gypsy woman present;
and on the occasion of my visit she consented, for the
first time, to meet the Gorgio wives of her husband's
friends. At that, Nitza, who was himself partly Jewish, never left his wife's side for a single moment,
afraid that she might break out in great fury against

the other women on the slightest provocation—the other women, who, it seemed to me, for this once felt that they had to stand together against their single enemy; though on no terms of great friendship among themselves. The French high-school teacher resented the insolent intellectuality of the Russian Jewess, and the Englishwoman reproached the Russian for the fact that her parents had lost all the savings which they had invested in Russian bonds. The Roumanian wife of Basili seemed much more concerned with asserting the fact that she was not a Gypsy but a Roumanian than with quarreling with either of the women, and was the only one who dared to go near Nitza's wife, and treat her on equal terms.

After the boisterous and over-rich meal, I realized that Tanasi had invited me to his home to explain to these other women why Gypsies were in no way inferior to them. He turned to Nitza's wife, and said:

"He can Raker Romanes as well as my father; and what he knows of our Tchiatras, even my father didn't know. And my father was his father's friend. These Gagicas think that we Roms are just dirt; when, as a matter of fact, he explains that we are at least as good as the others, if not better. Why," Tanasi called out, sticking out his chest, "he has shown me in a book that we are Hindus, princes, maharajas . . ." And with typical Gypsy exaggeration, he first praised my authority on the subject, then elaborated so on the little I had told him, I was afraid I had let loose a Frankenstein monster.

During the discussion, the Russian woman, refusing to forget that she was Russian, was carried away by her innate Slav contradictory spirit; and dangling her intellect, she shouted that she belonged to the intelligentsia, and contradicted and argued every point. It amused me, for Tanasi, her husband, was both angry and proud; angry that she should contradict the beautiful things I said about the Gypsies, and proud that she could discuss with me on so deep a subject. Perhaps she, herself, wanted only to show off her learning to her husband. What she said was meant more for him than for me. She didn't trust the authority of any learned man who was not Russian; and I, knowing that, refused to quote a single Russian authority on the subject of Gypsies, although there are many, and not a few of them of the best. But when I made the mistake of quoting a Roumanian authority, the Russian Jewish Intelligentsia sneered.

A moment later, I had to lend my own handkerchief to wipe the lady's tears, for she had received a resounding smack from Tanasi because she had insulted Roumania. Bedlam broke loose. The lone Gypsy woman, Nitza's wife, was jubilant because Tanasi had not been intimidated by a Gorgio woman and had dealt with her as women should be dealt with. The Roumanian wife of Basili seemed to be divided in her opinions of the subject. She resented the indelicacy— a woman should not be slapped in the presence of other people—but felt that the insult to Roumania had to be avenged. The French wife of Aurel make believe she hadn't seen anything, and slipped tactfully away to another room. The English lady disappeared, never to come back again to her Gypsy lover! Horrified, she walked out. When her husband and the others began to look for her, she was nowhere to be found. I later heard she had gone back to Birmingham, and refused to return to the Gypsy husband.

So important an accident did not break up the meeting. Some Russian Gypsies, musicians, dropped in to visit their Roumanian friends. Meanwhile, the Russian Jewess had quieted down, after muttering terrible threats. These Russian Gypsies brought their wives with them, six of them, each very beautiful in a semiwild way, with striking eyes and crow-black hair. The discussion flowed immediately into political channels. The Russian Gypsies were in many respects superior to my Roumanian friends. They were better acquainted with the political situation of the world, and had about them an air of ease and sociability, which contrasted very strongly with that of any other Gypsies I had met before. The Russian Gypsies were, of course, strongly pro-Russian, although they were anti-Bolshevik. Because they were such Russian patriots, the Roumanians could do no less than they did. Soon the discussion became so violent, I feared my friends would come to blows. All this time, Tanasi's wife, though eager to join the Gypsy Russian patriots, kept wisely still, while the Roumanian Gypsies sneered at the Russian Gypsies, and the Russians growled and insulted the Roumanians. I thought of the strangeness of the encounter; that Gypsies, so persecuted by the people they lived with, should faithfully and warmly defend the countries that had persecuted them.

And then the climax was reached. Tanasi threw himself on someone who had insulted the Roumanian queen. At that moment, an older Russian Gypsy interposed himself. With one grand gesture, he ranged the six Russian women to one side, the men to another. He whispered softly a single word, raised his hands in the air, and the Gypsy choir began to sing the great song of brotherhood.

When the first song was finished, the Gypsies were in tears, kissing and embracing one another, begging one another's forgiveness. Even the Russian Jewess forgot what had happened only a little while before, and let herself be kissed by her husband. The French-woman and the Roumanian fell into one another's arms, awed by the terrific intensity and sadness of the song and the people about them. The Frenchwoman called out:

"Never will we understand them! He is so good to me, and your husband is so good to you, and Tanasi is always so good to Vera; and then, suddenly, they do something! We shall yet be knifed one day while we smile at them . . ."

I tell this story because it illustrates many points at once. It is in many ways the quintessence of things I have told before. Civilized man may correctly contend that other nations were within their rights when defending themselves against an alien people, which, being unassimilable, brought with it a form of life entirely antagonistic to their own, a people whose habits were incompatible with their own habits, and whose manner of living was such that it upset their own, and their civilizations.

The wealth of a country consists of the products of its soil, grain, and raw materials, and in the willingness of the people to extract these products and to transform the raw materials into finished objects. The nomadic habits of the Gypsies make them an unproductive people. Only a small percentage of the Black Brother-hood is working at productive trades, like coppersmith-ing and blacksmithing. Even these trades are practiced only intermittently between points of wandering. Out of a Gypsy population of 1,000, only 300 would be engaged in handiwork. But I venture to say that in any population, there are not more than 300 out of 1,000 doing really productive work. Out of every 1,000 hard-working Americans, Germans, Frenchmen, and Englishmen, 700 are engaged on tiresome and tedious tasks—pasting labels on cans, clerking in banks, shipping, amusing, vending, railroading, and a hundred other occupations—in which they are really no more productive than the 700 idlers out of 1,000 Gypsies. Only the unproductive occupations of civilized people are more honorable than that of the Gypsies.

We are accustomed to laugh and scoff, though we are intrigued, at Gypsy fortune tellers and palm readers, magicians and sorcerers. Yet a good deal of this magic and sorcery and fortune telling and palm reading parades in the civilized world in the guise of learning and science. How many years are wasted on the benches of colleges and seminaries, listening to the gospel of learned men, scientists and professors, whose knowledge and information is derived from other men at whose feet they first sat, and whose knowledge had in a similar way been derived from others who had had no contact with life and living problems?

The reproach that the Gypsies refuse to settle down is only one of envy. The desire to travel is greater to-day in the civilized world than it has ever been. Everybody wants to travel, to go from country to country, to do as the Gypsies do. We really envy the Gypsies their willingness to travel now instead of wasting years to accumulate the wherewithal with which to travel under comfortable conditions.

The cost of manufacturing automobiles, airplanes, trains, cars, when put together, forms the most considerable financial unit of any industry in the world. A third of the world's workingmen is employed digging ore, coal, cutting trees, and shaping the raw materials to manufacture means and vehicles of travel. Another third of the population of any country is continually traveling under a thousand pretexts. In other words, more than sixty per cent of the population of any industrial country is employed to manufacture means of traveling, and traveling. Still the civilized world does not consider itself a nomadic world. The number of miles covered in the lifetime of any civilized man is infinitely greater than the number of miles covered by a Gypsy caravan. The essential difference between the Gypsy and the so-called civilized man is that the aim of the civilized traveler is to get somewhere, to reach a definite point in the speediest manner, shoot through thousands of miles like a bullet from a cannon, on the fast express trains or on the wings of airplanes, while the Gypsy, being more poetical, is charmed by the traveling itself. The Gypsy travels for the sake of travel.

He is the real Epicurean. What matter that the food put before us be of the highest quality when it is consumed only for the final end—that of alleviating hunger? The Gypsy, a true Epicurean, thinks regretfully of the point of satiation, while he consumes his food slowly, with relish and for the joy of eating. To the civilized man, everything becomes an aim, everything a definite goal toward which he runs. The speed with which we go through life reveals our impatience to reach the end. The Gypsy thinks of the end as a sad

Gypsy fortune-tellers and palm-readers. (Chapter IX)

The Gypsies of Persia like bright-colored garments that
can be seen from a distance. (Chapter XII)

and inevitable moment. Meantime, while he lives, he loves and sins and sings.

Already a great number of people no longer await the day when they might travel in comfort. Every summer, there are thousands of poor, rickety automobiles, loaded with people in comparatively poor circumstances who tear themselves away from their jobs and shops to go a-gypsying and a-camping on dusty roads and on the shores of rivers.

It is quite possible that the civilized world will exterminate the Gypsy by compelling him in devious ways to live in cities, and housing him between stone walls. I have already pointed out the great number of cases of tuberculosis among Gypsies living in cities.

The civilized world will succeed in pinning these butterflies on the walls to study their coloration and the transparency of their wings; but by that time the dead Gypsies will have taught the world a greater lesson than the one it might learn looking at their corpses— that of the beauty of the sun and the open road.

It would be idle to speculate when the Gypsies first appeared in Russia. They seem much more indigenous to that country than to Spain, and even more than to Roumania. The Russian Gypsies are an integral unit of the general population of the country, one of the nations forming the Russian Empire, the only difference being, that while every nation of Russia has more or less its own boundaries, the Gypsies are everywhere. Because of their physical and spiritual superiority over the Russian muzhik, because of their higher intelligence and adroitness, the Russian Gypsies have never been made to consider themselves the pariahs of the country, and have never been treated as such. The Gypsy colorfulness, gaiety, and cleverness not only has appealed to the Slav spirit, but also has molded it to a great extent. There has never been instituted any special persecution against the Gypsy of Russia; and he has at all times, because of his special talents, fared much better than the general population.

At fairs in Moscow, as well as in the Nizhni Novgorod and Kief, the Gypsy has been a welcome guest, and has been less persecuted and hunted than the Jewish traders who appeared there. The rare villages and hamlets studding the wide Steppes have, for centuries and centuries, expected the Gypsies to bring some joy to them. Gypsy acrobats and prestidigitators, Gypsy ventriloquists, tight-rope walkers, and Gypsy fiddlers have been passing these lone villages and amusing the people, who welcomed them to while away some of the long winter days and nights. More than once some of the more courageous youngsters have followed the Gypsy caravan on its journey, preferring the risks and hardships of the road to the loneliness and weariness of the village.

The Russian song, Russian folk-lore, Russian literature are so crammed with Gypsy lore that one thinks there was nothing else worth while writing and singing about than these birds of passage. Not a Russian poet of note, not a Russian writer that hasn't written about the Tzigane. The old Russian aristocracy was not averse to taking to its bosom a Gypsy; and there is hardly a princely house that is free of the Gypsy strain; the Tolstoy family not excluded. Whatever color there is in these otherwise placid Northerners has been injected by the Gypsies.

There are between one hundred and fifty and two hundred thousand Gypsies in Russia, of which at least one-half live in settled districts outside the large cities. A hundred thousand Tziganes travel in tremendous caravans of five to six hundred souls each, led by a *Tziganski Ataman,* Gypsy chief, whose power over them equals that of the autocratic ruler of any country, and was, in a sense, molded on the autocratic power of the czar over his people. The Russians have forever clamored for democracy and equality; but what they have really always wanted, and needed, was an iron hand to rule them. Even the gruesome Ivan the Terrible has many more admirers today than some of the weaker and kinder Romanov emperors. A strong hand has ever been more admired in Russia than anywhere else in the world; and even the Bolsheviki now in power admire more the stronger men among themselves than the wiser ones. Russia is the country of the *"Kulack."*

The craving to be ruled by a strong hand has communicated itself to the Gypsies in Russia, who picked their leader not for sagacity or wisdom, as in other countries, but for recklessness and ability to rule. Even those who felt they were unjustly treated preferred suffering at the hands of a strong man to being let alone by a weak one. The Tziganski Ataman is, among other reasons, chosen for his imposing face and stature. He is the handsomest and the strongest of all. The Steppes of Russia have seen such leaders wielding whips, the handles of which were wrought of solid gold, with silver and gold buttons on their long coats and silver spurs on their boots. There have even been Atamans who rode on horses shod with silver. There must have been times when the Gypsy tribes were terribly hard up for money, living as they do from day to day, without provision for the morrow, but they have preferred cold and starvation, disposing of everything they possessed before touching the riches with which the chief adorned himself.

This romanticism in the Russian Gypsy has produced among the Black Brothers something which no Gypsy in any other country possesses. I am speaking of the female Gypsy choirs of Russia, so justly famous all over the world. To my knowledge, Gypsy women elsewhere have not shown any particular aptitude for music. The female of the species has not been known to possess the same musical gifts as the male. Here and there, of course, a Gypsy woman possessed a voice of better quality or rarer timbre than her sisters, but this was in no way more frequent than in women of other races or nationalities. But the *will to sing* of the Gypsy woman is so strong, the urge so powerful, almost all the Russian Gypsy women have agreeable voices; those who have been trained to sing have voices of a quality so differently dramatic from the voices of most women that one can really speak of a racial Gypsy voice.

Of course, the gifts of singing of the Russian Gypsy woman has been capitalized and commercialized until there are many so-called Gypsy choirs that give an entirely false idea of what the real thing is. Like many commercialized gifts, it has been diluted through the speeding-up process. Even the Gypsy singers in Russia have been compelled to sing too many new songs to please and give variety to the steady stream of visitors to the Russian cafés, the inns of Moscow and Leningrad. The strain of Gypsy melody is no longer pure.

The real Gypsy melody has the wildness, the sadness, and the intensity of the desert, the forest, and the mountains. There is no melody so powerful, so elemental, so gripping. The manner in which these songs are sung is so unique, it is almost impossible to transcribe them correctly on paper. I have heard choirs of twenty-four women in which each member of the choir was singing an independent melody, the singers weaving these melodies so wonderfully together into one strand, I never realized I was listening to the most complicated contrapuntal, polychromic music. Not only was the melody independent, but the rhythm of each singer was different. One song, "Reading a Letter," illustrated the twenty-four ways in which one and the same letter could be read, giving the same words twenty-four different meanings, according to the intonations and rhythms of the reader. It is a form of choral singing which the Gypsies particularly enjoy because of the possibilities it offers for subtle irony.

These Russian singers, living in districts set apart for them on the outskirts of Moscow, Leningrad, and other large cities of Russia, are the aristocracy of the Tziganes. They are wealthy people. Their homes are feathered, like the nests of certain birds, with the most glittering decorations upon walls and beds, and hangings of the most expensive silks and damasks. These Tziganes are so proud, it is easier to penetrate a royal palace than the home of a Russian singer. Many a Russian nobleman has learned how costly it is to place oneself on equal footing with Russian Gypsy singers, male or female, who are perfectly willing to sing for pay at given hours. The insane pride of any civilized artist is of no consequence compared to the artistic pride and aloofness of these people.

Within one half-hour, I have gone back and forth a dozen times on a street inhabited by these singers before a young boy of ten took notice of my existence. When I addressed him in his own language, expecting to startle him, he measured me from head to toe, and announced, through the narrow crack of a door, that some poor Roumanian had talked to him in a language he only half understood. I was aware somebody was peeping from behind the curtain of a window before I was asked to step in. For fully an hour, I was treated like a poor relative, met with questions detailed and adroit, before I was invited to stay for luncheon. In spite of the hospitality of Gypsies, it was at least a week before they introduced me to neighbors and members of their families. No social climber ever met with greater difficulties than I met in the attempt to pass the doors leading to the homes of Russian Gypsy musicians.

Their Byzantine fastidiousness is so gorgeously fantastic, a Gypsy lover of one of these singers took an oath not to return to her home before he had accumulated enough gold to cover his beloved's body from her neck to her toes. He returned fifty years later, the day she died, and buried her in the gold he had brought from America and France.

Passion, joy, gaiety, mingle, breathe, and exude from these Gypsies like mixed perfumes of living flowers.

The town of Kief, on the Dnieper River, with its fantastic Byzantine turrets, towers, and churches that seem more like Indian houses of worship than Christian, is more the heart of the traveling Gypsies than either Moscow or Leningrad. Listening to nomadic

Russian Gypsies anywhere from one border of the empire to the other, or to those who have migrated to other countries, you would conclude that all Gypsies come from Kief, or have at some time been there. The stalwart Ataman chiefs are elected there. All the friendships and rivalries of tribes begin and are ended there. There Voivode Stanko, one of the most famous of the Tziganski Atamans, once attempted to unite all the traveling Tziganes under one banner; his. For two years, Gypsies everywhere fought one another wherever they met, the women and children taking part in the battles as well as the men. Finally, after long and protracted fighting, most of the leaders were eliminated, and there remained only two, Stanko and Ivan.

Stanko gathered his followers, twenty-five thousand strong, and made ready to take them to the Crimea at the beginning of the spring. But there were too many. The villages and the towns were too far from one another to support such a tremendous number of passage birds. The Gypsies dug out the seed potatoes from the ground, and ate them. Instead of the advantages of numbers which Stanko had promised to his followers, they found themselves handicapped wherever they passed. Merchants closed their stores; and fairs, which had been scheduled to take place at given times, were suddenly postponed.

The Gypsies now began to grumble against their chief, laying at the flap of his gilded tent their difficulties and poverty.

To impress them with his authority, Stanko ate from gold plates, and used only silver knives and forks. The spurs on his boots and the stirrups on his saddle were of gold. Some Gypsy story-tellers say that his horses were shod with gold. And the inner part of his tent was gilded.

Now, when most of the money had been spent buying food for themselves and fodder for the animals, the Gypsies, finding nothing but closed doors before them, realized their folly. Even wolves regulate their packs according to the quantity of prey in the neighborhood. And yet, the Gypsies were drunk with the prestige they acquired traveling in great numbers. People were afraid of them. This was new to the Gypsies. The question was how to find means to retain power, and at the same time obtain the measure of prosperity enjoyed before.

At about that time, another Gypsy, Marco, who, realizing the folly of Stanko, saw the ruin and destruction of his people in the attempt to unite them all in one big traveling mass, gathered several thousand Gypsies, proposing to smash Stanko's power and force the disbandment.

Like all great generals, Stanko was no mean politician. He kept the reason of Marco's enmity a secret from his followers, and told them that Marco wanted to gather the reins of power in his own hands.

Two weeks later, the two rival bands were camping opposite one another on the banks of the river, waiting for the day when the waters could be forded. Marco and his people were possessed of a religious zeal, and looked to the people on the other side of the river as to misguided brothers and not enemies. They were unwilling to attempt force and hoped to convince them with words.

Nobody outside the Gypsy camps knew what was going on, although the Russian peasants and villagers

wondered and speculated on the reason for the formation of such immense bands. Finally, Marco, accompanied by his young wife and two of the older men of
the tribe, decided to cross the river, unarmed, to parley
and explain the reason of his coming to Stanko and
his people. Like all religious zealots, he believed that
if he but had the privilege of being listened to, everybody would understand his irrefutable arguments. But
bullets are dumb, and find their mark much more easily
than logic and understanding. Marco fell dead in the
rowboat between his friends. The two elders then
veered the boat to return to their people. But Marco's
wife, Yonka, threw herself into the river, and swim-
ming to the other side of the shore, carried the battle,
single-handed, against the powerful Stanko. Meanwhile, the people from the other bank, rowed, swam,
and paddled across.

The battle lasted for a week. As Stanko's people
didn't all know each other, in the night they killed each
other, burned one another's tents, took one another's
horses and wives and cattle. The battle came to an
end only after Stanko's people had had an opportunity
to listen to the reason for Marco's interference.
Stanko's people possessed themselves of their leader
and brought him, in golden chains, before a Gypsy
tribunal.

Her people had all they could do to prevent Yonka
from throwing herself at Stanko, and tearing him with
her own hands. At the end of the first day's trial,
Yonka asked for the privilege of watching the pris-
oner, lest he run away. But neither Yonka nor Stanko
were to be found the next morning. They had disappeared as if the earth had swallowed them. Two of the

fastest horses were also missing. And so the Gypsies disbanded again, a woman's love for a man having accomplished what Marco had not been able to do.

Fights between hordes and hordes and Atamans and Atamans have been going on for centuries among the Russian Gypsies. It is because of the rivalry between these powerful chiefs that Gypsies have migrated from Russia into the neighboring countries, and even far into the west of Europe. It is quite possible that some of the Gypsies who appeared in the western part of Europe at the beginning of the fifteenth century were of Russian origin, and had been compelled to leave their own habitats because of rivalries for leadership. Without being a warlike race, the Gypsies throw themselves with as much abandon into war as they do into music or love affairs, their intensity being such that when they are once launched, they are hardly able to keep themselves back.

The number of Slav words among the English Gypsies leaves but little doubt that their ancestors had sojourned long with the Muscovite clans; and even in the Spanish Gypsy language, one finds enough Slav words to hint of their possible origin. The Gypsies now living in Sweden, Finland, Denmark, and Norway are undoubtedly of Russian origin, and do not belong to the Lalere Sinte of the Germans, as is thought by many students of Gypsy life and lore.

The tricks of the Gypsy horse traders are known by horsemen the world over. One of the best thought-out horse thieveries was related to me recently.

A certain Russian boyar owned two of the finest horses ever seen in Muscovite-land. In conversation with a Gypsy, the boyar asserted that no Gypsy would ever be able to steal these horses from him. This spurred Vlad, a famous horse thief, to come to the village adjoining the boyar's estate. The boyar was immediately apprized of the famous Gypsy horse thief's arrival, and people at the inns began to bet for and against; the older peasants and even some boyars maintaining that no one could keep horses once Vlad had made up his mind to steal them, while the boyar and his friends' money was laid against the Gypsy. The boyar set a whole army of watchmen around the stable in which these two horses were kept. Driving daily through the village his pair of black horses, the boyar had beside him two men armed to the teeth, and his own pistols were worn handy for use. Vlad was being teased: "Look, the boyar still has his horses!" Every morning, the boyar drove his horses. Vlad sat at the corner table of the inn, and drank sparingly from his bottle of vodka.

And then, one day, while the boyar was enjoying his dinner, servants rushed in to tell him that Vlad had run away with one of his guest's horses and carriage that had been standing at the door. Only one road led to the border of the country. Calmly, the boyar looked at his watch. He knew how fast the horses Vlad had stolen could go, and knew how fast his own horses were capable of running.

"We shall not start until after we have finished our coffee," the boyar announced, "and then we shall overtake the Gypsy at the Nievsky village."

He ordered that his own horses and carriage be prepared. An hour later, he started on his way leisurely. When the horses were on the road, he whipped them

up to their fullest capacity. The three men, his guests,
had not known horses could run so fast. The wheels of
the boyar's carriage were in the ruts made by the carriage Vlad had stolen. Two hours later, Vlad's vehicle
came into sight. The boyar slowed up his horses.
There was no need to drive at top speed now. They
were gaining foot by foot. Vlad suddenly stopped his
horses, and raised his hands to surrender. The boyar
drove up beside him. The Gypsy was seized, tied
hand and foot, and thrown into the boyar's carriage,
while one of the guests took possession of the carriage
the Gypsy had driven. Exultantly, the boyar stopped
at an inn to refresh himself and his friends, and to boast
of his horses. The Gypsy was left, securely bound, in
the carriage at the door.

But their joy didn't last long. Vlad had figured out
exactly what the boyar would do. With the help of a
sharp blade which he had kept hidden under his
tongue, he cut the rope which bound his hands; and
leaving to the boyar the slower horses, he ran off with
the faster ones to the border. The boyar looked at his
watch, and proudly announced to his friends that they
could not catch the faster-running horses with the
slower ones. Vlad had won out.

When Vlad had reached an old age, this same boyar
took the Gypsy to his castle to live with him—and
watch his horses against other thieves.

The advent of the war, and afterward the advent of
the Bolsheviki, has changed the manner of life of the
Gypsies in Russia. The iron-bound rules of the Bolsheviki régime, like the iron-bound rules of the Germans, in a desire to make people happy and cultured—

to drive happiness with an ax into the people's minds, as Zola once expressed it—have compelled the Gypsies to settle in towns and villages, forcing them to abandon their nomadic life. A short ten years of enforced settled life has caused such changes in the health of the nomadic Gypsies that the Black Brothers are fleeing the Muscovite Empire, claiming that the secret agents of the Bolsheviki poison the Gypsies' food to get rid of them. Should the Bolshevik régime continue, and continue to act with the same intensity, within forty years there will not be one full-blooded Gypsy left in Russia.

But whatever of Gypsy blood will flow in the Russian people will maintain to a certain extent that degree of color and wildness which has given to Russian art and Russian music, to Russian literature and Russian dancing that startling character which has attracted more sympathy than economic changes and the Revolutionary ideas. Whatever is colorful and beautiful in Russia has its origin in the Black Brothers. It is well to think of the flower as well as of the bee when one tastes honey.

From Russian Gypsies, I heard the story of how Catherine the Great had once watched a tall, dirty, bedraggled, bearded Gypsy passing up and down below her windows. She ordered Prince Potemkin to bring that Gypsy to her apartments.

An hour later, the Gypsy was ushered into her presence. But he had been bathed, perfumed, and his beard had been shaven. Instead of his rags, he wore beautiful garments. Catherine was furious. "I wanted him as he was, and not as he is," she cried out.

The Gypsy looked at her steadily, and then, recalling

to Catherine her humble origin under which he had known her, he said: "And I, too, have wanted you as you were and not as you are."

Incensed by the remark of the Gypsy, Catherine ordered that he be stripped nude and made to stay outdoors overnight, chained to a warmly dressed soldier. It was forty degrees below zero. In the morning, Catherine went to see what had happened. The soldier was dead, frozen stiff, while the naked Gypsy was snoring peacefully beside him.

X—The English Gypsy

N MAY, 1596, UNDER THE PROVISION OF THE
statutes against Egyptians or Bohemians (as
the Gypsies were then called in England), a
company of one hundred and ninety-six persons was brought before the justice in Yorkshire. One
hundred and six, being adults, were condemned to
death; because, as the document set forth, they were
idle persons, some of them the queen's natural-born
subjects and descendants of good parentage, who led
idle lives wandering about the country in company
with these Gypsies, using a speech that was not understood by the other inhabitants of the realm, and obeying
laws that were not the laws of the realm.

During the execution of some of those found guilty,
the children cried out so piteously, beseeching reprieves
for their parents, that the Right Honorable Lords who
had condemned them obtained her Grace's pardon for
the offenders, on condition that the company mend its
ways and agree to settle down somewhere at the honest
pursuit of some trade or occupation; the non-Gypsies
who had traveled in their company were to go back
to their families. It was also stipulated that the Gypsies should be returned to the last place of habitation
where they had dwelled within three years. Then the
whole company was charged to one William Portyngton, who was commissioned to conduct each one to his
last place of habitation.

There are numerous versions as to how long this trip

of the Gypsies through England, in charge of Mr. Portyngton, lasted; it could by no means have lasted less than three months, during which time the Gypsies fell off from the company one by one, anxious to avoid the place where they had lived, and bent on choosing where they intended to live, or from where they wanted to leave off as soon as the sheriff turned his back.

What a merry jaunt that must have been for people who had just escaped the gallows! Mr. Portyngton wished his errand might continue for another three years; for who knows better how to make life count than the one who has just escaped death? It was the middle of summer; the meadows were green, the forests were in full foliage; the towns and villages they passed through had been enjoined by the authorities to procure ample food for the tourists! The Gypsies could foresee, after this outbreak, a long period of quiet. There was music, song, dance, love.

Though this document is in a certain sense one of the oldest documents in England dealing with Gypsies, it does not establish the time when they first came to England. No mention is made that the Gypsies did not know the language of the country, although mention is made of their speaking another language also. There were Gypsies in France as early as the eleventh century, and it is highly probable that they began to enter England in small companies before the end of the twelfth century. The Channel separating England from France could not have barred them longer than one century. And once a small group had crossed the water, it must have found means to communicate with the brothers on the other side.

What most probably happened was that the first

appearance of the Gypsies in England was less spec-
tacular than their appearance in France or in Germany
in the fifteenth century. Having sensed a degree of
unfriendliness on the part of the authorities of
England, the newcomers made themselves as unobtru-
sive as possible. This was especially facilitated because
at that time in England there were numerous groups
of wandering people of English, Celtic, Scotch,
Welsh, and Irish descent; and tinkers and kettle-
makers, wandering field laborers, and others who
traveled with their families throughout the country.

Even a cursory study of the history of England
informs of these numerous groups of wanderers. Yet
what is most astounding in this Glamorgan document
relating to the proceedings of the justice of Yorkshire is the mention made of the natives of England
of good families who were found in the company of
these Gypsies. In other countries, natives who associated with Gypsies were always from the lowest social
strata—fugitives from justice, thieves, highway robbers, and such—who sought refuge with the Gypsies,
or intended to use the Gypsies as tools for their own
purposes. Who could they be, these gentlemen, these
first Romany ryes? The document mentions that
they were people of no mean learning, and even possessed of sciences. What had driven them to associate
with Gypsies? And had the Gypsies been denounced
by the families of these gentlemen?

Though the English temperament is reputed to be
the most phlegmatic, the most unromantic of any in
Europe, there emerges from its midst occasionally the
most romantic idealists, who for sheer daring and recklessness have never met their equal anywhere. It is

only a Byron that could have run so valiantly to the
defense of Greece; only a Shelley could have sent floating bottles on the water, containing sealed manifestoes
intending to free the world from its woes. Richard
Burton, George Borrow, Livingstone could not have
descended from any other parentage and heritage than
British. Small wonder then that in the sixteenth century, and probably a century before, persons of "good
parentage" should have been found in the company
of Gypsies, attracted by the wild and romantic life in
the open, the uncertainty of the morrow and the
glamour attached to the wanderings of an unknown
race.

The drab and colorless Englishmen and English-
women have frequently shed all their drabness on the
edge of the Channel when on their travels. People of
no other nationality are as anxious to wear the costumes
of the people they visit as the English are. The first
day of an Englishman or an Englishwoman in Spain
is spent acquiring colorful costumes and rags they
would never dare wear in their own country. Has
there ever been an Englishman who did not long to
wear the flowing robes of the Arabian! Who but a
Lawrence would have dared to wear the Arabian costumes he wore for years? It is said Lawrence
"Arabed" himself because of political necessity, but
the tale of his exploits proves that political necessity
was very much in the background, an excuse. Lawrence's life and doings in Arabia was urged by a mystic
romanticism, romanticism akin to that of Byron and
Shelley.

I fancy the Romany ryes found with the Gypsies in
1596 had so completely merged with the people they

lived with, the justice condemning them must have found it rather difficult to distinguish the sheep from the goats. Now, had there been only one or two among the Gypsies, there would have been no mention of them anywhere. The prominence given to their presence in this document proves there were perhaps a score or more. Undoubtedly, they had married into the tribe. No mention was made whether they returned to their parents with their wives and children. If they did not, their children remained with the Gypsies and dispersed all over the face of England. This may account for the quantity of English blood now flowing in the veins of Gypsies; for undoubtedly there had been Romany ryes before, and undoubtedly the Gypsies intermarried with the Scotch, the Welsh, and the Irish wanderers they met on the road.

W. J. Thompson, in his account of Gypsy marriages in England, comes to the conclusion that at least seven out of twenty Gypsies marry out of the tribe. I have met a number of Englishmen in certain professions—horse dealers and shoemakers—who have married Gypsy wives. I have also met Gypsy men who had married out of their tribes, but who have returned to the wandering ways of their people after a few years of sedentary life. It is because of this admixture that the names of most Gypsy families in England are Smith, Boswell, Robson, etc. The original names of the families have by now been completely forgotten. I have no intention of showing that the blood of England is mixed with the blood of the Gypsies as is the blood of the Brazilians or Roumanians; but one must come to the conclusion that a good deal of Gypsy blood flows in certain strata of English society.

The attempts to rid England of Gypsies were not confined to that particular instance in 1596. Sometime later, a large group was forcibly expelled back to France whence it had come; and a little later a still larger number were exiled beyond the ocean to the Barbados. The attempts to compel the "Egyptians" to settle down were as numerous as the accusations for pagan and heathenish customs, sorcery, and cannibalism, which rose from time to time, coupled with charges of kidnaping, treachery, and lechery, which were continually leveled against the wanderers. Although refuted or dismissed because of lack of proof, these accusations took hold of the imagination of the people; and there were times when the Gypsies found it more expedient to hide than to show themselves, and sometimes more expedient to leave the country altogether; when accusing fingers pointed, and they were driven by shotguns and received with pitchforks and axes for the perpetration of imaginary crimes.

The fiction about Gypsy kings and queens has found more believers in England than anywhere else. As in all democratic countries, the only king dethroned or robbed of his autocratic powers is the one on the throne. This done, the populace then elects a hundred other ones—king of the beggars, king of the Gypsies, king of copper, king of rubber—merely another way of replacing the legal wife by half a dozen mistresses.

Perhaps the "Life and Adventures of Bamfylde Moore Carew, the King of the Beggars," giving an account of the origin, government, laws, and customs of Gypsies, the method of electing their king and a dictionary of the cant language used by community of Gypsy "mendicants," is the most amusing book about

English Gypsies. In this book, Bamfylde Carew, or whoever wrote the book, after imparting information never acquired anywhere or which had never been imparted to him in good faith, tells how he was initiated into the "mysteries of the society, which, for antiquity, gives place to none, of one of the most ancient and learned people in the world"; and how the old king, called Claude Patch, having died, the grieved Gypsies flocked to London from every part of England, holding the vote between their teeth, and how, after a difficult and learned process of elimination, he, Carew, the stranger, who was not a Gypsy, was elected their king.

Carew's book gains in importance when studied closely for the few remarks thrown in inadvertently by the person who wrote it. One phrase, "whether Homer himself might not have been of this society, will admit of a doubt, as there is much uncertainty about his birth and education, though nothing more certain than that he traveled from place to place . . ." is especially exciting for interesting speculation.

Whether Homer ever lived is still questionable, but the figure of him as described points to the probability of Gypsy origin. No other Greek poet of that stature and power traveled from place to place, twanging the lyre and singing his songs. The very colorful quality of Homer's poetry is so alien, so strangely foreign to other Greek poetry, so unlike Greek in its character and lack of restraint, that the suspicion that this wandering, blind minstrel was of other than Greek origin is justified. Homer was the first one to speak about Gypsies and call them by their own name, Sygynes, the first one to say that Vulcan loved them because of their ability at the forge. It is quite possible that other

Greek poets jeered at Homer because he was a stranger, and the Greeks reproached him for the use of foreign locutions.

The dictionary of the cant language appended to Carew's book is composed of words of the thieves' language, with only a very thin sprinkling of words that might have Calo origin.

After the appearance of the Black Brothers in England, the word "Gypsy" was made to indicate every wandering people, and thus many sins and depredations committed by others were attributed to the real Gypsies, persecuted and killed for the sins of others.

A few years ago, I visited England during the Derby. In spite of the heavy downpour of rain, hundreds of Gypsy tents and Gypsy wagons were spread all over the field; the Gypsies indeed were the most conspicuous element in the whole crowd. While watching the race, I had one eye on a caravan tent which held a number of beautiful and fascinating women, evidently not belonging to the same family nor the same race. These young women, between the ages of seventeen and twenty, were all dressed rather gaudily, with colored kerchiefs covering their hair and long earrings dangling to their shoulders. "Gypsies! These are Gypsy women . . ." I looked at the women's plump and heavy hands, at the short stubby fingers, and knew immediately they didn't belong. Presently they cleft the crowd sidewise and I saw them perform dexterous pocket operations, under the supervision of a tall, broad-shouldered ruffian leaning on a heavy cane. Suddenly, a woman cried out: "Thief! Thief!" Never before had I heard such yelling and screaming. Never before had I seen such gesticulations. A tremendous crowd formed immediately around the lady; but while the crowd was pitying the poor woman who had been robbed, the Gypsy women were lifting the pocketbooks of the people held under the spell of the young wench who clamored that her purse had been snatched. I learned later that the "victim" was also one of the gang.

I remained on the Derby field after most of the crowd had departed homeward, and walked in rather deliberately upon the tent these so clever pocket lifters belonged to. There were only three men to the twelve or more women, and they were fighting among themselves as to the distribution of the loot.

"We be Gypsies," one of the men informed me.

I learned from him the newer meaning of the word "gypsying." The broad-shouldered ruffian asked how "gypsying" was going on in my country; and by "gypsying" he meant pocket lifting.

"And be there many of you?" I inquired.

"Yes, a few hundred . . ." Everything was "suitable" except that there were too many black foreigners a little to the back. These black foreigners were the only real Gypsies on the Derby field.

As night was falling and the women were still lingering about the tent, my host ordered the wenches to work; and for want of a better name, their work was also called "gypsying."

The same night, I discovered in another tent one of the Gypsy scholars roaming through England. Attached to one of these pseudo-Gypsy tribes, the rye knew that their claim to Gypsydom had no foundation in reality. This gypsying gentleman scholar repeated word for word opinions on the origin of the Gypsies as expressed by Samuel Roberts in a book printed in London in 1836. In this book, the author claimed that the Gypsies were the descendants of the ancient Egyptians, dispersed among all nations for their sins in many ages, to be finally restored to the land of their forefathers, as foretold by the three great prophets, Isaiah, Jeremiah, and Ezekiel. Samuel Roberts drew a comparison between Gypsies and Jews, both peoples originally driven out of their homeland by the wrath of the Almighty; the Egyptians shunning society and disregarding wealth, while the Jews, dreading obscurity and poverty, flocked to the most powerful cities pursuing wealth, which they cannot retain after they obtain it. Other proofs in this book that the Gypsies are the ancient Egyptians are the similarity between ancient Mexican and Toltec monuments. How the Gypsies got to Mexico, Mr. Roberts doesn't tell us; but he does defend the Gypsies, saying that they never apply for parochial relief, that they have abstemious habits, are rarely, if ever, seen as common beggars, and that the female Gypsies are rarely, if ever, prostitutes.

These Gypsy virtues were enumerated to me by the scholarly Gypsy in the very tent where lived people who committed these very sins.

Though there are not more than twelve thousand Gypsies in all England, so many papers have been written about them and so many studies made, it seems that all England has at some time or other gone Gypsy-hunting, in much the same way school children go out in the fields butterfly-netting. We can learn no more about the butterfly after we have netted it than we can learn about the Gypsy settled in a camp. Like the butterfly, the Gypsy has to be studied in his flight;

his very manner of flying is probably the most interesting study of all.

In "Guy Mannering," Sir Walter Scott wrote: "They're queer devils—they're warst when they're warst guided. After a', there's baith gude and ill about gyspies." Or, as Arthur Symons says, in "In Praise of Gypsies": "They are changeless: the world has no power over them. They live by rote and by faith and by tradition which is part of their blood. They go about in our midst, untouched by us, but reading our secrets; knowing more about us than we do about ourselves; prophets, diviners, soothsayers. They are our only link with the East, with mystery, with magic." Mr. Symons, who has known them well, sees among other things that the Gypsies do few things but do these things better than others; that they create nothing but perpetuate; that to restrain the Gypsies and fight against their instinct is to cut out of humanity its rarest impulse.

But Symons errs when he says that the Gypsies are nearer to the animals than any other race, because of the freedom, abandon, and physical grace of some of their gestures. Yet this does not prove their nearness to animals. Because Symons does not understand their language, he claims that their lilting voices are unacquainted with anything but the essential parts of speech: all that we should need if we lived in the open air and put machines out of our hands and minds. As a matter of fact, the Calo is a rich, flowery, and expressive language. Especially is this true of the Calo spoken by the Gypsies of England. The other Gypsies consider the flowery manner of the Romany proof that the Gypsies of England do not belong to the same race; for only sedentary people have the leisure to say things so slowly. A wanderer's language is both brief and expressive; it has to be understood on the run.

But Symons says beautifully that all their faults can be explained, if not wholly excused; that their thieving is merely the necessity of taking what they need, and that they reject instinctively what is of no use to them. Europe was from the first against them. Although the Gypsies have said time and again that they would rather die than live under a roof, the lawmakers of all countries, considering this unnatural, have wanted to compel them to live in the unwholesome quarters where the poor of the world have always lived. The Gypsies are considered unnatural because they are wanderers, when as a matter of fact nothing is more natural than to take whatever road one comes upon without thought of destination.

But in England, where the poor have always worked so hard for so little, the Gypsies who turned their backs on factories and smirched cities were hated by the very people for whom they should have served as models.

"There has been great talk," Mr. Symons goes on to say, "of degeneracy, decadence and what was supposed to be perversities; such as religion, art, genius, individuality. But it is the millionaire, the merchant, the money-maker, the sweater, who are the degenerates of civilization, and as the power comes into their hands all noble and beautiful things are being crushed out one after another, by some mechanical device for multiplying inferiority. Civilization, as it was thousands of years ago, in China, in India, was an art of living, beside whose lofty beauty we are like street urchins scrambling in a gutter. We live to pick up scraps; they lived a tranquil and rational existence. . . . The Gypsies have escaped . . . contamination for thousands of years. Are we to allow the slave-masters to get hold of them at last?"

Among the English Gypsies, one frequently hears of the arrival of Russ and Ungars, who bring news of the East, or, as Borrow's celebrated phrase goes, on the "Affairs of Egypt."

In 1913, the London newspapers spoke of the arrival of some eighty coppersmiths under the chiefs Gregory Maximoff and Philipoff. They immediately took houses in Ilford; and though the resident population gossiped of the wealth of the wanderers, some of the Gypsies immediately applied for poor relief. The inhabitants of Ilford then complained that their prosperity was being ruined by the presence of the Gypsies, that the value of real estate was decreasing because of them, and that these foreigners had no beds, lived in unsanitary houses, houses that were not even supplied with water. When three of the Gypsy children died, the villagers compelled the strangers to leave immediately. Some of the Gypsies then removed to Walthanstow, a few only remained in Ilford, while others went in search of more generous hospitality.

Now, these coppersmiths, originally from Russia, who had lived a sedentary life in Norway, would have settled down to a sedentary life in England, had the population not been so set against them. Small and large communities have compelled them to take to the road again, then denounced and reproached their wandering instinct. I have met with several of these people who had come to England under Chiefs Maximoff and Philipoff. Most of them were half-breeds; and denying they were Gypsies, pretending to be Russians, they did their best to lose themselves in the lower strata of the population of London. Three of the younger men had already married white women; and two of the women, working as seamstresses, had married English citizens of foreign descent. Yet upon the discovery of the young man's origin, one wife left him, and sued for divorce on the ground that she had not known his nationality when she was wedded to him.

I have also met Roumanian and Serbian Gypsies in London and Manchester, anxious to lose themselves in the midst of the general population, avoiding associations with Gypsies in England, there being very little sympathy between the English Gypsies, the Welsh, and the Ungars or the "Russ," as they are commonly called by the Romanies, Boswells, Smiths, etc., the English Gypsies being as insular as the English themselves.

English Romanies have divided England among themselves, and an unwritten law keeps every tribe within a designated border line. The Blackpool colony of Gypsies, which is practically sedentary, is so well known to the other Gypsies that when one of the tribe happens to be in London, he is considered to be on a short visit, and his movements are checked up by the others, lest he be the forerunner of an invading army upon disputed ground. There is a group of seven hundred Gypsies at New Forest, and another group at the foot of the Malvern Hills; and they, being flower growers and sellers, will have nothing to do with the half-sedentary Welsh Gypsies who employ themselves fishing and rowing visitors on the lakes.

The Gypsies of the settlement of a dozen families of Boswells, near Arlington, living in broken-down railway cars, vans, and tents, have never been farther than a few miles from their homes. There are Gypsies living in the outskirts of Manchester, and others near Dublin, who not only are sedentary but seem riveted to the place of their birth, and consider the near-by as outlandish country. In the attempt to become sedentary, they have chained themselves to the wheels of their vans and the doorposts of their homes. And yet, within, there is a tremendous freedom. The spirit of those who actually live in freedom is not as free as that of those who dream of freedom. Freedom of action is only conducive to greater restraint. The Puritans, leaving England because they could not obtain enactment of religious freedom, upon reaching America satisfied their wish by enacting laws of freedom; and then, content that what they desired above all things was upon paper, they settled down to a more reactionary, intolerant life than the one left behind in England. I have seldom heard songs of freedom except from people who were anything but free. The spirit of freedom is expressed much more strongly, with much more powerful accents, in a camp of English sedentary Gypsies than by Gypsies of roaming Roumanian and Hungarian tribes in the Carpathians, where nobody sings of freedom: because he possesses it.

In a paper written by Eric Otto Winstedt about the above-mentioned coppersmiths, the writer tells of witnessing a Gypsy trial, *Romani Kris,* finding it very informal—or perhaps it was his presence that made it so. The judge was the culprit's father; the injured party was absent. Only his brother was there, and he did not seem the most bitter of those present. There were no formal accusers, because the offense, an intrigue between two young people, was not denied. The Gypsies at the trial were the jury, the judge seldom speaking. Women were out of the discussion; they soon left the room. Part of the jury followed, leaving only the culprit's family and the relatives of the erring wife.

The penalty most considered was banishment, but the view was taken that the condemned man would wander from one company to another. The culprit said that being an artist, he must belong to some company. There was another, and ridiculous, alternative of taking the culprit to the Russian consul for imprisonment. The verdict was similar to one given in English courts when the husband does not wish a divorce: if an illegitimate child is born, a sum of money is to be paid; and the husband thrashes his wife. A *Romani Kris* can sentence offenders to death.

Other customs of these coppersmiths are: The coins are removed from a woman's hair before she gives birth to a child, in order that they may not become defiled. For three weeks before childbirth, the woman sees no man other than her husband. When the child is born, all cups, plates, and utensils that have been used by the mother are broken; her bedding is burned.

Not only after childbirth is a women considered unclean. Eating utensils are defiled if she steps over them, and are destroyed. This extends even to water-pipes passing underground: if it were discovered that a woman passed over them, the Gypsies would inconvenience themselves to find another source of supply, even for washing. While making a shirt for a Greek

Gypsy whom the coppersmiths met in South America, a woman's dress caught fire and she thrust the shirt between her legs. Nevertheless, she gave the shirt to the man.

He wore it for about three weeks, during which time his wife was ill. Had the coppersmiths told the man that his shirt had been defiled, he doubtless would have demanded a money settlement. Because of the danger of defilement, men's and women's shirts and other clothing are washed separately. A defiled bucket is used no more. An apron is worn to avoid pollution of objects by contact with the defiled parts of women's clothing. When women are permitted to eat with other Gypsies, they must have their own plates, spoons, and glasses. Women outcasts have their plaits of hair cut off.

If their parents can afford it, children are married at the age of twelve. A father wishing a wife for his son goes to the *diwan,* carrying a bottle of wine, round which a kerchief is wrapped. He says: "I have lost a little cow." Someone with a marriageable daughter replies that he can have the lost animal for such a sum of money. A three-day feast follows an arrangement. The last day of the feast, the bride goes around with a kerchief to gather money "to build a little house." If she doesn't collect enough the first time, she tries again, saying the walls are built but she needs money for the roof. Divorce is not uncommon. If the husband is to blame, the dowry is returned.

A hare must not be eaten because it is a vampire. The leg of a fowl must not be eaten by children, for they will become liars if they do. Children with fathers cannot eat the hearts of animals, because it would be like eating their father's hearts. The hedgehog is never eaten except as a ceremony or medicine. Coppersmiths always bare their heads to the new moon.

The English Gypsies assert that the coppersmiths coin false money; but this may be a charge made by the Romanies, who resent the intrusion upon their soil by these foreigners. Most English Gypsies refuse to believe that they and the Russ are of the same race.

Before long, however, these weird customs, refined, changed, will filter through to the tents of most of the Gypsies of England.

While in New York, I met a family of Romanies belonging to the Stanleys, near Christchurch, one of the most remarkable Gypsy tribes of England. To my surprise, on a Friday, an old Gypsy woman blessed in Hebrew seven candles in as many brass candlesticks. What had introduced this Jewish custom into Gypsy tents? Well, it was very simple. One of the Stanley women had served as a wet-nurse in a wealthy orthodox Jewish family, where the mother blessed seven candles every Friday evening. Mary Stanley arrived at the conclusion that this sorcery was responsible for the wealth of the Jews. She lent her ear to the mutterings of the weekly officiant, caught the sound of his words, and lifted the whole procedure for her own people. And then things happened! Whatever Mary's family touched turned to gold. They had never made so much money, had never had so many good turns happen to them. The words of the incantation before the candles were guarded carefully, though five hundred dollars, and more, had been offered by other Romanies for the secret.

Who knows how many Gypsy customs and traditions have been borrowed from peoples they have lived with! The Calo takes what he needs, or thinks he needs, and makes it his own. Another custom, another superstition, is like one more trinket on the necklace of his beloved. To trace such customs as were really brought from India in the long ago, you would have to sift through a fine sieve the genuine from the false, the gold from the sand in the river.

Noticing the love of the English for the dance in the last century, the Romanies have stretched tents on the outskirts of English villages, announcing, by large posters, balls, dances, and promenades every Saturday evening. Admission to the camp was threepence. And there were side-shows to the main tent; selling medicines for men, women, and cattle, fortune-telling booths, miracle workers, etc. One clever poster announced in large letters that the camp was "open till time to close, for people with more money than sense." Of course, the older people of the village did not look with favor upon the recreation the younger element sought in the Gypsy tents and booths. Accusations of theft and prostitution flowed freely, and were frequently taken up by the authorities, town-meetings, and clergymen. It is very difficult to convince the average man of the purity of Gypsy women, when all outward signs advertise the contrary. The pellmell kind of Gypsy home feeds the belief of most people that Gypsies are promiscuous, polyandrous, polygamic, and absolutely amoral. Even Gypsy solidarity is misinterpreted that way. The peasant cannot understand that one, sexually a stranger, should risk his life and wealth for another man or woman.

In 1539, according to the records of Staffordshire,

two Gypsies were condemned to death by government authorities; the crime being "lawless existence, etc." The Gypsies moved heaven and earth to free their friends, and succeeded only after paying a bribe of three hundred pounds sterling, a tremendous sum in those days, particularly for a tribe of poor Gypsies. As five women seemed more interested than the other Gypsies in the freeing of these men, people immediately came to the conclusion that they were all wives of the condemned, and the victims were not better off when free than in jail.

In Scotland, probably because of intermingling with the pugnacious type of tinkers they met and mixed with upon their arrival there, the Gypsies led a lawless and agitated life. Encouraged and abetted by the landed gentry, with quarrels to settle among themselves, Gypsies robbed and pilfered peasants and wayfarers under the wing of their protectors. Two tribes, the Shaws and the Faas, having declared war against the Browns and the Baillies, the opposing camps met at Romano, near Dunbar, in June, 1675, and engaged in a pitched battle, resulting in many deaths and crippled: a battle that has become a living legend now, a legend growing and changing with the years.

It is customary to talk of the cowardice of the Gypsy, yet to the honor of the race be it said that not all Gypsies of military age waited to be conscripted. Those of the New Forest volunteered in the early days of the Great War; the same is true of Welsh Gypsies —in particular, the Roberts family. In France, I met with two Gypsies, one armless, the other with only one leg, whose wives had pinned their husbands' medals on their own breasts. Both these Gypsies belonged to

the Faas of Scalloway, and had come back to France
with their families to show them "where the war had
been." The manner in which these fellows talked
about the big fight was as casual, as romantic, as if it
had been a little quarrel between themselves.

"The war would have ended long before. The
trouble was, *pralǫ,* there were too many Romanies on
the other side. And they won't give in, as you know;
they are that hard-headed."

There were many Gypsies, and there still are, in the
boxing game in England: bare-fist fighters. Gypsy
boxers did not fight in a modern arena, attended by
seconds and handlers. An enterprising Gorgio arranged a match to the finish, paying the loser only so
much for the rounds he stayed and a bonus to the win-
ner. The two boxers were usually from distant camps,
to insure fair play for the audience, and had never
seen one another. One-Eyed Smith, a two-fisted terror,
was engaged by a manager to box a Gypsy whom he
had under contract and wanted to punish, and who did
not know who his antagonist would be. At the hour
set for the fight, while the audience was filling the
tent, Smith arrived on horseback, tied his mount to a
post outside, pulled his shirt over his head, and ducked
bare to the waist under the rope where his antagonist
was waiting for him—a brother who had strayed from
the tribe.

While the two boxed furiously, One-Eyed Smith
talked to his brother, and persuaded him to return
home with him. To get as much money as possible
from the manager, the younger brother stayed forty
rounds, until even the hardened onlookers begged them
to stop. They had cut one another to shreds in the heat

of the fight. When the tent was empty again and the money had been counted out to both of them, the younger one sank dead to the ground. One-Eyed Smith charged his brother's corpse on the horse, and returned home to give it decent burial.

Speaking of Gypsy burials, I must mention the account given by D. M. M. Bartlet of the funeral of "Isaac Heron," who died at Sutton-on-Trent in 1911. All the clothing and personal belongings of the deceased were inclosed in the coffin. What could not be put in was destroyed and burned. Even the horse of the deceased was slaughtered. The laying out of the body, the burning of candles, the fasting of the mourners, and their demeanor were such that the astounded onlookers could verily believe that time had slipped back several thousand years, and the earth revolved so that the scene happened somewhere in India, and not in peaceful, prosaic England.

With slight variations, the burial customs of Gypsies are the same everywhere—in Serbia, in Germany, in Russia, in England. The variations are arbitrary, and are frequently only variations added from the burial customs of the people the Gypsies happen to live with. As to the traditions regulating the demeanor of the direct mourners, they are as fantastic as the tribe happens to be imaginative; and are, on some occasions, little short of the old practice of the Hindu, where the wife is buried alive beside her dead husband. On two occasions, I have witnessed the simulacrum of immolation, where the stark-naked wives jumped into the grave, to lie down for a brief moment near the corpse. When a woman does that, she becomes impure and can never marry again.

Compared to the dancing Gypsies of Spain or Hungary, the English Gypsies of today are "footless," to use a Gypsy expression. But it has not always been so. One of the earliest documents (1514) regarding Gypsies in the British Isles refers to them as having "danced before the King in Halyrudhous"; and though they were banished afterward from court, they continued to play the part of entertainers where entertainment was desired. There were many famous Gypsy dancers in England—Addie Lee's family at Yarmouth. There was also a company in Scotland, who danced before the king in 1530; and a famous danseuse with her two Gypsy daughters caused a great furor, and several scandals, in the England of 1689. There was a time when Gypsy dancers were so famous in England that they appeared in the music halls of the large towns. When Oliver Cooper and his brother Dooley danced, sons of "Fighting Jack Cooper," the Gypsies charged as much as a guinea for public admission.

The Gypsies living today in Norwood can still hoof with the best of the world. Yet, as a rule, English Gypsies are not at their best when dancing; and though they play the fiddle, and some of them have won renown with the bagpipe, they do these things only indifferently well, having adapted both their dance and their music to their audiences, and not trying to express themselves. The English Gypsy expresses himself best artistically in tales and legends. The beautiful variation of "Jack and the Beanstalk" is only one of a thousand:

There was once an old woman whose only son, Jack, said to her one day:

"Give me a cake and a blessing, mother, and I'll go out and look for work."

Before long, Jack met with a farmer, who asked him: "Can you plow?"

"Yes," said Jack, "I can plow through the eye of a needle."

"But that's impossible," marveled the farmer.

"It's quite easy," said Jack. "I can do it!"

So the farmer took Jack to his house, gave him something to eat and drink; and after filling his belly, led him to a large field, in the middle of which a tree was growing.

"Shall I plow the tree up?" asked Jack.

"No," said the farmer. "Plow up to it, but let the tree stand."

As soon as the farmer left, Jack took hold of the plow and plowed as straight as a die toward the tree. There, instead of stopping, one horse went on one side of the tree, the other horse on the other side, and Jack drove the plow straight through the middle of it, splitting it into two halves, which fell down, one on each side of the plow.

When the farmer returned to see how Jack was getting along, he drove Jack from his services.

"All right," said Jack; and dropping the reins, he left the horses where they were standing, and set out for home.

After Jack had rested a few days, he again asked his mother for a cake and a blessing.

"Oh, mother, but I'm tired of looking for work! Instead, I'll go to the fair and sell the cow."

"If you can get a good price for it, go ahead," his mother answered.

Before he got to the fair, Jack met with a farmer, who asked him how much he'd take for the cow.

"Fifteen pounds," answered Jack.

The farmer said, "Too much!" But he offered to give Jack all the money he had in his hands.

"How much might that be?" asked Jack. The farmer wouldn't tell, whereupon Jack called the bargain off.

"Well, then," said the farmer, "how would it be if I was to give you fifteen beans?"

"That would be grand," said Jack; "for they'd be better for us than fifteen sovereigns would. We have a bit of a garden, and we'd soon have a lot of beans."

His mother, seeing him coming home without the cow, was delighted; and asked him what kind of bargain he'd made. When Jack told her he'd sold the cow for fifteen beans, she scolded him; but he assured her they'd do more good than fifteen sovereigns would.

"Waste no more time crying, but help me plant the beans!"

So the beans grew; they grew so high you couldn't see the tops of them; they were lost in the heavens.

One day, Jack thought he'd climb to the top to see what was at the end of the stalk. So he took off his shoes and stockings, tied his kerchief around his middle, and climbed and climbed, till at last he came into another country, and found himself in a big room, filled with gold and silver things. He grabbed a beautiful crown to take back to his mother.

"Just try this on, mother. It's for your head. See how it suits you!" So the old woman put on the crown. "Oh, my mother! You look like a queen."

But Jack, not satisfied, went right back to the place

where the treasure was, and found watches and chains, and seals, and all manner of jewelry. Tying the watches and chains around his middle, he fastened up the bottoms of his trousers to drop the other things down inside of them; and when he could carry no more, he began to climb down the beanstalk.

When he had got no more than half-way down, he saw an old woman coming after him. The old woman had been in the room all the time, and had seen him taking the jewels.

"Mother," Jack shouted. "Come, take these things from me!"

His mother came running into the garden. Jack threw the things down to her as fast as he could. Then, when he had got rid of the last thing, he climbed to the ground, and with an ax chopped clean through the beanstalk. Down it tumbled, with a tremendous crash, the old woman with it. Her neck was broken, and she died. So Jack was the end of her!

Shakespeare undoubtedly knew many Gypsies. Still believing that they were Egyptians, he used them as a model in his description of Cleopatra. Really, the Egyptian queen is made to look, speak, and act like a Gypsy wench highly romanticized by a dramatic poet. The English curse, which calls a man the son of a four-footed female, first used by Shakespeare, is also of Gypsy origin—of Turkish Gypsy origin, to be exact. The Mohammedans, considering the dog to be a very impure animal, could think of nothing worse, more unclean, than to call a man the son of so impure a quadruped.

The Gypsies tell among themselves how one of their

Northwood men dealt with a doctor, who, having saved the life of his child, demanded as payment the price of the cow belonging to the father.

"Very well, then," said the Gypsy. "I shall take the cow to the fair, and turn over to you the price she fetches."

The doctor agreed, and sent one of his own men, lest the Gypsy cheat on the bargain.

The Northwood man then took a live chicken to the market along with the cow. Soon, there was a crowd around the Gypsy. And one of the farmers, who had just come hunting for a cow bargain, asked:

"How much for the cow?"

"Half a crown," answered the Gypsy.

Thinking the Gypsy a fool, the farmer decided he could acquire the fowl for a penny, so he asked casually, as he put out his hand for the cow's halter:

"And the chicken?"

"One hundred pounds," answered the Gypsy.

"How's that?" the man sneered. "So I buy only the cow. Here is your half-crown."

"But I *won't* sell the cow without the chicken; and I *cannot* sell the chicken without the cow."

At the end of the fair, the bargain was closed, and stood as follows: Half-crown for the cow, and eighty pounds for the chicken. Thus, the doctor was punished for his greed, while the Gypsy kept his agreement with him.

Quick bargaining wit is also illustrated by another tale, in which the cleverness of one Gypsy is pitted against the wit of another.

A Gypsy had a very lame horse he wanted to sell. He dragged the animal to one fair after another, but no buyer wanted it. Deciding to unload the crippled horse on another Gypsy, the owner drove a nail obliquely through one of the horseshoes in such a manner that it appeared the horse was lame because it was badly shod. Along came a Gypsy, looked at the animal, saw that the nail was badly driven, and bought the nag at a ridiculously low price.

The bargain closed, the limping horse led away, the former owner of the horse laughed to his heart's content. Unable to contain himself, he walked up to the tent of the man he had fooled to jeer at him. There the Gypsy and his friends were celebrating. Seller and buyer looked at one another for a second; then, both began to laugh.

"Have you looked well at your horse?" the former owner asked.

"And have you looked well at your money?" the other answered.

Then only the Gypsy looked at the coins he had received in payment: they were all counterfeit.

Such tales are heard daily in Gypsy camps: some true, most of them invented and served as exercises to the young ones—"Gypsy Latin" . . .

Since the majority of Romanies in England were, and are, horse traders, there are also heroic tales of men who loved their horses more than anything in the world, and tales of horses which loved their masters so that they died of broken hearts when neglected.

At May Hill, Gloucestershire, I heard a tale of how, when a "darling" horse was stolen from the master it loved, the mare committed suicide by throwing itself and its rider down a cliff, preferring death to another master. Of course, such stories have to be taken

with more than one grain of salt, the English Romanies being inclined to overstatement, to say the least.
Coppersmiths speak of kettles so big they could cover
Westminster Abbey; horse traders, of horses so fast
they could outrun bullets and even rays of the sun. I
have heard tales of dancers who danced so long they
discovered themselves on the seventh day atop the
church steeple—and these honors and prowesses are
claimed by both the Grays and the Shaws, each calling
the other liar.

And what is one to say to Tommy Boswell, who
claimed that his father, Lewis Boswell, once played
against Paganini; and added modestly that the honors
were judged fairly divided! Ten years from now,
some other descendant, scraping a fiddle indifferently
well, will tell an enraptured audience around a camp-
fire that Paganini cried listening to Lewis Boswell, and
was so moved by his playing that he gave him his fiddle.
And the story-teller will point to the fiddle in his lap.
Though everybody will know the fiddle was bought
for twelve shillings at a London pawnshop, eyes will
gleam, hands will stretch out reverently toward the
"Paganini" fiddle—to touch the priceless instrument.
The story-teller himself will believe his fancy more
than his memory. Fancy always outstrips the memory
of Gypsies.

Of such gossamer stuff is the soul of the Gypsy.
Childish? No. Wise! The Gypsy subconsciously
knows that fancy is more than fact, and does not have
to ponder over heavy tomes, like Schopenhauer's "Die
Welt als Wille und Vorstellung."

Yes, but they are swindlers, fortune-tellers, liars,
and non-producers! In a world with forests of black

chimneys against a gray sky, they shun work, and avoid the responsibilities of civilization? Well, what of it?

Their petty swindles are more amusing than the wholesale swindles of great financiers, whereby widows and orphans are despoiled of the money a foreseeing husband and father has provided.

Their fortune-telling? Don't we all love to hear what we want? It has never done more harm than the usual flattery we lavish upon those who crave flattery. And don't actors, artists, and others pay publicity agents to sing their praises in the press and in books, though they know the man who has written the words does not believe them, and would not have written them had he not been paid for doing so?

A world-famous tenor would not sing unless his own paid claque was in the audience. To avoid mishaps, he traveled with the chief of his claque and the few chosen ones whose hands were calloused by clapping for him. He once dismissed this "chef claqueur," because he had betrayed the master and clapped his hands for someone else who had paid for the services: the priest untrue to the trust divinity reposed in him.

The fortune-telling of the Gypsies is, at its worst, less harmful than the slightly more scientific prophecy of our psychologist and psychoanalysts, indulging in the same art under the protection of the law and respectability. The Gypsy fortune-teller is the psychoanalyst of the poor. How often has an old wrinkled Gypsy changed a gray day into a rosy one for a despondent maiden and the love-sick man! And how much more romance-inspiring is an open camp, a tent, than a doctor's cabinet.

Granted.

And as to their non-productiveness. It is an untrue

accusation. Only they refuse, because of physical and spiritual inability, to work in factories and shops. Why should we persist? Are there not enough people working in England and elsewhere? Are there not enough things produced in these smoky hells of our industrial towns? And who will do the work of the Gypsies when they are squeezed into our factory doors? And who will do their work as well? as gaily? Whose red laughter will echo in the glen and the valley?

The civilized world recognized the rights of conscientious objectors during the late war. England was harder pressed for men to man the trenches than she is today, or ever has been, to man the factories and farms. Yet, she respected the scruples of conscientious objectors. Well, the Gypsies are the conscientious objectors to factory work, to all the soul-killing inventions of a haphazard civilization. They have existed as they have for thousands of years, and are physically not inferior to most peoples. Two thousand years hence only, if the steel and smoke civilization lasts as long, will mankind be prepared to draw conclusions as to whether the Gypsies were right or wrong—unless none survive.

The Gypsy tents and caravans on the sides of the luscious, green-hedged paths of rural England give the finest note to the landscape. To see one of these Gypsy maidens, balancing herself on the hips as she walks townward, kerchiefed brown head high over a delicately chiseled neck, makes one think of a fairy flower that has detached itself from the soil, to be carried along by a low wind over the dust of the road. And if they are not the most devout church-goers, the Gypsy Christmas carols sung in Herefordshire are still of the finest of old England.

That they are not the lawless people they have been depicted, can be seen from the following figures:

BRITISH GYPSY CRIMES, APRIL–DECEMBER, 1907

1.	Sleeping out, or sleeping in tents	10	
	Damaging turf, etc., by camping	19	
	Camping on the highway	30	
	Allowing horses to stray	43	
	Obstructing road, tethering horses in road, etc.	9	
	Making fires within 50 feet of road	11	
	Setting fire to gorse	4	
	Want of water-supply or sanitary accommodation	18	
	—		144
2.	Careless or furious driving	6	
	Cart or van without lights	4	
	No name on cart or van	6	
	Dog without name on collar	5	
	Hawking without a license	1	
	—		22
3.	Poaching	15	
	Taking wood, sticks, ferns, etc.	21	
	Breaking pound	2	
	Fortune-telling	1	
	Hoaxing, with fortune-telling	2	
	—		41
4.	Cruelty to horses	6	
	Begging, or causing children to beg	8	
	Cruelty to, or neglect of, children	3	
	—		17
5.	Assault (2 serious charges, 11 females)...	35	
	Drunkenness (sometimes in charge of horses)	11	
	Disorderly conduct	6	
	Obscene language	8	
	Using threats	5	
	—		65

6. Small thefts	28	
Larger thefts (viz., horse & trap & bicycle)	2	
Obtaining goods by fraud	1	
Stealing by ruse (not fortune-telling)....	2	
	—	33
7. Abduction (the girl proved to be over 20)	1	
Attempted suicide	1	
	—	2
	—	324

Since all nomads are classed as Gypsies, Gypsies are blamed for many crimes performed by white vagrants. Both Gypsies and white tramps complain they are unfairly judged. The above report was taken from newspapers. Only 143, or 44 per cent of the 324 persons accused had surnames mentioned in Leland's list ("The Gypsies," pp. 304-309). And Leland recognized many families possessing only half or quarter blood.

Serious misdemeanors are always mentioned in newspapers; and that this list is comparatively free testifies to the orderly life of the British Gypsies.

Sections 1 and 2, including more than half the charges, are violations which could have been committed by anyone living like a nomad.

Section 3 shows the difference between Romany and white codes of morality.

Sections 4 to 7 are more or less disgraceful; Gypsies would think so, though, "mumply tramps" might take a laxer view. The two "larger thefts" were obviously not committed by Gypsies.

Even disregarding the inclusion of non-Gypsies and the fact that three dozen of those accused were acquitted, it is not so shameful a list!

The English Gypsy is a mixture of the nomadic element of several races—English, Scotch, Welsh, and Irish—superimposed upon the original Gypsies who arrived on the Isles in the eleventh or twelfth century. I know of no better blood combination than the one that is theirs by inheritance: ruggedness, ability, lightheartedness, imagination, and artistry. Hey, ho, the Gypsies are coming . . .

OME YEARS AGO, I ATTACHED MYSELF TO A tribe of Gypsies going westward from New York. The tribe, about a hundred strong, had already traveled in the United States and Canada ten years when I first met them. The men were coppersmiths; the women plied very successfully the trade of fortune-telling. They were Russian Gypsies. During that winter, the men had been earning good money working in the shops of New York City; and the women had found enough believers in their charms and sorceries to buy themselves immense strings of pearls, heavily diamonded rings and earrings, and yards and yards of loud silk of the finest quality. Yet when spring came, they left their almost comfortable homes, dumped themselves, with their children and belongings, in rather uncomfortable vans, and started out westward.

The joy of being on the road again was so intense and so overpowering, the first day was spent driving on while singing and laughing. When the horses were being fed, the Gypsies, with their women and children, instead of sitting down to a meal, danced wildly around an imaginary camp-fire, and rolled themselves on the grassy slope. Girls and boys, desiring an even closer contact with the earth, took their clothes off to feel the coolness and "the velvetness" of the grass upon their naked bodies.

That evening, by the camp-fire, after the dinner of

broiled meat, I asked Chief Marco the question that had been on my lips the whole day: "Why did you come to America? What made you come here?"

Marco looked at me. The question had never been put to him before. He had never put the question to himself. And then suddenly he answered with a hundred questions.

"And why shouldn't I have come? Because there was a strip of water between this country and the one I was last in? Why did you come here? Why does anybody come here? The only difference is that everybody else will stay here, while we will go on further; and tomorrow somebody will ask me in another country: 'Why have you come here?'" Marco called out to the other Gypsies: "See what he asks me—why have we come here?"

So they all laughed aloud and made fun of me because I had asked such a foolish question.

"Ha-ha—he asks why we have come here! He-he —he asks why we have come here! Did you hear what he asks? He asks why we have come here! And he says he is almost a brother!"

So the word was passed from one to another, until I felt I had never put a more ridiculous question to a human being. No people on earth have the sense of the ridiculous so strongly developed as the Gypsies; they can ridicule to death the most serious question or situation. Sense of humor, sense of the ridiculous! The Gypsies deserve first place in that.

Merriment continued late into the night. When they were tired of dancing and singing and rolling themselves on the ground, they continued to make me the butt of their ridicule, by repeating:

"He asks why we have come here . . . Ha-ha . . . ho-ho!"

It was well after midnight when I dragged myself to sleep under a van. Before I closed my eyes, Lenta, the chief's very beautiful daughter, chucked me under the chin, saying:

"Why do you ask such foolish questions?"

I was angry with myself to have appeared so stupid before her. She was so splendidly built. The skin of her body was the color of ripe honey, kissed by molten amber.

We were up bright and early the following morning. The Gypsies seemed to have changed completely overnight; they were all so serious. The day before, we had passed villages and towns without stopping; now our vans stopped everywhere, and the women spread fanwise through each village, canvassing every door, telling fortunes, selling baskets; while the men, whose trade instinct had been reawakened on the road after a winter of work in shops and factories, were buying and selling goats and calves and dogs and cats and horses.

The second nightfall found us with a rickety old Ford, which grunted, shook, and snorted every time it was made to go. I fell asleep immediately. We had camped outside of Albany. No bed had ever been so welcome as the bare ground under me that night. Women and children were sleeping all around me; some of them had fallen asleep while eating, they were so tired.

Yet in my sleep I heard the snorting of the rickety little piece of machinery. At daybreak, when I opened my eyes, I saw half a dozen men busily engaged about the Ford. They had been working the whole night to put it in order. When it was again started, it ran as smoothly as it had run in its early youth.

Before the third sun had set, we had three automobiles, among which was a huge invalidated Packard car, dragged behind one of the Fords. And that Packard was made to run smoothly before the night was over by the Gypsies, who displayed the same ingenuity in repairing broken-down old cars as they had displayed for centuries in puckering up and spiriting up broken-down horses.

It took us three weeks to reach Toledo, Ohio. By that time, there wasn't a single horse or van in the tribe. The four-footed animals had all been traded and sold and bartered for automobiles. Chief Marco and his people had become motor enthusiasts, and had, in three weeks, learned all about machinery and its possibilities. No car had been with us longer than two days. There was continual bartering, exchanging, and selling. Everyone helped; even the women, who had hitherto been busy telling fortunes, were neglecting their profession for the newer and more exciting one of second-hand automobile trading. But somehow, the colors of the dresses of my Gypsy women friends had become subdued. When we reached Toledo, there was not a single scarlet scarf around the women's heads. At least two hundred American words had gone into the Calo language which my friends had been speaking among themselves. The Gypsies were still very gay, very spirited and happy; but it was a different sort of gaiety. With the change from horses to automobiles, something had gone out.

Even Marco, the chief, had seen the change in his

people; for one day looking at his people, whose hands and faces were smeared with blackened grease, he asked me, "Why have we come to this country?" And pointing out John, his son, and a very good violinist, who had developed into the best mechanic of the tribe: "How will he ever play the violin again with fingers coarsened by the touch of steel and iron?"

In Toledo, I decided to give the adult crew of the tribe a treat. I knew that they had been to see moving pictures, but I found that they had never seen a theatrical performance. My friends, Spring Byington and Mary Vincent Stephens, were, I discovered, playing at a local theater in "Smiling Through." I bought twenty of the best seats in the orchestra; and, returning to the camp, I told the Gypsies to prepare themselves to go to the theater with me that evening. The people of Toledo will never know how much money was saved them that day by a theater party; for instead of telling fortunes and gathering in the shekels, the Gypsy women and the Gypsy men spent money freely in the shops, buying new shoes and stockings and new shawls and new jewelry.

I don't know what the management thought when they saw me arriving with twenty of the most violently colorful creatures Toledo has ever been blessed with. Even in their subdued way, the Gypsy women outcolored and outshone everything and everybody coming that evening to the theater.

My troubles, however, were only beginning. During the play, when the villain shot and killed the heroine, my Gypsy friends sprung up like one man in their seats, ready to throw themselves on the stage and tear the villain to pieces. I cried, and explained that it was all make-believe, that the heroine was not dead and that the villain was not as bad as he looked, that he was paid to play the part of such a bad man. They sat down again, but shifted seats so that all the men were seated together. At the end of the act, I remained with the Gypsies to explain to them what a play really was. When things had been more or less cleared up, I found out that the young men had decided to wait for the villain at the stage door. The conversation among them had been whether they should shoot him or knife him. Before the end of the play, Spring Byington, who had looked through the peep-hole and seen me, had sent for me. I had meant well, but I had almost upset the whole show, players as well as audience.

In another few days, I had to leave my friends; two of the automobiles had become ambulant stills, and I had no desire to have any business with revenue officers. Before I left, however, Lenta told me she was to become an American and go to school to learn to read and write. Indeed, they were all going to remain in this country; for nowhere else could they make as much money telling fortunes, trading automobiles, and selling drinks. It was a good country.

"But look, *miri pen*," I told her, "it's two weeks now since any of you have danced or sung!"

She was quick with her answer:

"Dancing and singing aren't the only ways to amuse oneself."

"But it always was your way," I retorted. "And it's probably the best way."

That made her very sad. She repeated my words to the others, and they were all very sad when we parted, saying, "We have neither danced nor sung in two weeks." And they talked lovingly and regretfully of the horses they had sold. Yet I know that many things had gone with the horses, many beautiful things had gone with them, and many an evil for the Gypsy had come in with the automobile.

I have since traveled in the United States with other Gypsy tribes: Hungarian Gypsies, Roumanian Gypsies, Brazilian Gypsies and English Gypsies, all of them crossing and crisscrossing the roads of this country, going south in the winter, and west in the summer. Only the newcomers, the late arrivals, traveled the old-fashioned way. Those who have been here a season or two take to automobiles, singing, laughing, dancing less, spending all their time bartering and trading, still thinking in terms of horses, each one hoping to return soon to his own home and buy for his dollars living horse-flesh. But more of them settle in more or less permanent ways in large towns and cities. The number of English words entering the Gypsies' language, excluding so many Calo words, also excludes so many concepts and ideas of life. Love for possession, for money, comes into their souls with every new word in their language.

In Chicago, all about Jane Addams' Hull House, there are hundreds of Gypsy families, living in the old decrepit houses of the district, alongside families of Mexican, Polish, and Russian laborers. When I visited in Chicago lately, I found the younger element of Hull House tremendously interested in the Gypsies; some enthusiasts had even gone to the trouble of learning their language, and were already acting like young

George Borrow; only where Borrow had desired to bring the contents of the Bible to the knowledge of the Gypsy, the Hull House people desired to impress upon the Gypsy a new kind of Americanism. Young Gypsies were exhibited, talents were discovered, Gypsy songs were being sung in evening classes; and one young Gypsy, who for some reason or other had taken up drawing, was being exhibited to each and all as a future Picasso, Picabia, El Greco combination. Some of these well-meaning enthusiasts told me: "If we could get these people to settle down permanently, what genius could be made to flower!"

And these reformers were also blind to the fact that the great number of deaths from tuberculosis among the Gypsies of Chicago was due primarily to the attempt to settle in one place. The old story of caging swallows. The same errors are independently committed all over the globe by a thousand different groups.

And yet even these Gypsies of Chicago have only outwardly accepted the semblance of Americanism; for their chief, Bimbo, still wields his great authority. When one of the young girls of the tribe had eloped with another Gypsy against the chief's will, the couple was brought back from Los Angeles to Chicago, and the young man was made to divorce his wife. However, he was permitted to remarry her six months later, after he had obtained the chief's permission and recognized his authority. *Leis prala,* the law of the brotherhood, was not to be broken lightly.

I have occasionally met these Chicago Gypsies on the road. They act as if they have escaped from a jail. Other Gypsies look upon them with suspicion; the length and degree of that suspicion depending entirely on the length of time a Gypsy has spent in Chicago among the white people.

As mentioned elsewhere, the first Gypsies. came to this country about the end of the eighteenth century. A group of Gypsies exiled by the English government were embarked on the good ship Virginia, sailing for Barbados, whose governor had been instructed to dispose of them in the easiest and quickest manner. But somehow, while still on board ship, the Gypsies learned what was awaiting them. That ship never landed where it was supposed to land. The Gypsies disappeared, saving trouble to the governor.

I have heard it said by Gypsies that this first batch of people of their blood landed, mingled with the Indians and were absorbed so well by the red men that their blood is now an integral part of the blood of the Indian tribes. There being no evidence to the contrary, I am inclined to accept this seemingly impossible version of the fate of the first Gypsies who arrived in this country. My inclination to accept the version is due to its seeming impossibility. The whole story of the existence of the Gypsies seems so impossible that one impossibility more or less doesn't matter really. What is a miracle more or less between Gypsies?

The year the English tried to rid themselves of the Gypsies, the French made a similar attempt and exiled a few hundred of their Bohémians to Louisiana. Only, the governor of Louisiana not having been instructed to rid himself quickly and quietly of these newcomers, the Bohémians were allowed to land. They lived and thrived so well they are still there, traveling up and down Louisiana, distinguished from other Gypsies, speaking French as it was spoken two centuries ago.

In appearance, these French Gypsies are unlike other Gypsies. In the long ago, they evidently crossed themselves with a blond race in France, quite possibly the Cagots, a race probably descended from the Merovingians, living in the south of France. But their habits and customs and traditions are as strongly Gypsy as ever. I once witnessed a wedding feast. It differed only in minor details from similar feasts I have witnessed in France, in Roumania, in Spain, and in Hungary. The Louisiana Gypsies profess to be good Catholics. The couple was married by the priest. The real marriage ceremony, however, took place with the chief of the Gypsies officiating; and the oath was not "I take this woman unto wife until death do us part," but was the same old Gypsy oath, "to leave her free to seek happiness elsewhere as soon as love has left my heart." A wedding is not considered a wedding until the right wrist of the man and the left wrist of the woman have been incised and tied together, so the blood of the two cuts mingles.

These Louisiana Gypsies seldom leave Louisiana; and while it is true that many of them have settled as farmers, and others as traders in towns and cities, their longing for the road overtakes them frequently when they are most needed at home, in the midst of the harvest or before a fair.

I have heard very little song among these Gypsies, but they dance as well as the Spanish Gypsies. By some curious twist, old dances now completely forgotten in France are being danced by these exiled Gypsies thousands of miles away from the country that had

persecuted them. I fancy that choreographists studying the old French dances would find better examples
among the Gypsies than among the Frenchmen. Just
as philologists, anxious to study the old Castilian
tongue, have to visit Constantinople, Athens, and Bucharest, where the descendants of the exiled Spanish
Jews have kept the old Castilian pure, so will philologists in a few years have to go among the Louisiana
Gypsies to study the old French tongue. A language
is kept in a purer state by an illiterate people than by
a literate one. Literature refines and corrupts a language. Literary people only seldom have ears for the
speech of the people, and invent an idiom of their
own, as different from the national one as a city garb
is from the national costume.

Spain and Portugal attempted to rid themselves of
the Gitano difficulty by exiling these people to Brazil.
A Brazilian authority on the subject, Professor Moreno, has come to the conclusion that not one prominent
Brazilian family today is free of Gypsy blood. There
are different versions as to how this happened. The
first one is that the Gypsy tribe arriving in Brazil was
composed of more women than men, while in Brazil
there were many more men than women. This being
the case, the Brazilians bought wives from the Gypsies.
It is within reason that the bewildered Gypsies, arriving in a new country after so many hardships, should
have felt less aversion to white people who treated them
well than they had felt in Spain or Portugal to people
who had treated them so miserably.

Another version, however, maintains that it was the
Gypsies who arrived there with fewer women than
men, and that, having rapidly acquired a considerable

part of the wealth of the country, they bought themselves into the best of the Brazilian families.

Be that as it may, the fact is that while what Professor Moreno said about the Brazilian blood is true, there is not a single Brazilian Gypsy tribe that is without white blood in its veins. The Russian, Roumanian, Hungarian, and Spanish Gypsies consider them impure and, because of that, will not intermarry, or indeed have anything to do with them. I have heard English Gypsies in America deny the Brazilian ones' blood completely, saying they were Negroes who had intermarried with the Portuguese in Brazil.

In the last twenty years, hundreds of these Brazilian Gypsies have come to the United States. I have met with them in San Francisco and Los Angeles, in Seattle and Chicago, in Philadelphia, New York, and Detroit. They are not as sympathetic as the others. They are very acquisitive, quarrelsome, quick with the knife, sing very rarely; and Gypsies claim that the Brazilian Gypsies never laugh, which is the greatest of all sins.

Not long ago, a tribe of Brazilian Gypsies settled for the winter in a street of the lower East Side of New York. Almost a hundred of them lived in a half-dozen empty stores in one row on the right side of the street. Opposite them, another row of empty stores housed a tribe of Hungarian Gypsies. While there has always been enmity between Gypsies of different countries, I have never seen such as between the Gypsies of Hungary and Brazil. The Hungarians accused the others of more crimes and of more unclean habits than they themselves have been accused of by other peoples. And when a young Brazilian Gypsy offered a considerable sum of money to buy for wife a Hungarian Gypsy girl, the audacity of the offer alone caused a series of riots which resulted in the expulsion of all the Gypsies from that street. No Southern family could have felt as insulted if a wealthy Negro had sued in marriage the daughter of one of the oldest Virginia families.

Irving Brown, who has written so beautifully about the Gypsy in Spain and the Gypsies he traveled with in America, told me recently a very amusing incident.

Some friends of his, to whom he had spoken very enthusiastically about Gypsies, asked the privilege of dining with them. Brown arranged a dinner with the Gypsies at Sherry's. Before bringing the Black Brothers to the restaurant, Brown had a distinct understanding with them and paid a stipulated amount to the Gypsy women to read the fortunes of the guests free of charge. There was to be no asking and no begging on this particular occasion.

Appareled in their gaudiest—the women with all their silk shawls about their bodies and all their jewels hanging around their necks, the men dressed in their Sunday best—the Gypsies appeared at Sherry's, and behaved with dignity during the dinner, entertaining the guests with song and dance and fortune-telling, and giving Brown's guests the treat of their lives.

But suddenly the host began to notice that the silver was disappearing from the table. His eye having been sharpened by his contact with Gypsies, it didn't take him long to discover in whose pocket most of the silver had gone. He took the man aside, and told him:

"Remember what we agreed. There was to be no begging and no extra charge. I've paid you for this entertainment. In taking the silver, it's as if you were taking it from me. Now, you wouldn't do that to your host, would you? Please put everything back on the table!"

The Gypsy replaced the silver reluctantly; then, turning about, he faced Brown and said:

"It's true I wouldn't take anything from a host; but when a host displays that much silver, it's a different question!"

And Brown fancies he has lost the friendship of this particular group of Gypsies; that they will never again look upon him as an equal, or brother, since in such a matter he placed himself on the side of the other people, and protected their wealth. They were not stealing, they assured him; but they did need silver badly. I want to state here that no Gypsy has ever taken anything from me in all the years I have known them.

A few weeks ago, on the East Side of New York, a friend of mine took me to a Gypsy family which had had a child run over and killed by an automobile truck. The unrestrained despair of the mother was like a storm, or a fire, in its intensity. I had never seen anything to equal such abandon, in joy or despair.

That night, I was dining in a restaurant where Gypsies foregather occasionally on Sundays and holidays. I found about twenty of them when I arrived, all dressed in their best. The wine had flowed freely; still they were silent, while the mother of the dead child was weeping quietly. Suddenly, she called out to one of the young men, "Sing!" From under the table, another young man pulled out an accordion. The bereaved woman, still young, beautiful, and exceedingly well-built, began to dance with as great abandon as she had wept in her despair a few hours before. She danced until she literally exhausted herself, when she collapsed on the floor in a heap of colored silks. Now the other Gypsy women, disregarding the comfort of the other guests, pushed the tables aside to make a wide circle around the exhausted woman, and danced in a ring about her, springing in the air, executing the most fantastic steps, hypnotizing her into insensibility by the incessant movement, the dancing, color, noise, which turned and swirled about her. During this intense performance, the husband of the woman was standing quietly aside. When long after midnight the dance had ceased, they were all exhausted, except the husband, who carried the woman, sleeping peacefully like a child in his arms, around the block to his home.

For two weeks, the whole tribe was doing nothing but trying to entertain the bereaved mother; to give her moments of forgetfulness, "so that she might conceive another child without thinking of the dead one," an old Gypsy woman explained.

I don't know whether such behavior is customary among Gypsies or not, for I have never seen it done before, nor have I heard any Gypsy or Gypsy student refer to it. Yet it seems to me that it could not have originated spontaneously for this particular occasion only. The death of children, I knew, had always been taken very seriously by bereaved parents; but I have seldom known a tribe of Gypsies to take such an active part in the sorrow of one of their members, except for the traditional cult of the dead to which they are all addicted.

In aristocratic countries, the Gypsy chiefs have always styled themselves dukes, judges, atamans. But in democratic countries, like England or the United States, the Gypsies, having psychologized the people, decided to call their chiefs "queens" and "kings." There are neither kings nor queens of the Gypsies in Hungary, Roumania, Russia, Germany, or France; but there are plenty of kings and queens of Gypsies in England and the United States. The Americans and the English expect a good deal more romance outside themselves than they have inside themselves. Those who live romantic lives seldom read romances. Every once in a while, you read fantastic tales of wedding feasts and funeral processions of such and such a Gypsy king or queen. On these occasions, the power of the king and queen is elaborated upon, fantastically out of proportion to whatever truth there is in it.

In addition to the Brazilian, French, and southern European Gypsies roaming in the United States and Canada, there are a great many Eastern Gypsies from Syria, Persia, and even some who have lived the last few generations in Egypt, who have come to live here the last twenty years or so. There are also five to six thousand English Gypsies, or a mixture of English, Welsh, and Scotch Gypsies. But these Eastern Gypsies are mostly acrobats and showmen, and live not in tribes but in single families, working the fairs and amusement places of the country. No contact is as difficult as contact with them, for each and every one denies his ancestry, pretending to be Arabian, Egyptian, Persian, etc. Yet not one of them hesitates to point out the other one as a Gypsy. One of these acrobats who wanted to prove that not his but a neighbor's family was Gypsy, gave me details, names of father and mother, the town of birth, the date of birth, and the date of his friend's marriage and birth of his children. Investigating, I found the information correct; only it applied to the fellow himself; it was the history of his own family and not that of the other.

There are always at least two dozen families on Coney Island during the season, and I fancy there are more than a thousand individuals working the vaudeville circuits, billed under Greek, Persian, or Arabic names. These Eastern Gypsies are much more primitive than even the Balkan Gypsies in their habits; and left India or Persia much more recently than the other Gypsies. That they live in single families instead of tribes, is no proof of a more advanced civilization, but that they are still under the delusion that it is possible to lose themselves completely in the white population without being noticed.

In California, I knew of one acrobat family that was bleeding itself white to maintain a young son and daughter in luxury in the hope they would eventually marry into white families. Gaya, the girl, who had taken the name of Gwendolyn and pretended to be an Egyptian princess, finally did marry a young "extra" from one of the moving picture lots, only to find out on the day of her marriage that he was a Gypsy—perhaps the only male Gypsy in captivity in Hollywood. Having known the two youngsters and known of their courtship, I had taken it for granted that each one was aware of the other's descent, and had let it go without mentioning it to either of them. Before the wedding, Stephan suggested to his bride that they go to Glendale, where his mother lived. Then only he told his wife that his mother was a Gypsy and that, while he was trying to take Valentino's place (the ambition of every dark-eyed young man after the movie actor's death), she lived in a tent in Glendale, far away from Hollywood, because she couldn't bear to live in a house. And then Gaya revolted. "A Gypsy! The marriage is off. There isn't going to be a wedding. It's all off!"

However, her brother's sense of humor saved the situation. He laughed and laughed, so loudly and so peculiarly that Stephan looked at him squarely, and looked at his bride. Suddenly, he addressed them in Calo; a Calo they did not completely understand, for Stephan, though born in this country, was of Hungarian descent. So they laughed together.

I was called in on that affair. The question was whether Gaya's parents should be told the truth or not. As the parents were working their way eastward, and it would be a full year before they would see their children again, I suggested they should be left in ignorance until things worked out somehow. A few weeks later, Goru, Gaya's brother, who had taken the name of Gordon, was married—to Stephan's sister, also trying to break into the movies. All of us adjourned to Glendale to Stephan's mother, where we had an old-fashioned Gypsy wedding feast, with song and dance and a lot of pork, while the old woman chattered, making a hundred different incantations and prayers to the sun and moon for the happiness of her children.

Fancy not that this is an isolated case; most attempts of these Gypsies to lose their identity are thwarted by their highly developed sense of affinity. Nine times out of ten, they stumble upon one of their own kind, or someone in whose veins there flows some of the Black Brothers' blood. The present immigration laws restrict the arrivals in this country of these Orientals; still, some do trickle in from time to time on six-months engagements as artists for vaudeville circuits, etc.

The ones already here will eventually be absorbed first by the non-Anglo-Saxon population of this country. It is easier for independent families to hide their identity than for those living in large groups. The offspring from such mixtures will inherit such sensibilities and the country will be the better for the absorption of their blood.

But what about the English Gypsies, or the Gypsies whose last home has been in England, in Scotland, in Ireland, or in Wales? They have been coming here for the last hundred years, and they continue to arrive in large groups, in single families and singly. Blacksmiths, coppersmiths, shoemakers, traders—watch them at horse-fairs, at races and occasionally at prize-fights. Rough fellows, though good-natured, these English Gypsies. And bluff and blarney—none like it in the world!

During the winter, they live everywhere, in industrial towns, mingling with the rest of the population and working at all kinds of trades, their real national identity unknown to their neighbors and fellow workers. I found dozens of English Gypsy families in the silk mills of Paterson and in the steel mills of Pennsylvania. Even while working in shops and factories, they are not backward in practicing their individual little trades and tricks—card sharping and fiddling; while the women practice "phrenology," or sell to some wealthy ladies the "last bit of lace brought from Ireland, which has been in the family hundreds of years."

Spring no sooner arrives than they are on the road,

stringing their tents along the Hudson River from the mouth to its very source in the Adirondacks. Clean, trim, sprightly, the girls, with just a touch of red ribbon in their hair, sell woven baskets to automobilists who stop to rest for a minute, or offer cold water to the thirsty ones. These English Gypsies do not mingle with the other Gypsies. Indeed, when an Ungar caravan is announced, they hide; they prefer not to be seen by the people of their blood whom they deny, lest they be confused with them. Moving their vans but once in a week or so, the Romanies wend their way northward, entering Canada sometime in August. As they are not so shy as other Gypsies, it is quite easy to get near them and establish relations of semi-friendship. Though they are willing to talk and tell others what they pretend to know of themselves, they take a special delight in mystifying. Feigning ignorance, I have collected from them about two hundred words, of which not one word's correct translation was given me. The youngest of children has taken special delight in mystifying me: "When you next meet Romanies, tell them so and so, and you will be accepted as a brother by them." And the Calo words they told me were: "Throw cold water upon him; he is another fool."

Two years ago, I met a rather large caravan belonging to a Smith clan, claiming to be of the first to have arrived to these shores. They had just returned from a trip up the St. Lawrence River. They had camped for a few weeks near an Indian reservation. I thought of the terrible winter the Indians had before them; I could guess the number of Indians on that reservation from the number of blankets, coats, saddles, boots, and moccasins the Gypsies possessed. I asked the leader of the tribe whether they hadn't compelled the Indians to spend the last of the summer in the water; for they must have been left absolutely naked. He answered jestingly:

"Them Indians are clever people. They can get their hair to grow to their feet, and cover themselves with it, can't they?"

One clan of these English Gypsies has a curious custom. When a member of the tribe dies on the road, the body is sent to the local undertaker, with instructions that it be embalmed and kept until called for. Every spring, this tribe meets at Atlanta, Georgia, in its own corner of a cemetery. Then the coffins of the dead are brought and buried in holy ground. I have often tried to find out the reason for this terrific waste of money. No one wanted to give any explanation. So much money was spent on undertakers' bills, the tribe was kept in continual poverty; and yet not one of them thought of an individual burial somewhere else in the States or in Canada. The cult of the dead did not seem to apply in this particular case. When I did find out the reason back of it, the childishness and the naïveté surprised me so that I am not fully convinced. It appears that the founder of the clan here, about a hundred years ago, had suddenly "got religion," and was as fantastic in that as he had been in everything else. He became convinced the day of the awakening of the dead was not very far away; so, to take advantage of the white population (a real Gypsy's chief concern), he ordered that all the members of his clan be buried in one and the same place, as close to one another as possible. On the day of judgment, at the sound of the first trumpet, his clan being all together, in one huge band, would be able to assert their power over the other ones, mostly strangers to one another; and he being the chief, the Gypsies would take the reins of power in their hands and dominate the world again, as they had dominated it before in some remote past.

Neither Russian nor Hungarian Gypsies, Spaniards nor Macedonians, could be made to follow such a cloudy idea; they being in general much too realistic for that. But there has evidently been a large flow of Celtic, Irish, and Scotch blood in the veins of these Gypsies.

While I was away from the States for a few years, one of my colleagues had married. When I returned, he told me he was already the father of a child a few months old. He invited me to dinner one evening at his home to meet his wife.

"Isn't she a fantastic creature?" he repeatedly asked me.

Indeed, I found her that; oval face, large dark eyes, and that touch of Spanish frequently found in people of Irish descent. Had I but looked at her hands, I might have guessed; but her hands were never displayed. About ten o'clock, Bob's tongue began to hang a little thickly in his mouth. His conversation, though spicier, began to be more interesting. The bell rang. His wife went to open the door; a commotion, as if a hundred people were trying to jam their way through the narrow door, was heard. When it was all over, just two people appeared, the father and mother of the lady; and it was unmistakable. They had no sooner looked at their son-in-law than the mother said in Calo to her daughter:

"Don't let him have any more wine!"

Bob was explaining them to me:

"Gosh! They talk Celtic as if it were an every-day language. Marvelous people. My wife talks Celtic, too."

Mrs. Bob asked her parents quickly not to *"basher Romani* for the Gorgio is not deaf." But we quickly formed a party, of which Bob, whose eyelids had become as heavy as his tongue, was not a member. This was the fourth daughter they had married to a Gorgio. Two of them had been on the stage. One was teaching. (This was a very doubtful explanation, considering how the two old people looked at one another and then at their daughter when they gave it to me.) Another daughter was going to school in Newark; "bringing her up to be a lady." But I could obtain no invitation to come and see them in their home. Before saying good night, as we had all been looking rather deeply into the glasses put before us, mother and daughter had in a spirit of fun taken from me several pieces of silver—"cross my hand with silver that I may read your fortune." Good Romanies; they weren't giving up their little tricks even with a friend of the family.

To any Gypsy student unable or unwilling to travel far from home, the United States affords the best chance to study the Gypsies of all countries—their individual evolution, as well as the changes in the language. For here, anyone with eyes and ears can find Gypsies of all countries, of all trades, of all clans, of all stations. Horse dealers, blacksmiths, coppersmiths, fortune-tellers, musicians, pure-bred and half-bloods, quarter-bloods, and eighth-bloods, *Dias, Didicais.* I have never yet taken an automobile trip for a day without meeting a caravan, and sometimes two or three; their adaptability being such there is no work they cannot learn, no place they cannot extract a living from. And what a gay, full life they lead! I have met dozens of Gypsy girls in the sweat-shops of New York; manicurists in barber shops, having learned sufficient Italian to fool even the owner; actresses, acrobats, models, plasterers, musicians, plumbers, horse traders, automobile traders, veterinarians, insurance agents, book venders, and carpet sellers. Not a trade, not a profession which they have left out. But when spring comes, they can be known by their absence. There isn't one Gypsy boy or girl who doesn't know how to read the patteran well enough to find relatives who may already have started on the road.

And yet, the same quarrels between them, the same distinctions as among the other peoples of the United States. The Roumanian Gypsy refuses friendship with the Hungarian Gypsy, and the two of them consider the Russian Gypsy unbearable. The Spanish Gypsies, the aristocrats of the road, refuse to have anything to do with the Brazilian ones, and consider the English to be impostors, not belonging to the race at all. In this respect, they are very much like the Jews, who, though of one and the same root, make the same distinctions among themselves, considering the superiority of the people they have lived with until now as their own, and refusing to mingle with Jews of countries culturally inferior to the countries they themselves were born in.

What do you think will happen to the Gypsies here? Absorption seems so imminent, one is first tempted to say that it is the only thing; but remember that fifty

years ago Charles Godfrey Leland, who was a much
better student of Gypsy life than George Borrow, wrote
that in another twenty or thirty years we should see
the last Gypsy. It is now fifty years since, and we have
not by any means seen the last million of them. Sixty
years ago, George Borrow practically said the same
thing; and yet while the number of Gypsies has not
greatly augmented, it hasn't diminished either. In the
United States, especially, the number has not diminished. Every year there are hundreds of caravans of
white people stringing along the roads, from the At-
lantic to the Pacific coast: first and second generations
of Czechs, Hungarians, Slovaks, Russians, Poles and
Irish, who take to the road in the spring and go a-gypsying with their families. You will get as many expla-
nations for this gypsying as you will meet families doing it. There are many who play at being real Gypsies
and assure the inquirer that they do; they are proud
of being what they claim to be. The number of families going gypsying increases as the automobiles become cheaper and the roads more practical. In some
mysterious way, these people pick up a few Calo
words; enough slang of a kind to make up little songs
and nursery rhymes. Many of these pseudo-Gypsies
remain on the road the whole year round, traveling
south in the winter, and westward and northward in
the summer; "seeing the sky" for the first time; discovering that it isn't necessary to work eight hours in a
shop to earn a living, that one can pick up a living on
the go. These traveling Americans have no objection
to intermarrying with Gypsies. I have indeed met
some who have already married their daughters and
sons into Gypsy tribes, and feel as if they had bought

themselves into the very aristocracy of the road; much the feeling that some Americans have when they have married their charming daughters to impecunious French and Italian noblemen.

If traveling is one of the characteristics of Gypsies, the people of the United States are the most nomadic people on earth. Perhaps only because their immediate ancestors were the most adventuresome of their blood. Perhaps because of the nature of the country. The average American covers more miles in one year by train or automobile than any Gypsy has ever covered in a lifetime. I fancy that if the immigration laws were not what they are, we should have attracted hither all of Gypsydom living in the more or less civilized world. And they would repay any small infractions against the law with an infectious gaiety and lightness of heart, song and dance, and inject a new kind of leaven into the all-grain dough which will eventually grow into the loaf this country will offer on the altar of civilization.

N ADDITION TO THE COLONIES OF GYPSIES DE-
scribed in the preceding chapters, there are
smaller groups of Gypsies in every part of
the world.

In Sweden, the Gypsies of Linköping, there now for
several generations, have so thoroughly acclimatized
themselves and assimilated, only a native could distinguish them from the rest of the population. Their
vivacity having been toned down in the course of generations, it is now only a little above that of the Swede;
but since like everything else vivacity is a question of
relativity, the Swedes consider the Linköping Gypsies
an extremely vivacious and hysterical people, although
they do not appear so in the eyes of one who has met
with Gypsies of other lands.

The northern climate not being very favorable to
traveling, one could hardly call the Swedish Gypsy
nomadic; "restless" would probably be the better word
to distinguish them from the others. When some of
these Gypsies migrated with a group of Swedes to New
York, they lived for years in the Swedish colony without outsiders being aware of the difference of nationality between them and the Swedes.

Roumanian Gypsies who visited them refused to believe they were blood-brothers, and denounced them
as impostors. As a matter of fact, the two groups denounced each other as impostors; for the Swedish Gypsies refused to believe that they were kin to the "gesti-

culating, colorfully dressed, loud-speaking rabble from the East."

The Gypsies of Norway—there are over a thousand —are not easily distinguishable from the Gypsies of Sweden. As a matter of fact, there is no more difference between the Gypsies of Norway and the Gypsies of Sweden than there is between the people of Norway and the people of Sweden. They are hard-working, trading people, following the fairs and markets, dealing in cattle, and working as coppersmiths, iron-forgers, and blacksmiths. Indeed, these occupations are so much identified with the Gypsies of Norway that in the popular language anyone working at these trades is called "Tzigani" or "Heiden" (pagan), even though he may not be a Gypsy.

Still, because of this slight restlessness, they have constituted a problem both for Norwegian and for Swedish authorities: thwarted, because their Gypsies have at no time submitted readily to local and state rules regarding the compulsory education of children. Tradition among the Norwegian Gypsies demands that everyone belonging to the race live at least two weeks of the year in a tent. An infant dead before having had the opportunity to live for two weeks in a tent is considered as having died outside the race, and is buried without the ceremony attending Gypsy funerals.

The Gypsies of Finland live in larger caravans than the Gypsies of Norway, Denmark, or Sweden. Most of these caravan Gypsies are cattle herders, and many of them have even gone to Lapland, where they have become reindeer herders. There are tribes who own thousands of deer. Reindeer herders must continually move from one place to another in search of new grazing lands, and this is ideally suited to the nature of the Gypsy. Though reputed to be the cleanest Gypsies living under the sun, the Finnish Gypsies, no less than the others, are accused by the rest of the population of all the evils, and of uncleanliness to boot. On general principles, every theft committed in Finland is laid at the door of the Gypsy, even if for years there hasn't been a Gypsy in the vicinity. Hard-headed, hard-working, close-lipped Finns look with disfavor upon this more or less easy-going people. Envying their freedom, they accuse them of laziness, when, as a matter of fact, none but Gypsies could do the nerve-racking work they do, rounding deer and cattle as well and as efficiently, doing so much work besides—and still have time for song and dance.

Gypsies are known by the population of Sweden, Denmark, and Finland as "Tartars," because this was the first name by which they were identified; and the belief has implanted itself so strongly that the younger generation of Gypsies themselves think they are Tartars, whose ancestors had separated themselves during the fourteenth century from the army of Tamerlane when the fiery conqueror led his people against the whole world.

The first Gypsies appeared in this northern country about the end of the fifteenth century. There was a forced expulsion of the "Tartars" from Sweden in 1512, and another one in Denmark in 1536, the accusations against them being the usual ones: paganism, immorality being more emphasized than in any other country. The question as to when they got back into these northern countries still remains unanswered, except that they were never completely weeded out, and that groups of families remained hidden on the shores of fjords and dugouts in the mountains until the fury against them had somewhat spent itself. In Sweden, as well as in Denmark, popular organized hunts treated the Gypsies no better than wolves.

Today they are living more or less unmolested; and except for an occasional report on the Gypsy problem by the Commissioner of Education, one hears very little against the "Tartars," who have almost forgotten their original language, and use a deliberately reverse Swedish as the secret language among themselves.

It seems the original root of these three groups was composed of a branch of the Gypsies who entered Germany, but took refuge in Sweden when the persecution against them had become unbearable. This original tribe mixed with another branch, which probably came a hundred years later, of the Gypsies who had first settled in Russia but had roamed as far as Finland. Because of the extreme cleanliness of the Finnish Gypsies, Swedish investigators pretend that the Finnish Gypsies came from Sweden, and not from Russia. In addition to persecutions as Gypsies, the Black Brothers have always had to suffer because of the people they formerly lived with. In Hungary, the Roumanian Gypsy is hated the more, because he is a Roumanian. The like happens to the Hungarian Gypsy in Roumania.

There are close to ten thousand *Zingaros* roaming through Italy. Though the Gypsies living in Italy have seldom, if ever, been molested either by the authorities or by the people, there being no reproach against them either for uncleanliness or for refusal to send children to public schools, the Zingaros of Italy have developed neither music nor dance to the degree to which these arts have been developed by the Gypsies in countries where they have been pursued and persecuted. Tenting freely everywhere, mingling freely with the population, but living their own lives unmolested, uncensored by anyone, the Zingaros have kept themselves racially pure (except in Sicily, where they have frequently intermarried with the peasants). The Zingaros of Italy, cattle-dealers and iron-forgers, have for centuries been the minstrels and showmen of the country, exhibiting trained bears and learned monkeys, while the Gypsy women work spells, witchcraft, sorcery and practice medicine far more extensively than medical science has ever been practiced in Italy. Working upon the superstitious minds of the Latins, the Gypsy women have reawakened the *vecchia religione* that had been lying dormant in the people, below the surface of Christianity.

The Italian peasant and villager to this day believe more in the sorcery of the Zingaro women than in the blessings of the priest, when building a home or making an important decision.

As most masons in Italy are Gypsies, there is a curious custom which, in a sense, parallels the simulacrum of immolation of which I have spoken before, whereby a Gypsy woman lies down for a few moments in the grave beside her dead husband. This superstition is that no home can withstand the force of the wind and the anger of the soil, dug deep for the foundation of the walls, unless a human body has been buried underneath it. The anger of the earth must then be propitiated with a corpse. But as the law will not allow the sacrifice of a human being today, as soon as the foundation of a building is laid, the Gypsy mason, or his wife, watching the road, tape measure in hand, takes the dimension of the shadow of any man, woman, or child passing by. Then the tape, the exact length of the shadow, is buried under the foundation, and the work continues. The person whose shadow measure was buried will die within a year. This shadow burying is from a leaf of the *vecchia religione,* the old belief in Italy. The Gypsy is being heavily paid by the builder of the house; for since the measurement of the shadow is taken when the person is unaware, his own shadow might be measured if he did not pay the Gypsy sufficiently.

Some years ago in Brescia, a wealthy Italian had the house of a neighbor demolished and the foundation dug out and the ground filled in, because he had been informed that the shadow of his only daughter had been buried under that house. The Gypsy masons had a lively time of it, fleeing in all directions; and it would have fared hard with them and with the builder of the house if the Gypsies hadn't uncovered the secret that the father of the girl, upon building his own house, had charged his mason to bury the measure of a shadow underneath it. The Gypsy mason threatened to divulge whose shadow he had measured. Such information would have caused an endless blood feud in Brescia. The people would have gone around killing one another, for no doubt such shadows had been buried under most of the houses; and at the death of any man, the charge could have been leveled against anyone who had built a home the preceding year.

It will be remembered that "officially" the first Gypsies appeared in Italy in 1427 or 1428, at Romano, where the persecuted clans of Germany assembled in the spring for a conference. No doubt, many Gypsy families never returned from that conference, but remained in a country where they found such fertile ground to spread their superstitions. The Italians had willing ears, eager for whispers of sprites and genii, of shadows and souls living underground, deep in the bowels of the earth, from which they emerge at nightfall through all the wells and cracks in the mountains. Neither is the air free; for according to Gypsy sorcerers and witches, millions of unseen bodies, unseen shadows, our own and those of our enemies, are continually accompanying us overhead. When Onoria merely thinks of killing Victoria or Vincenzo, his shadow overhead immediately sets out to accomplish the deed, floating over space in search of the unseen double of the victim, henceforth to travel in the air a dead body, and cause disease and pestilence in the country. These murderous wishes and thoughts are exploited by the Gypsy sorcerers in their fortune-telling. What Italian has ever lived without wishing to avenge some real or imaginary wrong upon another one and, unwilling to be imprisoned by law for the actual deed, has not lavished his thoughts voluptuously on all kinds of imaginary killings and punishments? The Gypsies know what the people they live with desire most secretly.

Darker than almost any of the other European Gypsies, with even more luminous eyes, fiercely burning, and bushy brows, their women molded of a more Junoesque statue than most Gypsy women, the Italian Gypsies are more vivacious, louder, and quicker than the Gypsies of England, or those of Spain, Roumania, or

Russia. Their bodies exhale such an enormous heat that being with a half·dozen of them in even the coldest parts in an open tent, one feels as warm as if there were so many burning stoves. The animal heat of an Italian Gypsy is one of the most curious phenomena of racial adaptability. The Zingaro has the faculty of controlling at will the heat of his body.

Generally speaking, the Gypsy of other countries is seldom jealous of his wife; first, because he has no reason to be, purity being traditional in his tribe; secondly, because he doesn't consider any love contact between his wife and a Gorgio possible in some cases, or of any consequence in other cases. Not so the Italian Gypsies! Most of the crimes committed by them are due to jealousy.

I knew one Zingaro who, after he had punished his wife, set out single-handed in search of the man who had betrayed him, and traveled practically all over the globe to find him. When I knew Cesare, he was a man of eighty, and had already been on the hunt for the guilty one for more than fifty years. During this time he had traversed every country, and been in every city of the world. Yet never for one moment had he forgotten the object of his travels. He practiced knife-throwing for at least an hour a day. He carried in his pocket a wooden bull's-eye; and, showing it to me, he explained:

"When the thing first happened, my aim was so uncertain I only hit the outer rim of the bull's-eye at ten yards' distance. Today I can hit it exactly in the center at forty yards, no matter at what angle it is placed." And so saying, he measured off his pace, hung the piece of wood on a tree, and hit the thing exactly in the center half a dozen times in succession, without the slightest deviation. "When the thing first happened, I was a weak man; perhaps that was the reason why it happened. Today, look what I can do!" And placing a walnut in the crook of his knee, and flexing his leg once, he crushed the walnut.

There was not a language Cesare could not speak well enough to make himself understood. There was not a trade he had not worked at.

When I suggested that the man he was looking for might be dead and buried long ago, the Zingaro looked at me so piercingly, I stuttered and mumbled a thousand apologies, saying that it was merely a suggestion, and that I wished it might not be so—that the man hadn't died and wouldn't die other than by his hand or knife. A few days later, however, I questioned whether he could recognize the enemy if he were to meet him suddenly on the street.

"I would recognize him in a thousand," the Zingaro affirmed.

Of course, my old friend had not looked at himself in the mirror in fifty years; and, not knowing how he had changed in appearance, he did not realize that the other man's appearance had probably changed so as to be unrecognizable.

That, also, is a Zingaro superstition. Women do look at themselves in mirrors, carrying several of them hidden in the pockets of their ample skirts; but men never do. I have seen Gypsies shave without looking at their reflection in a glass.

Old age came very suddenly to this old Zingaro; and I met him years later in New York, walking on Second Avenue, his body so bent it seemed the forehead would touch the ground. The people he lived with assured me that they knew the other man had died several years before; but they refused to tell this to their friend, who still practiced his knife-throwing an hour every day, and still walked several hours every day in search of the man he so hated. Cesare died practicing knife-throwing, when someone assured him the "other one" had died in Constantinople.

Of course, Cesare may be an extraordinary instance of vengefulness. Still, with less strength, it is very common among Zingaros. Women are as vengeful as men. Italian literature, and folk-lore as well, is replete with stories of Zingaro vendettas.

An Italian army officer told me that in the late war it happened that a Hungarian regiment, composed mostly of Hungarian Gypsies, was suddenly faced by an Italian regiment, at the head of which were a great number of Zingaros. For the honor of their race and their reputation in both countries, these people fought a war entirely their own, stubbornly, bravely, hand to hand, while the rest of the army watched the bloody contest.

In song-making, the Zingaros are unequaled. The melodies are trifling and generally patterned after some known Italian melody, but the poetry and songs in praise of natural phenomena are intensely beautiful, savage, and passionate, reaching Homeric heights in the descriptions of landscapes and battles, and still greater heights when cursing the enemy. It is said that when a betrayed Italian woman asked a Zingaro woman to curse the faithless husband, the curses invoked were so terrible the vengeful woman herself died of fright listening to them.

The Zingaro distinguishes himself from other Gypsies in that he is never bareheaded; to hinder such thoughts as are not uttered from flying out of the head, and to prevent himself from being reached by the thoughts of sprites and genii floating in the air. Whenever possible, even the horses' heads are covered. In the eyes of the Zingaro, certain kinds of horses, those which have a dash of Arab blood, are almost human, have their own god, their own religion, and their own doubles, sprites, and genii, which have as much power as those of human beings. Some of the Zingaros, living in the most southerly part of Italy, celebrate the nuptials of their mares and stallions with as much pomp as they do those of their children. The birth of a little colt is attended with even greater ceremony than the birth of a child. When hungry or thirsty, the Zingaro will think first of his horse, then of his children, then of his wife, and only lastly of himself. *"Li grai prima in tute."*

The belief of the peasant that a Zingaro can talk and understand a horse's language is only little short of true. There is a mysterious bond between animal and man. With my own eyes I have seen horses execute what the master wished silently; although he stood fully a hundred feet away from the animal.

In the long run, Gypsies begin to resemble in character the people they live among, with always a measure of exuberance added to that possessed by the natives themselves. One has but to look at the "Heiden," the Austrian Gypsies, to characterize them as Freud did: "coffee and milk Gypsies." There is something nice and smooth about them, almost effeminate. The grace, which has been spoken of as the grace of a tiger, becomes in an Austrian Gypsy the grace of a domesticated cat. The attempts of Maria Theresa and the emperor to civilize and settle the Gypsies had more or less been concentrated upon Hungary. The Austrian Gypsies, almost completely civilized, had degenerated and died out. Those who had survived are what they are.

In Poland, the Gypsies are nationally proud and antagonistic to all the other Gypsies who occasionally happen to pass through; and, like the Poles, their speech is full of politeness. When they address one another, they never forget the Polish *"pani,"* although what follows may be the filthiest Calo curse.

Besides the Gypsies in Europe and America, there are still large groups of Asiatic Gypsies, roaming from Persia to Turkestan, Afghanistan, Siberia, and Egypt, and there are tremendous hordes of Sudras in Arabia. Doughty, in his "Travels in Arabia," tells of meeting Gypsies in Arabia, plying much the same trades as everywhere else, blacksmiths and horse-traders. They are distinguished from the rest of the population because they always ride asses, and not horses as the Arabians do. And although these Gypsies have probably been there as long as, if not longer than, the present inhabitants, they are still considered strangers, hated, despised; and much the same accusations are leveled against them by the Arabs as by the Europeans: uncleanliness, kidnaping, eating foul food, and immorality.

Because of the shyness of the Asiatic Gypsy, their primitiveness and savagery, any approach by white people is almost impossible. What is known about them is more guessed and deduced than derived from close contact and scientific investigation. But one thing is known: that they are so nomadic that the Arabs consider them as nomads. If an Arab stays in one place three days, the Gypsy stays nowhere longer than that many hours, and is supposed to move his tent from one place to another even while he sleeps.

It is quite possible that these Arabian Gypsies are the direct descendants of those whom Timur overthrew, that they are of the same origin as the European Gypsies, though they bear very little physical resemblance to them. Their language is dissimilar to the Calo, used everywhere else, only in minor details. A Roumanian, Macedonian, or Russian Gypsy would understand their speech with very little difficulty within a few days, and would be understood by them.

Is it due to the atmospheric conditions of the desert, or is it due to other reasons that so many prophets have arisen there in the past, and that so many still arise today? There have been prophets, even among the Gypsies in Arabia, within the last century, prophets who have attempted to gather all the Gypsies under one flag and lead them back to their own country. Only thirty years ago, over thirty thousand Gypsies gathered in the desert, and pitched their tents around the tent of the prophet who was to lead them out of slavery. The affair would not have been as great a fiasco as it turned out to be, I was told by a Gypsy who had participated in that movement, if they had been able to agree as to where their homeland was. Many Gypsies of Asia believe they are Egyptians, while the prophet and those about him were convinced that they came from somewhere in Turkestan, somewhere between the mountains, where the homes their ancestors had left were still vacant and awaiting them—"not tents, but houses dug out in the mountains, and guarded against intruders by tigers and leopards." Such a thing sounds almost impossible to civilized ears, but one must remember that only a few years ago a band of little, parched, dark-skinned people appeared in Palestine, led by a prophet, who proved to the world they were Yemenites, who had taken refuge in the desert at the fall of Jerusalem, and lived there two thousand years, unknown to anybody, until he had shown them the way.

And what is one to say about the Egyptian Gypsies? To see them under a tent three feet high, which doesn't seem able to contain more than two people, and which is made to hold fifteen and twenty at a time, one has the weird feeling of seeing so many worms crawling out from underground. Most Egyptian Gypsies are so short-sighted, and have such bad eyesight, they can hardly see anything three or four feet from their noses.

The whole of Asia and Egypt seems to act like a huge sieve, sifting the people once so powerful on the Hind, and now spread over the whole world.

While there were large migrations of Gypsies from India thousands of years ago, hundreds of years ago, the trickling of small tribes and single families has never ceased. In a two-thousand-years-old, unending stream, the Gypsies have continually come down, associating with others they found on the road, always going farther down, farther down, from Asia into Turkey, from Turkey into Greece, with a longer stop in Macedonia, and from there over the face of the globe, led by the wind of fate and the enterprising spirit of individual members of families.

And always the Gypsies of the East have, among other things, been the showmen, the doctors, the sorcerers and astrologists.

Pallas considers that the language which the Gypsies speak resembles completely a language of Hindu merchants, the Multani, with a band of whom he happened to be acquainted in Astrakhan. Calo words are divided into three classes: root words, derivatives, and loan words. The foreign languages which have supplied the Gypsy language with some of its words are Turkish, Greek, Roumanian, Italian, Wallachian, Magyar, German, Slavonian, Kurdish, etc. The sun is called in Nuri *sam,* and in Hindustani *kam.* The name of silver in Nuri is *rup,* and in Hindustani *ruppa.* Hair in Nuri is *bal,* and in Hindustani *bal.* Head in Nuri is *cero,* and in Persian *ser.* Fortune in Nuri is *bakst,* and in Persian *baht.* Tent in Nuri is *catar,* and in Hindustani *catar.*

A Sasani, named Abu Dulaf al-Hazarigi al-Yanbu'i, has composed an ode, "The Sasanian Ode," in Arab Gypsy language. It is, however, impossible to quote specimens of this ode, because of the impropriety, wantonness, profligacy, and numerous foul expressions. But some of these expressions have found their way into the classical language of famous writers.

There are many eminent men of learning who have preserved a considerable amount of the language and manners of the Beni Sasan.

The Gypsies have different names in the different countries of Asia—Nawar in Syria; Gagar in the land of Egypt; Karbat in the neighborhood of Aleppo as-Sahba; Karatch in the mountains of Zuzan in the summer; Mutriba at El-Dast in winter; Gu'aidiyah in some villages of Syria; Ganganah in the vilayet of

Mosul; Kauliyah in the country of the Bedouin and the desert of Syria; Zutt and Zatt in the neighborhood of Busrah; Sahsawan in the north of Persia; Tat, Kufs, Kantchu, Posha, and a hundred other names.

The dress of the Gypsies in the country of the Arab does not differ from the garb of the people of the country; head-shawl or head-band with a long gown, girdled at the waist; over the gown a cloak. The dress of the women is like that of the Arab women, with a little more color, a bodice, and a veil. As to the Gypsies of Persia and surrounding countries, their dress is like that of the Kurds. But they like bright-colored garments that can be seen from a distance. For encamping they have a blanket which they also wear in the winter time.

The Beni Sasans' distinction is the dusky color or copperiness of their appearance, and the lankness and leanness of their bodies. The whiteness of their well-set teeth, the width of the jaws, the thinness of the lips, the equality of the nostrils, and the compelling power of their eyes, sets them apart from the rest of the population of Asia. Their eyes are black; the eye-sockets, sunken; the eyebrows, long and bushy. They are bright of face, thin in the legs, wasp-waisted, graceful, flexible, with long fingers and elegant joints. Lively of limb, graceful, with an ability for strange contortions and twistings, they are born acrobats. They train their children, female and male, from earliest youth to such things, just as they train them to sing, deceive, lie, steal, cheat, and flatter: everything needed to lead the life of an undesired wanderer, everywhere, in the marts of London, Paris, Rome, and at Bagdad, at the entrance of the mosques.

"They commit what thought does not imagine, and what does not come into the mind of man." Educated Moslems of Irak say that the female children of the Kauliyah are not born virgins. Arab investigators also maintain that the Kauliyah are the most immoral people on earth, that when a daughter has reached the age of puberty, her father teaches her debauchery. Often households sell their children, male and female, to seducers or travelers or those who make a living by an immoral life. A single tent, which does not exceed ten feet in length and four in breadth, is occupied by one or two families, whose numbers amount to ten. But then, Arab investigators have said the same things of Jews and Christians. If some people don't believe what they know, Arabs always know what they believe.

"Children, and especially males, are among the things which they covet in theft; so many little ones disappear, nor is a trace of them found. These wicked outlaws are the cause of the pangs of parents, and cause them grief that does not cease day and night." But of this, also, Arabs have accused every other people of the globe.

Final means for a knowledge of the origin of the Gypsies is the analysis of idioms, and the examination of its origin. European scholars have all come to the conclusion that it is of Sanskritic origin. The Gypsies have preserved this language in all European countries from north to south, and likewise in Anatolia, Egypt, Syria, Armenia, and Persia. But it is not unmixed with foreign tongues, like English, French, and Italian, and their grammar. The admixture of these languages increases or decreases in proportion to the tolerance shown to the Gypsies by the people they live with. In

Arab countries, the Gypsies speak a language resembling the Kurdish and the Persian tongues; in England, the Calo resembles English; in Roumania, Roumanian, and so on.

They sing songs praising the sheiks of the tribe of Al-Muntafik, and call them the famous ones of the country; and say that if one wished to recompense them for their brilliant deeds, there was no gift comparable with their rank, even though the gift were as great or as high as Mount Sengar. "Thou, O Sa'dun—the Sheikh of the tribe of Al-Muntafik, the most powerful, well known for his raids, his courage and his wisdom—O goader of princes; verily thou bringest us the spears of the people of the deserts, bundle by bundle . . ."

"Al-Hadididi yegawel al-mewla gawak Eblis ya mewla
w'hattalak ganahain yekun tsuf lak dirah wegnahain
Lew tsuf haulna men ha'd halhain al-humur al-yarman
rawagis al-gata."

But what it probably means is: "Dog of dogs, cruel, impure fool, shedding blood of people in the name of God!"

"Verily, God has said to every one of us: 'Let thy forearm be thy ally and thy belly thy wallet; what hast thou to do with a known house, and thy living on thy brother a thing destined?' "

The Kauliyah trace themselves to the Beni Tamim. In summer, they camp in Irak, and in winter in Abu Saida and Halis, and their neighborhood; and they have 1500 tents. The men are blacksmiths and fiddlers, and the women tell fortunes for a handful of rice and a few dates. Grellmann's investigations, however, proved that their place of origin is also Hindustan, and that they are also of the same ancestry as the Pariahs. These Kauliyah in Irak practice dancing and singing; this is their principal business in every country. Bands, both male and female, delight people by music and song. But the music is Arabic in character! We must not forget, however, that the songs of Gitanos are abridged from Spanish songs; fragments and sections in which loss and grief are abundant, from the poems known as *Polos* and *Tiranas* in the land of Andalusia, *Seguidillas* in La Mancha, *Totas* in Aragon. The Roumanian Gypsy songs are *Doinas* and *Sirbas,* and are Roumanian in character. Only in Hungary have the Gypsies developed their own music of ecstasy and intoxication.

The Gypsies have no religion, but adapt themselves to the religion of the country they live in. They do have certain ceremonies of their own, which they observe at birth, marriage, death, burial, and other special occasions; and some rule in domestic life regulating the familiarity of daily manners. But these customs and ceremonies are not uniform in all countries or in all tribes, but vary with the varieties of the people among whom they live, and the differences of their religions and rites—Moslems in the countries of Islam, Christian in Christian lands, they rely upon appearances that facilitate their existence.

The employments of Gypsies vary in different countries. The arts of the Karatch are sieve- and riddle-making, and the breeding of asses. The Mutriba make swords, daggers and knives, iron implements, and copper vessels. The Ganganah are blacksmiths, carpenters, burnishers, and makers of felt cloaks. The Kauliyah, in the district of Zahu, are agriculturists and breeders of cattle and domestic fowls. In Spain, the Gypsies are cattle-dealers; in Roumania, masons and musicians, gold-diggers and coppersmiths. In Hungary, they are musicians and showmen; in Russia, singers and cobblers. But they each and all have a strong aversion to tilling and sowing the soil; the very work the powers that be want them most to do.

In Transylvania, Wallachia, and Bulgaria, they wash and refine gold. In Spain, some of them keep inns, lodgings, and dining-rooms. In Castile and Aragon, La Mancha, Estremadura and especially in Andalusia, where they are widely spread, they own hotels. They are in great numbers in some quarters of Valencia, Murcia, the suburbs of Seville, and on the outskirts of Cadiz.

The Gypsies of Russia, Poland, and Roumania live in tribes, *taboras,* and their gains in everything are shared among them—able-bodied men, women, children, old men, and the sick. Yet there is no common purse amongst the Gypsies of England. The Spanish Gitanos are extremely individualistic, though they are generous to one another with their earnings.

But whatever Gypsies do, or wherever they are, there is some instrument of music in their hands, and they are almost always engaged in producing music, melodies, accompaniments, dance and mirth. And when the voices of their women are sad and beautiful, as in Russia, the combination is unsurpassable. And they are free.

Theories about the origin of the Gypsies are as many as there are Gypsies. One old theory held that they were remnants of a sect known as Atingants, who were heretics among the Greek Christians. Another theory maintained they are Persian Magians. Hafiz, the celebrated Persian poet, mentioned a people called Luli, noted for dancing and singing. Another opinion held they are from Sinkan, Africa, where they were known by the name of Zengitania, which had become corrupted to Zinganah, Ginkanah, Zingari, Gingari. Some say that the word "Tziganes" or "Tsiganener" is a corruption from "Saracens," under which name they were once known in Hungary. Proofs are not missing to show that they are Canaanites, whom Joshua, son of Nun, drove and scattered in all directions. Some authors have maintained that the Tchinganah are Cushites, from the loins of Cush, mentioned in the Old Testament (Genesis 10:6–7). Until Grellmann, Pott, Burton, and others unraveled the tangle, the most common belief was that they were Egyptians; or a cursed tribe of Israelites.

To this day, tribes and peoples known by various names, whose complexions are like those of the Gypsies, and whose language is identical with theirs, are to be found in North India. The name of *Rom,* the meaning of which is "man" or "husband," may have been derived from the Kurdish language, in which it means "man" generally, or "victorious life from such men"; or from a long sojourn in Roumania thousands of years later. An Arabic word *Rumm* has the same meaning. Nomads in Asia speaking a language akin to that of the Gypsies call themselves Siyah Hindu, "Black Hindus."

Wherever Gypsies encamp and wherever they roam, the chief is the master, not by heredity but by election. Merit is the only thing that counts, and women as well as men have been elected as chiefs, or kings; only the name is different; the authority is the same. If a woman possesses the qualities required, the woman is master. In the year 1860, the Gypsies in England elected as their queen a woman called Esther Faa.

XIII—The Tent in the Wind

AND NOW THE DEED IS DONE. I HAVE SAID ALL I know, and told what other people know, about the Gypsies. I have sifted my own knowledge and that of others through the sieve of my own temperament and prejudices, and bulked the whole in one lump—formidable in my eyes; slight, perhaps, in the eyes of others.

I have tried to prove that the Gypsies were in Europe long before the year authorities took notice of them; and while I did not go so far as to claim, with Bataillard, that they were the ones who brought bronze to Europe, I do believe that they brought the art of iron-forging, the dance of the East, and orchestral music to the shores of the Black Sea, to the Pont Euxine, when they first set foot on European soil.

When?

Alas! Wanderers make their presence known, but leave no lasting trace themselves. Were it not that inhabitants recorded the presence in their midst of this extraordinary people, so different from themselves, we should not know the little we do about Gypsies.

Did they come two thousand, three hundred years ago, imported by Alexander the Great, or a thousand years later, traveling of their own volition or driven by enemies? Who knows? For the strangest thing is that Gypsies are an even greater mystery to themselves than they are to us. Lost labor to whoever thinks of elucidating matters by questioning them—except in listening to their legends, the veiled, unconscious memory of their history and existence.

Here they were, in the long ago, living in a hundred or a thousand cone-shaped tents, spread in a large circle, in a world that was already living in brick and stone houses. Able. Hardy. Intelligent. Passionate. Organized. Prolific. Adaptable. Better endowed by nature than were the people who tolerated them in their midst. A prophetic historian would have had reason to believe they would in time be absorbed by growing civilization; that climate, conditions of life, geography, and propinquity would reshape them, as others had been reshaped and influenced. For, say what one may, the differences among European peoples are today more political than racial, more national than intrinsic. Culturally, Europe is composed of materials more or less sympathetic to one another. War and peace have had, and still have, the same power to bind two inimical people; throwing them together beside one another or on top of one another. Nationally, the friend of today is yesterday's and tomorrow's enemy. Dress, food, language, customs, are continually being reformed and borrowed from people we come in contact with—in love or hate. More English is being spoken today in Germany than before the war. The English speak more and better French. In France, German is studied more assiduously today than ever. In the United States, people began to learn Spanish after the Spanish-American War. England dictates the style for men the whole world over; France, the styles for women over the civilized part of the earth. Germany dictates the taste in music; Italy, the appreciation for art. And so on. A European is at home in every large city of

Europe; and so is an American, despite the ocean which caused a superficial national separation. We are what we eat, dress, speak, and think. Science is international. Literature and art are international.

But what has caused the Gypsies to remain an entity outside the pale of influence of the civilized world? It seems to me the fundamental reason for this is to be found in the fact that compared to the other inhabitants the Gypsies were already a superior group when they first appeared in Europe. Considering themselves abler, superior, they refused to adapt themselves to the method of life of the inferior native inhabitants in whose midst they camped, and thus prevented themselves from growing with them. To this day, the Gypsy considers himself superior to all peoples in wisdom of life, in ability, in artistry, in strength and intelligence, and refuses the formal school education, not because he is inferior to it, but because he considers the education of the Gorgio unworthy, ridiculous, and superfluous. Duty—private property—reduction of individual freedom . . .

But you will tell him:

"Look at yourself. You are poor, bedraggled, uncomfortable, ignorant."

And his answer, ready and prompt, will be:

"Yes, but I am happy. The contrary of 'poor, bedraggled, uncomfortable, ignorant' does not spell happiness!" And this answer is irrefutable. "And as to 'ignorant.' The things we know cannot be found in books. We know you better than you know yourselves."

"We live in houses; cool in summer, warm in winter. When we are ill, we call a doctor to cure us."

"We live in tents summer and winter. Yet we don't know the diseases you know. We have no need for doctors—until you compel us to live in houses."

And this answer is likewise irrefutable. Talk to a Gypsy of industry, and he answers you with talk of freedom. Talk to him of wealth, and he responds with a chant on the elimination of worry: the uncontrollable, unhealable cancer of the soul.

And should you launch forth on pride, he will point out that his tribal pride is of purer metal than any political pride of today. And there is no gainsaying this. He does not have to dress to look respectable. We need beautiful clothes to cover our ugliness. His beautiful body shines through the rags that cover it—to conform to our law. The Gypsy loves nakedness.

The Gypsy lies to preserve his integrity, and steals to maintain his inner honesty, which does not recognize private property. Did Proudhon hear the phrase *"La propriété, c'est le vol"* from the Gypsies living at the gates of Paris?

The tent-living Gypsies have seen the destruction and disruption of Palestine; and the Jews, once a nomad people, had lived in houses and had founded a civilization of their own that was leaning on what they had borrowed from Egyptians, Phœnicians, Greeks.

The tent-living Gypsies have seen the crumbling of Darius' palaces in Persia, the destruction of Babylon and the breaking down of Alexander's empire. They have seen Macedonia shrink from a cannon ball to an almost invisible grain of bird shot. Greece fell. Rome fell. The Byzantine empire was unglued by its own heat; and in more recent times they have seen the dismembering of empires that had been joined together by the flesh and blood of millions of men through centuries and centuries to give body to the illusion of some ambitious, power-thirsty day-dreamer. They have seen the rise and fall of many empires. . . .

"Wind that breaks and scatters the strongest houses is resisted by the bending tent. The wisdom of life is the continuation of life, and so the wisdom of the Gypsy is superior to that of the civilized world."

And so unyielding have the Gypsies been that thousands of years of life in surroundings contradicting their manner of life have influenced them but little. Oh, they have changed! They are not exactly what they were three or four thousand years ago. But they have changed according to their own native processes; from within and not without. They have accepted no religion, no customs, no laws, no traditions from the world outside their tents; and they have kept their own language, though they have been subject to a hundred differences in every generation. National entity! No other nation can boast of one as perfect as the national entity of the Gypsies.

Like the tent in the wind, the Gypsy does not stubbornly, openly, oppose the principles and the laws of the peoples he lives with. He bends this way and that. Yet when the wind has blown over, he stands as straight as before—while the wind still blows elsewhere. Moslems while in Turkey, Catholics in Spain, Methodists in England, Greek Orthodox in Russia . . .

And what of tomorrow? When shall we have seen the last Gypsy? Civilization, industry, economic pressure, science, hygiene, will they not force the Gypsy to adapt himself to new conditions? to walls, doors, and houses?

A thousand years ago, the world thought that that generation had seen the last Gypsy. Five hundred years ago, the French, the English, the Italians, and the Germans thought they had heard the last of him. George Borrow gave an account of them which reads like a custom-made epitaph for their tomb. Charles Godfrey Leland said the last of the Gypsy had already been seen—and there are a million tent-Gypsies today, as fierce, as passionate, as free as they have ever been—still bending under the wind.

And the Gypsy answers: "The last of the Gypsies will be seen when we return to India, picking our way amidst the scattered ruins of the world."

For they believe they are eternal; they believe in themselves, and not in us. For they still are convinced that theirs is the superior manner, that they are a superior race of cleaner and better blood—a superior people, oppressed by a hundred inferior ones.

"Bathe as frequently as you may, you only cleanse your skin. Our blood is pure; our breath is sweet."

But all this I have already said. Some of it I believe, and some I do not. Yet what is atavistically Gypsy in me responds to their claims, to their wisdom, to their passion for untrammeled freedom, and sings the song of the wood and the glen to the rhythm of the pebble-bottomed brook and the beat of my tramping feet upon the crust covering the heart of the world.

Yet—will they resist all pressure? Can they? Will history not repeat itself and absorb the Gypsies?

History does not repeat itself. Man repeats himself, and repeats the life of his ancestors, instead of continuing it.

THE END